Other Titles in the Irwin Library of Investment and Finance

Convertible Securities
by John P. Calamos

Pricing and Managing Exotic and Hybrid Options
by Vineer Bhansali

Risk Management and Financial Derivatives
by Satyajit Das

Valuing Intangible Assets
by Robert F. Reilly and Robert P. Schweihs

Managing Financial Risk
by Charles W. Smithson

High-Yield Bonds
by Theodore Barnhill, William Maxwell, and Mark Shenkman

Valuing Small Business and Professional Practices, 3rd edition
by Shannon Pratt, Robert F. Reilly, and Robert P. Schweihs

Implementing Credit Derivatives
by Israel Nelken

The Handbook of Credit Derivatives
by Jack Clark Francis, Joyce Frost, and J. Gregg Whittaker

The Handbook of Advanced Business Valuation
by Robert F. Reilly and Robert P. Schweihs

Global Investment Risk Management
by Ezra Zask

Active Portfolio Management, 2nd edition
by Richard Grinold and Ronald Kahn

The Hedge Fund Handbook
by Stefano Lavinio

Pricing, Hedging, and Trading Exotic Options
by Israel Nelken

Equity Management
by Bruce Jacobs and Kenneth Levy

Asset Allocation, 3rd edition
by Roger Gibson

Valuing a Business, 4th edition
by Shannon P. Pratt, Robert F. Reilly, and Robert P. Schweihs

The Complete Arbitrage Deskbook
by Stephane Reverre

Quantitative Business Valuation
by Jay Abrams

Applied Equity Analysis
by James English

Exchange-Rate Determination

Exchange-Rate Determination

Models and Strategies for Exchange-Rate Forecasting

Michael R. Rosenberg

McGraw-Hill

New York Chicago San Francisco Lisbon London
Madrid Mexico City Milan New Delhi San Juan
Seoul Singapore Sydney Toronto

The McGraw-Hill Companies

3 4 5 6 7 8 9 BKM BKM 0 9 8 7

ISBN-13: 978-0-07-141501-9

ISBN-10: 0-07-141501-7

McGraw-Hill books are available at special quantity discounts to use as premiums and sales promotions, or for use in corporate training programs. For more information, please write to the Director of Special Sales, Professional Publishing, McGraw-Hill, Two Penn Plaza, New York, NY 10121-2298. Or contact your local bookstore.

Library of Congress Cataloging-in-Publication Data

Rosenberg, Michael Roy, 1947-
Exchange-rate determination: models and strategies for exchange-rate forecasting / by Michael Rosenberg.
p. cm.
ISBN 0-07-141501-7 (hardcover: alk. paper)
1. Foreign exchange—Forecasting. 2. Foreign exchange rates. 3. Foreign exchange—Forecasting—Mathematical models. 4. Foreign exchange rates—Mathematical models. I. Title.
HG3821.R58 2003
332.4'56'0113—dc21 2002152449

CONTENTS

THE GUIDE TO EXCHANGE-RATE DETERMINATION

"Having endeavored to forecast exchange rates for more than half a century, I have understandably developed significant humility about my ability in this area...."

Alan Greenspan
Remarks Before the Euro 50 Roundtable
Washington D.C., November 30, 2001

"There may be more forecasting of exchange rates, with less success, than almost any other economic variable. Although measures such as real interest-rate differentials, differential rates of productivity gains, and chronic external deficits are often employed to explain exchange rate behavior, none has been found to be consistently useful in forecasting exchange rates even over substantial periods of one or two years."

"We at the Federal Reserve have spent an inordinate amount of time trying to find models which would successfully project exchange rates, not only ours, but everyone else's. It is not the most profitable investment we have made in research time. Indeed, it is really remarkable how difficult it is to forecast."

Alan Greenspan
Remarks Before U.S. Senate
Semi-Annual Monetary Policy Report
Washington D.C., July 16, 2002

Getting the exchange rate right is a critical objective of all international investors. Unfortunately, getting the exchange rate right on a reasonably consistent basis is far from easy. As anyone involved in the business of currency forecasting can attest, it can be a humbling experience.

Currency forecasts can go awry for a variety of reasons. For instance, if one's expectation of the direction in which fundamental-based forces are heading is flawed, so will be one's forecast of a currency's future path. Even if one's interpretation of the underlying fundamental forces were correct, currency forecasts might still go awry if short-term technical forces carried exchange rates far from their fundamental equilibrium path.

Scores of empirical studies have found that fundamental-based models tend to perform poorly in terms of explaining exchange-rate trends, particularly over short-term periods. However, fundamental-based models have been found to work better over medium and especially longer-run horizons. Unfortunately, most fund managers, whose performances are evaluated over relatively short time spans these days, are not often willing to risk significant sums of capital on the basis of longer-term, fundamental-based projections. That is why many market participants have recently turned their attention away from longer-run fundamental-based forecasting approaches in favor of shorter-term forecasting tools such as technical-based trend-following trading rules. In addition, there has recently been significant interest in flow, sentiment, and positioning indicators to determine the exposure of market participants to the individual currencies. Such indicators are often used as contrarian indicators to determine whether a currency is significantly overbought or oversold, and thus ripe for a correction.

Given the wide variety of forecasting approaches, we thought it would be useful to put together a guidebook that summarized each of those approaches in an easy-to-read format. Our intention was to create a user-friendly format where the written text was purposely kept to a minimum and where charts and tables would tell the story.

This guidebook recognizes that the tools required for short-term investors differ significantly from those needed for medium and long-term currency managers. Hence, the guidebook devotes separate chapters to the determination of exchange rates over short-, medium-, and long-term horizons.

The schematic diagram on the following page provides a convenient illustration of the layout of this guidebook and highlights the myriad of channels through which fundamental and technical forces jointly affect exchange rates. Some of those channels will tend to exert a more profound impact on exchange rates in the short run, while others will tend to have a more profound impact in the medium or long run. We explore each of those channels in the chapters that follow.

In Part One, entitled "Exchange-Rate Determination in the Short Run," we investigate the potential risks and rewards of using a variety of short-run forecasting tools in formulating short-term FX strategies. These include moving-average trend-following trading rules, sentiment and positioning surveys, FX dealer customer-flow data, information embedded in currency option prices, and risk appetite indices.

We find that moving-average trading rules would have generated significant risk-adjusted excess returns over relatively long periods for most major currency pairs, although losing trades tend to occur far more

Exchange-Rate Determination in the Short, Medium, and Long Run

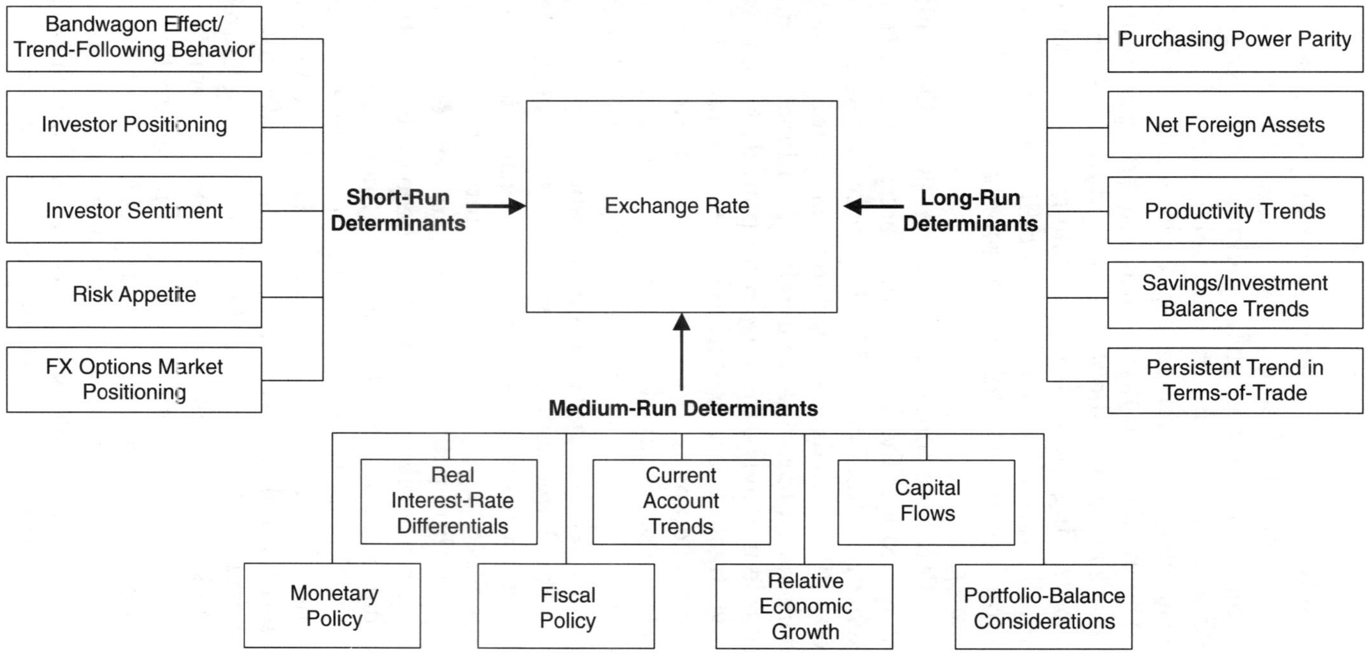

frequently than winning trades, in many cases by a factor of 3 to 1. The high frequency of losing trades suggests that moving-average trading rules can be risky over short periods. It also suggests that an investor would need considerable risk capital on hand to absorb such losses to stay in the game until exchange rates eventually become more highly trended.

The evidence on flow, sentiment, and positioning surveys suggests that these indicators should be viewed more as contemporaneous rather than as leading indicators of exchange-rate movements. We argue that such indicators can be useful as confirmation indicators in conjunction with traditional trend-following trading rules in formulating short-term FX strategies.

In Part Two, entitled "Exchange-Rate Determination in the Long Run," we explore the fundamental forces that give rise to long-term cycles in exchange rates. The chapter begins by noting that deviations from estimated PPP values have tended to be large and persistent, suggesting that fundamental forces other than relative national inflation rates have played a key role in driving the long-term path that exchange rates have taken. We investigate a variety of fundamental variables that have had some success in explaining the long-term path that currencies have taken, including relative productivity growth, persistent trends in a country's terms of trade, long-term trends in net foreign asset and liability positions, and long-term trends in national savings and investment.

In Part Three, entitled "Exchange-Rate Determination in the Medium Run," we investigate a wide range of cyclical forces that have caused currencies either to rise or fall on a medium-term basis relative to their long-run equilibrium path. In many cases, these medium-term deviations from the long-run equilibrium path have been quite sizeable and persistent. We find that medium-term trends are influenced by a variety of macroeconomic indicators such as the trend in real interest-rate differentials, current and capital-account balances, relative monetary and fiscal policies, relative economic growth, and portfolio-balance considerations.

Finally, in Part Four, entitled "Anticipating Currency Crises in Emerging Markets," we set out to identify those economic and financial variables that have had success in correctly predicting whether an emerging-market currency might be vulnerable to a speculative attack, and whether it is possible to construct an early-warning system that can successfully pinpoint when a speculative attack might occur. Empirical research finds that crises-prone currencies typically display a number of classic symptoms that warn of an impending attack. Those symptoms include excessive real appreciation of the emerging-market currency, weak domestic economic growth, rising unemployment, an adverse terms of trade shock, deteriorating current-account balances, excessive domestic credit expansion, banking-system difficulties, unsustainably large government budget deficits, overly expansionary monetary policies, a high ratio of M2 money supply to reserves, foreign-exchange reserve losses, falling asset prices, and/or a huge build-up in short-term liabilities by either the private or public sector.

The overall conclusion one draws from a variety of empirical studies is that the success of early-warning systems in terms of generating correct out-of-sample projections is mixed. While most early-warning models can point to a significant number of correctly predicted crises, those same models also have a tendency to generate a sizable number of false alarms and missed crises.

Perhaps all that one can say after reviewing all of the different approaches to exchange-rate determination is that no single approach has a monopoly on being right all of the time. Some strategy systems, such as moving-average trading rules and forward-rate bias strategies, appear to have a long-run track record of success, but one needs to be mindful that there were a number of periods in the past when significant losses were incurred from following these strategies. Likewise, some key fundamental variables may have closely tracked the trend in exchange rates in the past, but there is no guarantee that they will continue to do so in the future. If divergent trends begin to set in, fund managers must decide whether or not to disregard the trend in those key fundamental variables.

Although many fund managers might prefer to follow a rigid rule or trading system for formulating FX strategies, one should not sell short a judgment-based approach to currency investment management. In the end, successful FX management is based as much on "art" as it is on "science."

PART ONE

Exchange-Rate Determination in the Short Run

CHAPTER 1

Short-Run Forecasting Tools

Economists have come up with a wide range of theories to explain how exchange rates are determined. The overwhelming body of evidence from scores of empirical studies indicates that fundamental-based models, while useful in explaining long-term trends, have not met much success in explaining short-term exchange-rate trends. Indeed, the evidence suggests that for short-term horizons, a random walk characterizes exchange-rate movements better than most conventional fundamental-based exchange rate models.

One of the reasons why researchers have not been able to unearth any significant relationship between changes in macroeconomic variables and changes in exchange rates over short periods is that exchange rates often exhibit much greater variability than do macroeconomic time series in the short run. The often chaotic behavior of exchange rates is capable of generating so much noise that it may obscure any discernable relationship between macroeconomic time series and the short-term movement of exchange rates.

Bandwagon effects are also capable of causing exchange rates to wander away from fundamental equilibrium values in the short run. Survey studies find that FX market participants tend to have extrapolative expectations over short-term horizons and mean-reverting or regressive expectations over longer horizons. If investors have extrapolative expectations over short horizons, they may tend to accentuate and perpetuate exchange-rate movements in the short run far beyond the path justified by fundamentals alone. Indeed, if a significant number of investors engaged in extrapolative/trend-following trading strategies, exchange rates might tend to overshoot on both the upside and downside, which could further obscure the relationship between macroeconomic fundamentals and the short-term movement of exchange rates.

Because exchange rates can and often do deviate significantly from any semblance of fair value in the short run, investors have looked for alternative forecasting tools to help them formulate currency investment strategies over short-term horizons. Short-run forecasting tools that have attracted interest in recent years include technical-based trend-following trading rules, sentiment and positioning surveys, FX dealers' customer order flow data, information embedded in currency option prices, and risk appetite indices.

Investors who concentrate their energies on such tools presume that the market exhibits a tendency to tip its hand ahead of time as to which direction it intends to take exchange rates in the future. While technical models have been found to be profitable in the past, most of the other short-term indicators are relatively new to the FX arena and thus only a limited time series is available to test their predictive power. What evidence we do have, however, suggests that in most cases, these indicators are more useful as contemporaneous rather than as leading indicators of exchange-rate movements. Nevertheless, they may prove useful as confirmation indicators that can be used in conjunction with traditional technical-based trend-following trading rules in formulating short-term investment strategies.

WHY FX MARKET PARTICIPANTS FOCUS THEIR ENERGIES ON SHORT-RUN RATHER THAN LONG-RUN STRATEGIES

FX market participants typically fall into one of two camps:

1. Shorter-run technically oriented traders
2. Longer-run fundamental-based investors

Shorter-run technically oriented traders do not base their investment decisions on fundamental considerations. Rather, they rely on trend-following trading rules to determine their position taking: they buy when the currency is rising, and they sell when the currency is falling. In contrast, longer-run fundamental-based investors base their investment decisions largely on valuation considerations. If a currency is believed to be mispriced relative to its fair value, fundamental-based investors would buy those currencies that are believed to be undervalued and would sell those currencies that are believed to be overvalued.

Knowing precisely what exchange-rate level represents a currency's true equilibrium or fair value is not an easy task. Different exchange-rate models can and often do yield quite different estimates of a currency's long-run equilibrium value. In most cases, the marketplace will have only a rough idea of where a currency's long-run equilibrium value lies. Because of this, fundamental-based investors will not set their sights on an imprecise point estimate of fair value but rather on an equilibrium range or band. Within this equilibrium range or band, fundamental-based investors will presume that the true but unknown equilibrium exchange rate, $\bar{q}$, lies somewhere between an upper-bound, $\bar{q}_U$, and a lower-bound, $\bar{q}_L$.

The $\bar{q}_U$-$\bar{q}_L$ band has been referred to as the "band of agnosticism" in academic writings (see DeGrauwe, 1996, see also Figure 1–1). When exchange rates trade inside the $\bar{q}_U$-$\bar{q}_L$ band, fundamental-based investors tend to be agnostic in terms of their currency positioning, accepting the

FIGURE 1-1

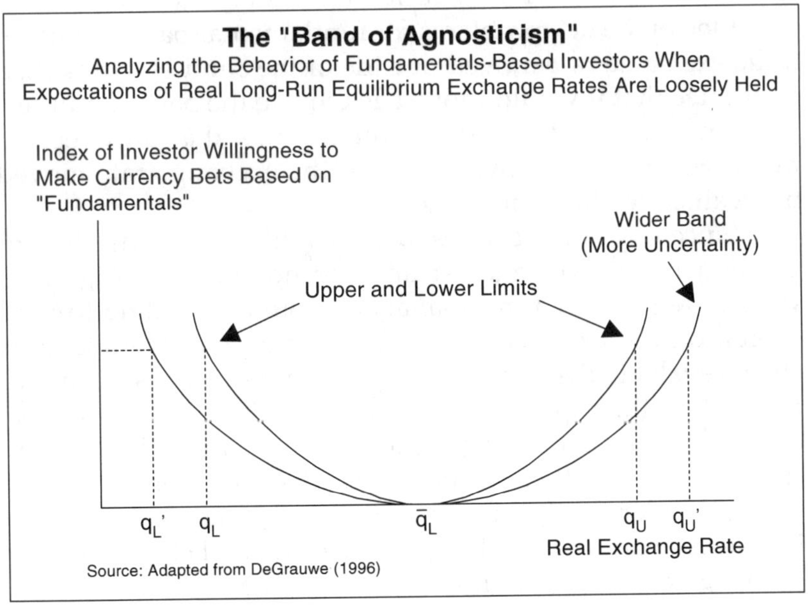

fact that the actual exchange rate is probably trading close to its fair value. Exchange-rate movements within the $\bar{q}_U$-$\bar{q}_L$ band are viewed as noise and therefore not worthy of serious investment consideration. Fundamental-based investors would thus not feel compelled to take on either aggressive long or short currency positions when exchange rates are trading inside the band. Instead, they would more likely adopt a neutral stance toward currency positioning.

When exchange rates fluctuate inside the band of agnosticism, trading tends to be dominated by short-term technically oriented traders since fundamental-based investors will refrain from joining the fray until the actual exchange rate moves outside of the band. When the actual exchange rate moves outside the $\bar{q}_U$-$\bar{q}_L$ equilibrium range, fundamental-based investors will tend to shed their agnosticism and become more willing to take on aggressive long positions if the actual exchange rate falls below $\bar{q}_L$ and aggressive short positions if the actual exchange rate rises above $\bar{q}_U$.

In times of greater market uncertainty, however, the band of agnosticism is likely to widen since investor confidence regarding estimates of fair value is likely to be less strongly held than in tranquil environments. In such cases, technically oriented traders would tend to dominate trading activity over even wider ranges ($\bar{q}_U'$-$\bar{q}_L'$ > $\bar{q}_U$ - $\bar{q}_L$). That, in turn, would likely lead to even greater FX volatility in the short run.

One of the key problems for fundamental-based investors is that even if the exchange rate moved outside of the band of agnosticism, there is no guarantee that it would move back inside the band anytime soon. Indeed, fundamental-based investors run the risk that an overvalued currency might get even more overvalued if the exchange rate moved deeper into overvalued territory, and vice versa.

Since large financial resources are likely to be needed for investors to position themselves against an overshooting exchange rate, one has to wonder how many fund managers would be willing to risk their clients' capital on the basis of long-run valuation considerations, particularly if clients evaluate their fund manager's investment performance over a relatively short time span. If fund managers view it as simply too risky to take on long or short currency positions on the basis of long-run valuation considerations, then there might be several occasions when exchange rates could wander far from any semblance of fair value, and yet very few investors would be willing to risk their clients' capital to bring the exchange rate back into line with fair value.

FIGURE 1-2

FX Dealers' Perception of the Role of Fundamentals in Explaining Exchange-Rate Movements

FX Dealer Survey Question—Do You Believe Exchange-Rate Movements Reflect Changes in Fundamental Value on an:

	Intra-Day Basis	Medium-Run Basis (up to 6 months)	Long-Run Basis (beyond 6 months)
Yes	3%	57.8%	87%
No	97%	42.2%	12%
No Opinion	0%	0.0%	1%

Source: Yin-Wong Cheung, Menzie D. Chinn, and Ian W. Marsh, "How Do UK-Based Foreign Exchange Dealers Think Their Market Operates?", NBER Working Paper 7524, February 2000.

HOW FX DEALERS VIEW THE DETERMINATION OF EXCHANGE RATES IN THE SHORT RUN

When FX dealers were asked recently what role fundamental factors played in the determination of exchange rates, 97% of the respondents felt that fundamentals played no role on an intra-day basis (see Figure 1–2). However, over medium- and longer-term horizons, FX dealers felt that fundamental forces did play an important role, with 57.8% of the respondents believing that exchange rates reflect fundamental value on a medium-term (within 6 months) basis, and 87% believing exchange rates reflect fundamental value on a long-term (over 6 months) basis.

When asked to rank the most important determinants of exchange rates on an intra-day basis, FX dealers indicated that bandwagon effects, speculative forces, and overreaction to news were the principal driving forces in the very short run (see Figure 1–3). On a medium-term basis, economic fundamentals and technical trading increase in importance from the dealer community's perspective, but FX dealers also continued to assign importance to speculative forces as a key determinant of medium-term trends in exchange rates. For longer horizons, FX dealers believed that economic fundamentals were the dominant factor driving exchange rates. However, a not insignificant number (11.3%) believed that technical trading was important even in the long run.

FIGURE 1-3

FX Dealers' Perception of the Most Important Factor That Explains Exchange-Rate Movements

FX Dealer Survey Question—Select the Single Most Important Factor That Determines Exchange Rate Movements on an:

	Intra-Day Basis	Medium-Run Basis (up to 6 months)	Long-Run Basis (beyond 6 months)
Bandwagon Effects	29.3%	9.5%	1.0%
Overreaction to News	32.8%	0.7%	0.0%
Speculative Forces	25.3%	30.7%	3.1%
Economic Fundamentals	0.6%	31.4%	82.5%
Technical Trading	10.3%	26.3%	11.3%
Other	1.7%	1.5%	2.1%

Source: Yin-Wong Cheung, Menzie D. Chinn, and Ian W. Marsh, "How Do UK-Based Foreign Exchange Dealers Think Their Market Operates?", NBER Working Paper 7524, February 2000.

The FX dealer survey also asked dealers whether they thought that exchange rates were more predictable on an intra-day basis or on a medium-term (up to 6 months) or long-term (beyond 6 months) basis (see Figure 1–4). FX dealers were asked to assign a rating of 1 if there was no predictability, a rating of 5 if there was a high predictability, and a rating of 2, 3, or 4 if there was low, medium, or better-than-average predictability, respectively. Since FX dealers tend to trade on an intra-day basis, one might have thought that they would assign a high rating to exchange-rate predictability on an intra-day basis. This was not the case. Indeed, 62% of the dealer respondents gave ratings of 1 or 2, to the predictability of exchange rates in the short run, while only 11% gave ratings of 4 or 5.

For medium and longer time horizons, the confidence in exchange-rate predictability increases, with 30.4% of dealers assigning a ranking of 4 or 5 on a medium-term basis and 35.1% assigning a ranking of 4 or 5 on a longer-term basis. The question that we need to ask ourselves is: If FX dealers are more confident in predicting exchange rates on a medium/long-term basis rather than on an intra-day basis, why then do traders concentrate their energies on very short-run trading? The answer might be that traders are in a better position to evaluate and manage FX risk on a short-term basis, which overrides their greater confidence in medium/long-term exchange-rate predictability.

FIGURE 1-4

FX Dealers' Perception of the Predictability of Exchange-Rate Movements

FX Dealer Survey Question—On a Scale of 1 to 5, Indicate If You Believe the Market Trend Is Predictable on an:

	Intra-Day Basis	**Medium-Run Basis** (up to 6 months)	**Long-Run Basis** (beyond 6 months)
1 (Least Predictable)	21.6%	5.9%	17.2%
2	40.3%	20.7%	16.4%
3	26.9%	43.0%	30.6%
4	9.0%	18.5%	20.9%
5 (Most Predictable)	2.2%	11.9%	14.2%

Source: Yin-Wong Cheung, Menzie D. Chinn, and Ian W. Marsh, "How Do UK-Based Foreign Exchange Dealers Think Their Market Operates?," NBER Working Paper 7524, February 2000.

CURRENCY FORECASTING USING TECHNICAL ANALYSIS–THE ADVANTAGE OF TRADING WITH AND NOT AGAINST THE TREND

Technical models generate exchange-rate forecasts by extrapolating past sequences of exchange-rate movements into the future. For example, if a currency begins to edge higher and rises above some critical value, a technical model will typically issue a recommendation to take a long position in that currency, the presumption being that the newly formed trend will continue to carry the currency higher in the future. Similarly, a sell signal would be issued if the currency began to edge lower and fell below some critical value.

Trend-following trading rules will be profitable as long as the ensuing trend does indeed move in the same direction as the preceding trend, which would be the case if exchange rates moved in broad, well-defined cycles. But that is not to say that exchange rates must always move in large swings for trend-following trading rules to be profitable. What matters for long-term profitability is that large exchange-rate upswings and downswings must occur on a frequent enough basis to overcome those occasions when currency movements are not highly trended.

Fundamental-based models tend to focus on whether a currency lies above or below its long-run equilibrium or "fair" value. Technical models, on the other hand, are not interested in whether a currency lies above or below its fair value. Rather, technical models are only interested in whether the trend in the exchange rate is upward or downward. As long as a confirmed uptrend (or downtrend) is in place, a recommended long (short) position will be maintained even if the prevailing trend carries the exchange rate well above (below) its long-run fair value.

THE IDENTIFICATION OF FX MARKET TRENDS AND REVERSALS

Trend-following trading rules come in many forms. But what all trend-following trading rules have in common is that they seek to identify the direction in which the *broad* trend in exchange rates is heading. One can visualize the trend in exchange rates as a series of primary and secondary waves (see Figure 1–5). The primary wave refers to the large, broad moves in exchange rates that carry the underlying trend in currency values either

FIGURE 1-5

Identification and Confirmation of a Valid Trend

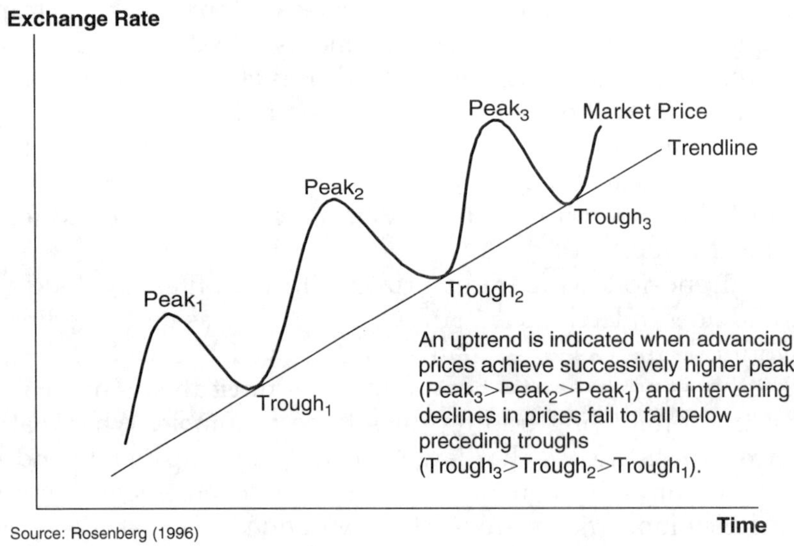

Source: Rosenberg (1996)

upward or downward. The secondary waves refer to the temporary corrections or partial retracements of the primary trend that typically take place over the course of longer-run exchange-rate cycles. What trend-following trading rules attempt to do is to identify the direction in which the primary waves are heading.

In a rising market, each rally and partial retracement will be higher than its predecessor. As long as advancing prices achieve successively higher peaks and troughs, they indicate that buying pressure is overcoming selling pressure. In such a case, the uptrend will be presumed to be intact, until a reversal is signaled. The opposite would be the case in a declining market.

Markets reverse in many different ways, but all reversals have one thing in common: All reversals of valid uptrends (downtrends) must be preceded by the failure of market prices to achieve successively higher peaks and troughs (lower troughs and peaks) (see Figure 1–6). In the case

FIGURE 1-6

Identification and Confirmation of a Market Reversal

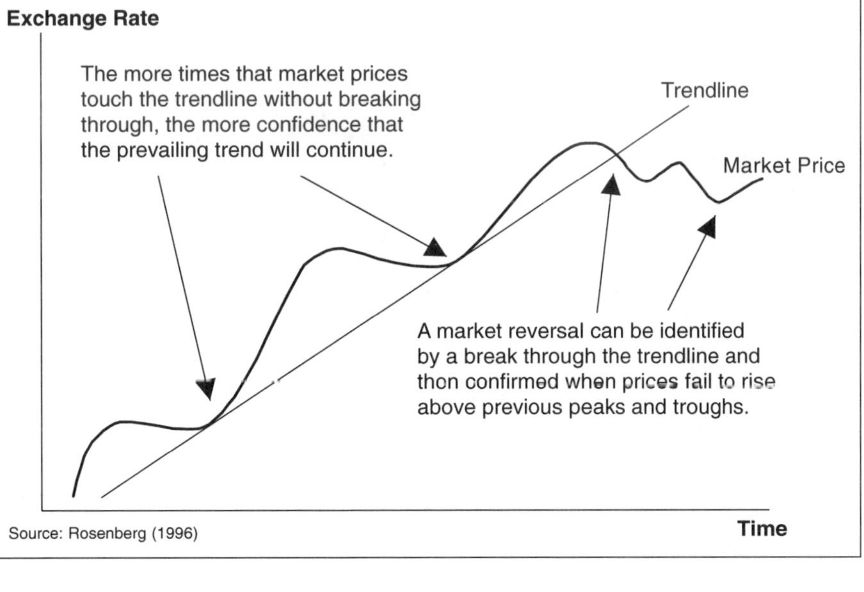

Source: Rosenberg (1996)

of a reversal of a previous valid uptrend, when the wavelike series of rising peaks and troughs is broken, it indicates that selling pressure is finally beginning to overcome buying pressure.

One of the most recognizable reversal patterns is the head-and-shoulders pattern (see Figure 1–7). A head-and-shoulders pattern is essentially a series of three successive rallies with the second stronger than the first, and the third weaker than the second. Because the third rally fails to carry as far as the second, the string of successively higher peaks is broken. This is an initial indication of weak demand, and the eventual drop in market prices to levels below the preceding trough (or neckline) is confirmation that a reversal is taking place. A recent Federal Reserve Bank of New York study (Osler and Chang, 1995) found that head-and-shoulders patterns have been successful in anticipating reversals in trend for the yen and Deutschemark.

FIGURE 1-7

Head-and-Shoulders Reversal Pattern

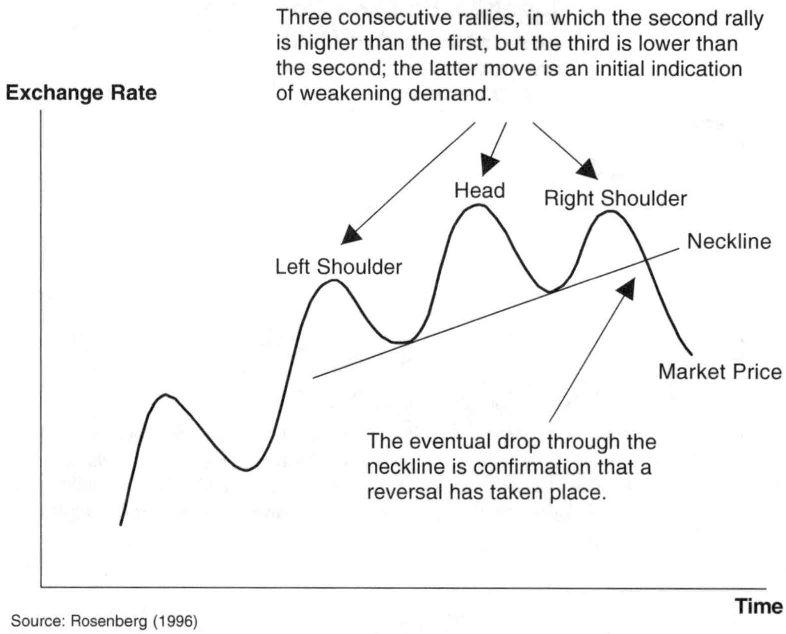

Source: Rosenberg (1996)

TREND-FOLLOWING TRADING RULES AND THE PRINCIPLE OF EXTRAPOLATION

A wide variety of trend-following trading rules abound, but by and large they all share the basic property of extrapolation. A chartist who monitors the behavior of market prices on a bar chart with a ruler and pencil will assume that an uptrend is intact as long as advancing prices achieve successively higher peaks and intervening declines fail to fall below preceding troughs (see Figure 1–8).

More sophisticated extrapolation techniques can be designed with the assistance of a computer. One popular computer-based technical model is the filter rule, which issues a buy recommendation if an exchange rate rises by $x\%$ above its most recent trough, and issues a sell recommendation if the exchange rate falls by $x\%$ below its most recent peak. Another popular computer-based technical model is the moving-average crossover model. By constructing longer-run moving averages of daily exchange-rate movements, one can more easily isolate the primary trend from short-run noise. If the short-run moving average of the exchange rate rises above its long-run moving average, it is an indication that buying pressure is overcoming selling pressure, and vice versa.

In each case, predictions of the likely future path that exchange rates might take are being generated by the extrapolation of the prevailing trend in exchange rates into the future. Essentially, it really doesn't matter which trend-following rule you use. Since a trend is a trend, all trend-following trading rules should roughly generate the same directional forecast.

Because all of these models generate forecasts by extrapolating the recent past trend of exchange rates into the future, buy or sell signals will be issued only after a currency has already started rising or falling. Although this means that trend-following trading rules will not capture the very top and bottom of market moves, they may nevertheless be profitable if the ensuing exchange-rate movements persist long enough and carry far enough to generate significant excess returns.

POTENTIAL PITFALLS FROM FOLLOWING TECHNICAL TRADING RULES

When exchange-rate swings are sustained and pronounced, the profitability of most technical trading rules will not be seriously undermined if the trading rule tends to be a bit late in drawing attention to a shift in market

FIGURE 1-8

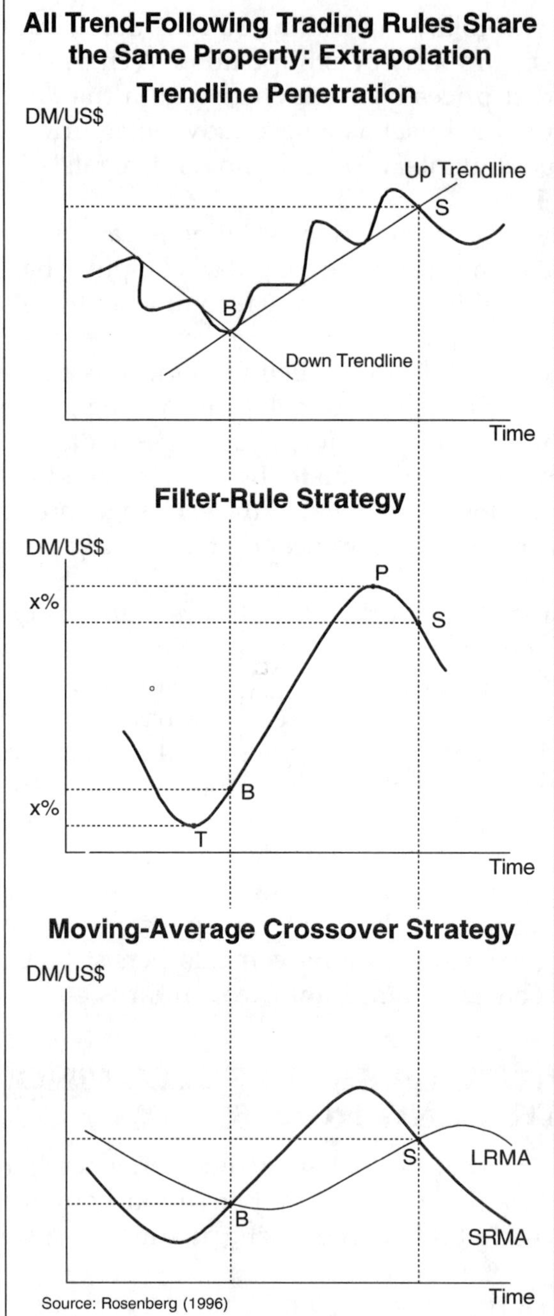

Source: Rosenberg (1996)

direction. Unfortunately, this market-swing requirement could prove in many cases to be a tall order. In markets that exhibit little overall price variation or are not highly trended, an investor who adheres to a trend-following trading rule will find his portfolio vulnerable to potential whipsaw losses caused by frequent false signals.

Consider the two exchange rate series depicted in Figure 1–9. The series on the left illustrates the working of a profitable *x*% filter rule trading strategy. A recommendation to buy dollars is issued at point *B* when the DM/US$ exchange rate rises *x*% from its recent trough at point *T*. The ensuing market action then carries the DM/US$ exchange rate to a peak at point *P*, but a recommendation to sell dollars is issued only at point *S*, when the exchange rate has fallen *x*% from its peak level. An investor who rigidly adhered to this *x*% filter rule trading strategy would have bought dollars at *B* and sold dollars at *S*, with the spread between *S* and *B* representing the profit margin per dollar invested.

The series on the right illustrates how losses can be incurred using a filter rule trading strategy. The series on the right behaves in a similar fashion as the series on the left, except for the fact that the dollar's upswing is less pronounced following the recommendation to buy dollars at point B_1. That is, the swing in the DM/US$ exchange rate from B_1 to P_1 falls short of the swing from *B* to *P* in the chart on the left. At P_1, the dollar's upward momentum is shown to lose steam far earlier than was the case in the series on the left. Indeed, the DM/US$ actually begins to lose ground soon after its initial rise and a sell signal is eventually issued at point S_1. Since the selling price (S_1) lies below the purchase price (B_1), a loss is incurred with the spread between S_1 and B_1 representing the margin of loss per dollar invested. Hence, the buy recommendation at B_1 proved to be a false buy signal, with the investor whipsawed in the process.

EMPIRICAL EVIDENCE ON THE PROFITABILITY OF MOVING-AVERAGE TRADING RULES

Studies on the long-run profitability of technical-based trading rules often find that simple moving-average rules would have generated significant excess returns over relatively long periods for most major currency pairs. We simulated more than 2500 sets of moving-average crossover trading rules for seven currencies versus the U.S. dollar—the Deutschemark, Japanese yen, Swiss franc, British pound, and the dollar-bloc currencies—over the 1986–2002 period, and unearthed the optimal moving-average trading rules listed in Figure 1–10. The criterion used to choose the optimal trading rule

FIGURE 1-9

Investors Who Follow a Trend-Following Trading Rule May Be Vulnerable to Whipsaws Caused by False Signals

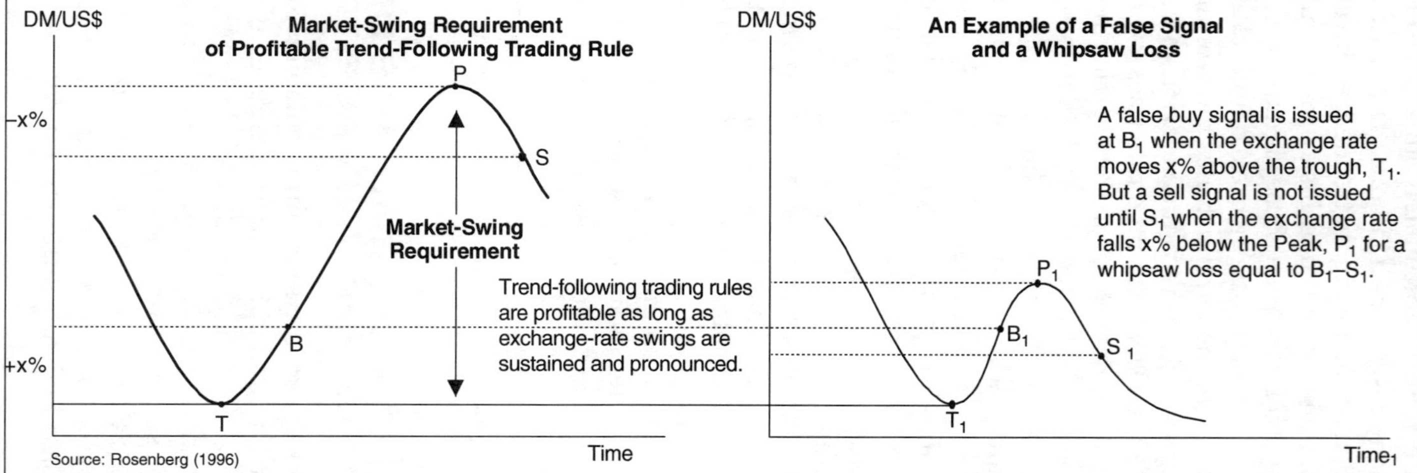

Source: Rosenberg (1996)

in each case was to identify the rule that yielded the highest Sharpe ratio (after adjusting for transaction costs) for the entire 16-year period.

For each exchange rate, there were a number of moving-average crossover trading rules that yielded similar attractive Sharpe ratios, and we list the top 10 trading rules for each exchange rate (see Figure 1–10). In each case, there was always one rule that eked out the highest Sharpe ratio, and it is shown in the column on the left. The moving-average crossover trading rules are ranked for each exchange rate and are listed from left to right.

Given the attractive Sharpe ratios reported in Figure 1–10, one might wonder why more investors do not rely on trend-following trading rules more regularly. One reason is that investors might have a fairly high Sharpe ratio threshold for committing capital to any particular trading strategy. For instance, many investors might not embrace a trading strategy rule unless it generated a Sharpe ratio of at least 0.50. And in some cases, an even higher Sharpe ratio might be required for an investor to add significant risk capital to a particular trading rule.

While the estimated Sharpe ratios may have been high on average for the 1986–2002 period, one should note that the Sharpe ratios were highly volatile when viewed on a one-year rolling basis (see Figure 1–11). Indeed, for most currencies, there are periods when risk-adjusted return performances are high and other periods when risk-adjusted return performances are downright poor. This was clearly the case for several key exchange rates in 2001, when one-year rolling Sharpe ratios fell sharply into negative territory.

FREQUENCY OF WINNING AND LOSING TRADES GENERATED BY MOVING-AVERAGE TRADING RULES

Most academic studies as well as our own work document the fact that moving-average trading rules have tended to generate attractive risk-adjusted returns over the long run. What is not often pointed out in these studies is the frequency with which winning and losing positions tend to occur. As Figure 1–12 illustrates, moving-average trading rules have tended to generate far more losing than winning trades on average. For example, in the case of the Deutschemark, Swiss franc, and the British pound, nearly three-quarters of the recommended trades generated by optimized moving-average trading rules end up as losing trades. Roughly two-thirds of the recommended dollar-bloc trades resulted in losses, and only the yen achieved a win/loss ratio close to 50%.

FIGURE 1-10

The 10 Best Moving-Average Crossover Trading Rules for 1986-2002

(Average Annual Total Returns and Sharpe Ratios for Selected Currencies versus the U.S. Dollar)
(January 1986-April 2002)

		#1	#2	#3	#4	#5	#6	#7	#8	#9	#10
DEM	**Mov. Avg. Days**	**1/32**	**1/33**	**1/31**	**1/28**	**1/30**	**1/29**	**1/34**	**1/20**	**1/35**	**1/19**
	Total Return (%)	5.01	4.89	4.38	4.20	3.96	3.88	3.98	3.58	3.43	3.13
	Std. Dev. (%)	11.06	11.06	11.06	11.06	11.06	11.06	11.06	11.06	11.06	11.06
	Sharpe Ratio	0.45	0.44	0.40	0.38	0.36	0.35	0.36	0.32	0.31	0.28
JPY	**Mov. Avg. Days**	**8/59**	**8/60**	**7/61**	**8/61**	**7/60**	**9/60**	**9/62**	**9/61**	**8/62**	**8/63**
	Total Return (%)	9.19	9.16	8.83	8.86	8.76	8.79	8.63	8.63	8.53	8.49
	Std. Dev. (%)	11.75	11.75	11.75	11.75	11.75	11.75	11.75	11.75	11.75	11.75
	Sharpe Ratio	0.78	0.78	0.75	0.75	0.75	0.75	0.73	0.73	0.73	0.72
GBP	**Mov. Avg. Days**	**1/19**	**1/18**	**1/20**	**1/21**	**1/22**	**1/16**	**1/24**	**1/15**	**1/17**	**1/23**
	Total Return (%)	5.80	5.45	5.36	5.32	5.28	5.20	4.91	4.82	4.80	4.49
	Std. Dev. (%)	9.46	9.47	9.46	9.46	9.46	9.47	9.45	9.47	9.47	9.45
	Sharpe Ratio	0.61	0.58	0.57	0.56	0.56	0.55	0.52	0.51	0.51	0.48
CHF	**Mov. Avg. Days**	**1/57**	**1/59**	**1/58**	**1/56**	**1/60**	**1/55**	**1/69**	**1/54**	**1/61**	**1/65**
	Total Return (%)	8.63	8.44	8.40	8.40	7.87	7.79	7.50	7.24	7.21	6.84
	Std. Dev. (%)	11.65	11.64	11.66	11.65	11.63	11.66	11.63	11.66	11.63	11.64
	Sharpe Ratio	0.74	0.72	0.72	0.72	0.68	0.67	0.65	0.62	0.62	0.59
CAD	**Mov. Avg. Days**	**14/199**	**14/200**	**14/197**	**13/197**	**14/198**	**13/198**	**15/195**	**15/193**	**15/194**	**14/196**
	Total Return (%)	1.88	1.88	1.86	1.83	1.82	1.81	1.75	1.66	1.64	1.59
	Std. Dev. (%)	4.81	4.81	4.81	4.81	4.81	4.81	4.81	4.81	4.81	4.81
	Sharpe Ratio	0.39	0.39	0.39	0.38	0.38	0.38	0.36	0.34	0.34	0.33
AUD	**Mov. Avg. Days**	**13/39**	**13/38**	**13/40**	**1/16**	**13/42**	**13/41**	**14/43**	**13/37**	**13/43**	**13/45**
	Total Return (%)	3.53	3.44	3.41	2.99	2.73	2.54	2.45	2.44	2.37	2.34
	Std. Dev. (%)	10.30	10.31	10.28	10.29	10.28	10.28	10.28	10.31	10.28	10.28
	Sharpe Ratio	0.34	0.33	0.33	0.29	0.27	0.25	0.24	0.24	0.23	0.23
NZD	**Mov. Avg. Days**	**10/17**	**11/15**	**10/18**	**10/15**	**11/17**	**14/196**	**10/16**	**11/20**	**11/16**	**11/14**
	Total Return (%)	5.20	4.99	5.10	4.76	4.67	4.28	4.28	4.41	3.85	3.38
	Std. Dev. (%)	10.79	10.80	10.78	10.80	10.79	10.14	10.80	10.78	10.80	10.81
	Sharpe Ratio	0.48	0.46	0.47	0.44	0.43	0.42	0.40	0.41	0.36	0.31

Note: A Sharpe Ratio measures the amount of return on an investment (less the return of a risk-free asset) per unit of risk, which is proxied by its standard deviation. Datastream is the source of the underlying exchange-rate data.

FIGURE 1-11

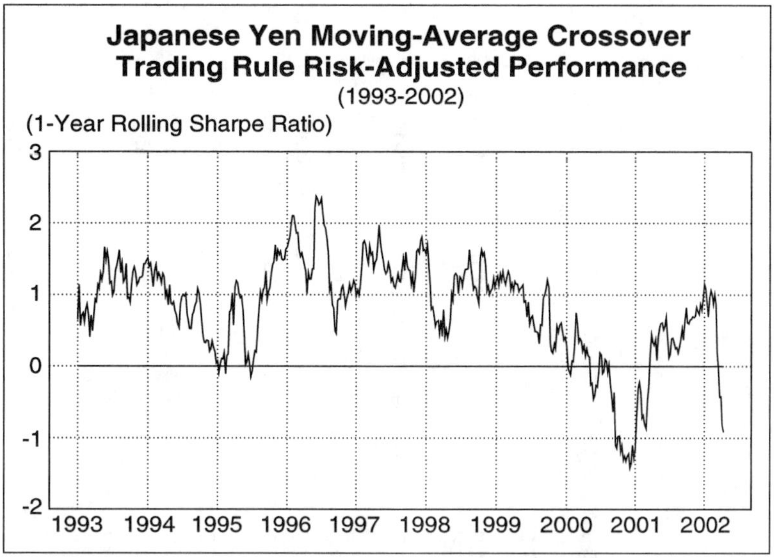

From a longer-run perspective, having a trading rule that generates such frequent losing trades does not pose a serious problem if the losing positions are cut quickly—so only a small loss is taken—and profits are allowed to ride on the less frequent correctly predicted winning trades. Indeed, this is often what is found to be the case. As shown in Figure 1–12, the average profit on the less frequent winning trades has tended to exceed the average loss on the more frequent losing trades by a fairly hefty margin. This margin of difference has been sufficient to allow moving-average trading rules to be profitable in the long run.

SHOULD MOVING-AVERAGE TRADING RULES BE VIEWED AS SHORT- OR LONG-RUN FORECASTING TOOLS?

The evidence on the profitability of technical trading rules suggests that there are often frequent runs of successive losing trades that have to be absorbed before a sizeable winning trade is generated. While positive returns are generated in most cases for the entire sample period, there are clearly uncomfortably lengthy intervals when frequent losses are incurred (see Figure 1–13).

FIGURE 1-12

Profit and Losses from Optimal Moving-Average Trading Rules

(Risk-Return Analysis & Winning versus Losing Trades of Selected Currencies versus the U.S. Dollar)

(January 1986-April 2002)

	DEM	JPY	GBP	CAD	AUD	NZD	CHF
Optimal Moving-Average Trading Rule Number of Days (SRMA/LRMA)	**1/32**	**8/59**	**1/19**	**14/199**	**13/39**	**10/17**	**1/57**
Average Annual Return	5.0%	9.2%	5.8%	1.9%	3.5%	5.2%	8.6%
Standard Deviation of Returns	11.1%	11.8%	9.5%	4.8%	10.3%	10.8%	11.7%
Sharpe Ratio	0.45	0.78	0.61	0.39	0.34	0.48	0.74
Total Recommended Trades	342	81	452	35	218	165	217
Wining Trades	91	37	126	13	61	58	57
Winning Trade Percentage	27%	46%	28%	37%	28%	35%	26%
Losing Trades	251	44	326	22	157	107	160
Losing Trade Percentage	73%	54%	72%	63%	72%	65%	74%
Average Profit on Winning Trades	2.97%	5.92%	2.27%	3.69%	2.03%	2.11%	4.63%
Average Profit on Losing Trades	-0.77%	-1.72%	-0.62%	-1.03%	-0.63%	-0.84%	-0.84%

FIGURE 1-13

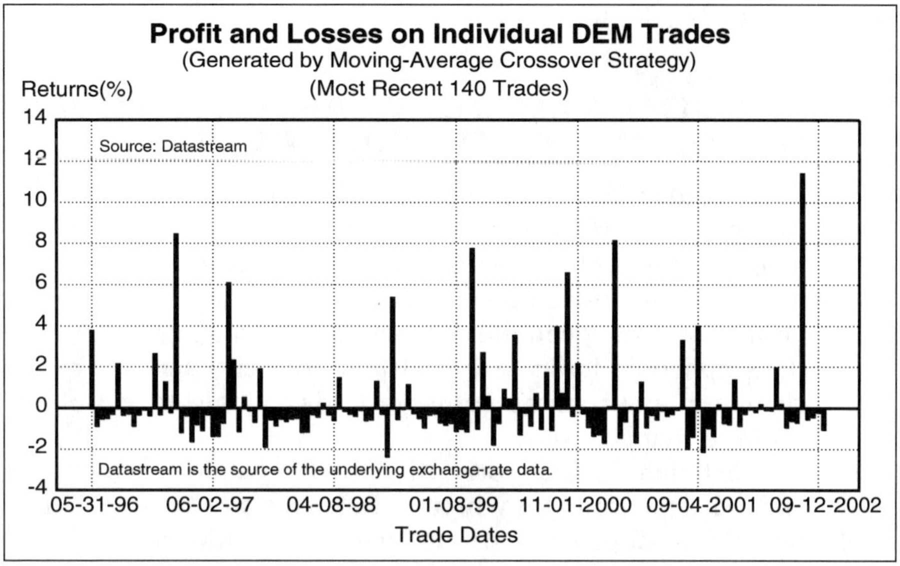

Our analysis raises several interesting issues. First, should technical-based moving-average trading rules be viewed as short-term forecasting tools, or instead would it be better to view such trading rules as long-term forecasting tools? The results here suggest that technical-based moving-average trading rules work best in the long run, not in the short run. Indeed, the odds that a moving-average trading rule recommendation will generate a profit appear to be no better than 25% to 35% in most cases in the short run. Second, it is possible that since the frequency of losing trades is so large, this might actually dissuade investors from using technical models in formulating short-term currency investment strategies. If investors shy away from using technical models because of the high frequency of short-term losses, this might explain why excess returns in the long run from technical-based models are not completely arbitraged away.

In order to successfully trade currencies using a technical-based moving-average trading rule, an investor needs to have staying power—considerable risk capital on hand to absorb possible frequent short-term trading losses—and patience. There might be other technical tools that could be used to cut down on the number of frequent losses on short-term trading positions, but one needs to be mindful of the fact that attempts to add "filters" or other types of technical bells and whistles to limit the frequency of false signals might hinder the upside potential of correctly predicted winning trades.

RANDOM WALK TESTS AND THE PROFITABILITY OF TECHNICAL TRADING RULES

Most academic studies have concluded that exchange-rate movements closely approximate a random walk process. A random walk (serial correlation) test seeks to investigate whether there exists a positive, negative, or zero linear relationship between today's change in the exchange rate and yesterday's change in the exchange rate. Evidence of a positive linear relationship would indicate the existence of trend persistence, since a positive change in a currency's value yesterday would tend to be followed by a positive change today.

Estimated serial correlation coefficients could vary between +1, 0, and −1 depending on whether there exists a strong positive relationship, no relationship, or a strong negative relationship between successive exchange-rate changes. The weight of evidence generally supports the view that for most currencies, the estimated serial correlation coefficients are often quite small and in many cases statistically insignificant from zero.

Although researchers often find support for the view that exchange-rate movements tend to fluctuate randomly on a daily basis, they also find evidence that exchange-rate changes are positively serially correlated when viewed on a monthly basis. Thus, although exchange rates may fluctuate randomly over very short time spans (that is, daily), they tend to rise and fall on a trend basis on a medium- and long-term (that is, monthly) basis. If so, this would imply that trend-following trading rules could be devised to profit from these medium- and long-term trends that exchange rates follow.

One of the problems with serial correlation tests is that they seek only to determine whether a stable "linear" relationship exists between successive exchange-rate movements. Although it might be the case that successive exchange-rate changes are linearly independent, they might nevertheless exhibit significant positive nonlinear dependence, which traditional serial correlation tests would not detect. This might explain why researchers have found that exchange rates follow a random walk, yet at the same time have found that trend-following technical trading rules have been profitable. Possibly there exists some form of serial dependency in successive exchange-rate movements; it's just that this serial dependence is not linear. If there exists some form of nonlinear dependence in successive exchange-rate movements, it would appear that trend-following trading rules are capturing this form of serial dependence.

ARE SENTIMENT AND POSITIONING INDICATORS USEFUL IN PREDICTING EXCHANGE-RATE MOVEMENTS?

Fund managers have turned to sentiment and positioning surveys in recent years as forecasting tools. In most cases, exchange rates move in the same direction that sentiment and positioning surveys are moving in the short run. For example, when sentiment toward the dollar becomes increasingly bullish—as reported in the weekly Consensus Inc. Survey of Bullish Market Opinion—the dollar tends to rise (see Figure 1–14). Similarly, when long U.S. dollar speculative positions are undertaken on the IMM (international money-market futures exchange), the dollar tends to rise as well (see Figure 1–15).

What does the empirical evidence say about the success of sentiment and positioning surveys in predicting exchange-rate movements? Our analy-

FIGURE 1-14

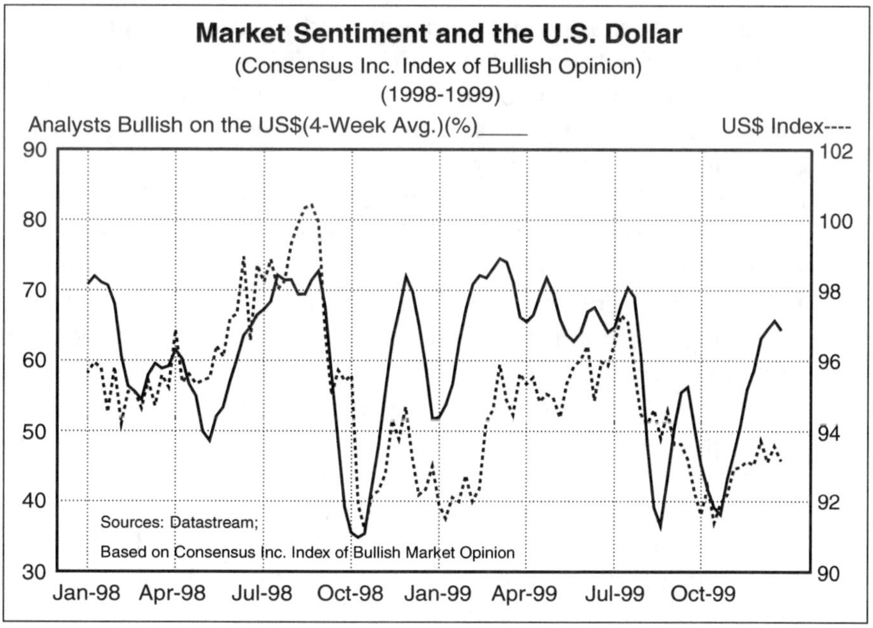

FIGURE 1-15

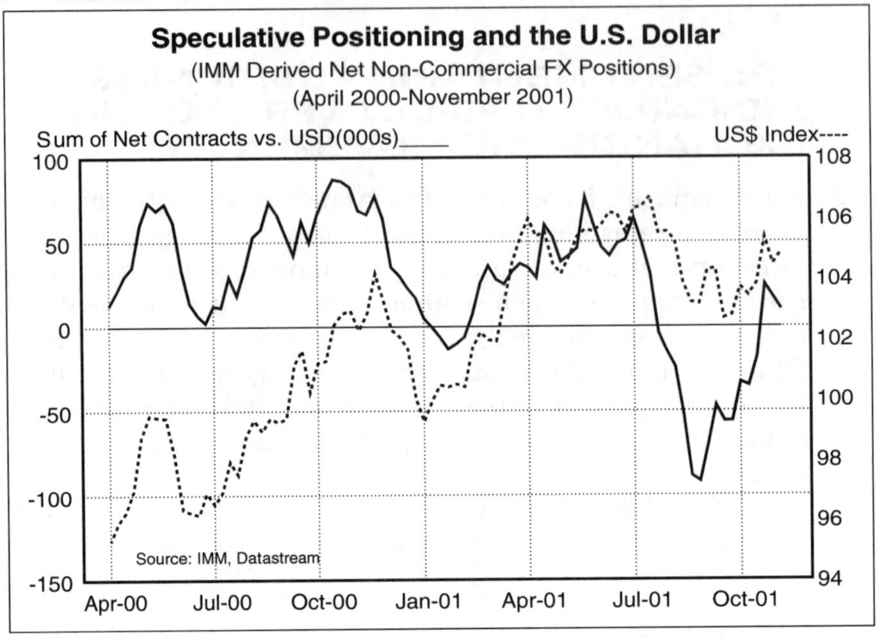

sis finds that changes in sentiment and positioning surveys are statistically significant, for the most part, in explaining contemporaneous changes in exchange rates. Lagged values of sentiment and positioning survey data, however, are statistically insignificant in predicting current changes in exchange rates. This suggests that sentiment and positioning survey data cannot be relied upon as forecasting tools.

What does the empirical evidence say about the usefulness of sentiment and positioning survey data as contrarian indicators? The trends in market sentiment and speculative positioning could be viewed as potential overbought or oversold indicators, if the rise or fall in each of those series appeared stretched relative to historical norms. Unfortunately, the empirical evidence suggests that there is no statistically significant relationship between overstretched sentiment and positioning surveys and subsequent changes in exchange rates. Based on these findings, it could prove risky to adopt a contrarian position simply because investors' FX exposures appear to be at extreme levels. History is replete with examples where overstretched markets have stayed overstretched for a considerable time. Perhaps all that one can say is that if one or more of those indicators moved into significantly overbought or oversold territory, then the *odds* of a reversal would have increased, but that it would not be possible to issue a definitive signal that an imminent reversal was at hand.

Although trends in sentiment and positioning surveys may not help us in forecasting future movements in exchange rates, they may nevertheless be useful as trend confirmation indicators. Because of the strong positive contemporaneous correlation between the sentiment and positioning data, on the one hand, and the trend in exchange rates on the other, sentiment and positioning data could be used in conjunction with a moving-average model to confirm whether an exchange-rate uptrend or downtrend is intact.

CAN ONE EXTRACT INFORMATION FROM THE CURRENCY OPTIONS MARKET TO PREDICT FUTURE EXCHANGE-RATE MOVEMENTS?

Investors often try to infer the market's expectation of future interest-rate movements by examining interest-rate futures contracts for various maturities or by examining the implied future path of interest rates embedded in yield-curve slopes. Similarly, investors often try to infer the market's expectation of future exchange-rate movements by examining the level of domestic/foreign interest-rate spreads, or the implied path of long-dated forward exchange rates.

Information on future interest-rate and exchange-rate movements can also be gleaned from the options market. Whereas interest-rate futures, yield-curve slopes, and yield spreads provide point estimates regarding expected future values, the options market provides a different piece of information—the market's expectation of the probability distribution of future interest rates and exchange rates.

For example, in the FX market, data on implied volatility for a range of maturities and strike prices are readily available. Implied volatility provides us with a measure of the marketplace's uncertainty regarding future exchange-rate movements. If implied volatility is rising, it "implies" greater uncertainty about future exchange-rate movements, and vice versa.

One could construct a forward implied volatility curve to glean expected future volatility movements by stringing together implied volatilities for a range of maturities with the same strike price. If the forward implied volatility curve were steeply upward sloping, the market would be pricing in the expectation of a future jump in currency volatility.

If the forward implied volatility curve were flat, the marketplace would be pricing in no change in the level of currency volatility in the future.

Does the forward implied volatility curve accurately anticipate future jumps in exchange-rate volatility? Because volatility jumps often occur suddenly and without warning, it is highly unlikely that the forward implied volatility curve would be able to consistently forecast future jumps in the exchange rate. Indeed, the Bank of England examined whether implied forward volatility curves anticipated the unwinding of the infamous yen carry (long dollar/short yen) trade in October 1998, and concluded that "forward volatility curves . . . did not expect the increase in volatilities (that occurred) in October 1998. Although (historical) volatility had increased throughout the summer, the forward volatility curve suggested that it would fall back towards previous levels." Indeed, in mid-September 1998, historical volatility was running around 22% to 26% and forward volatility curves were expecting implied volatilities to ease toward 14% in the October–November 1998 period. Instead, historical volatility soared to over 40% in early October when the yen carry trade was suddenly unwound (see Figure 1–16).

FIGURE 1-16

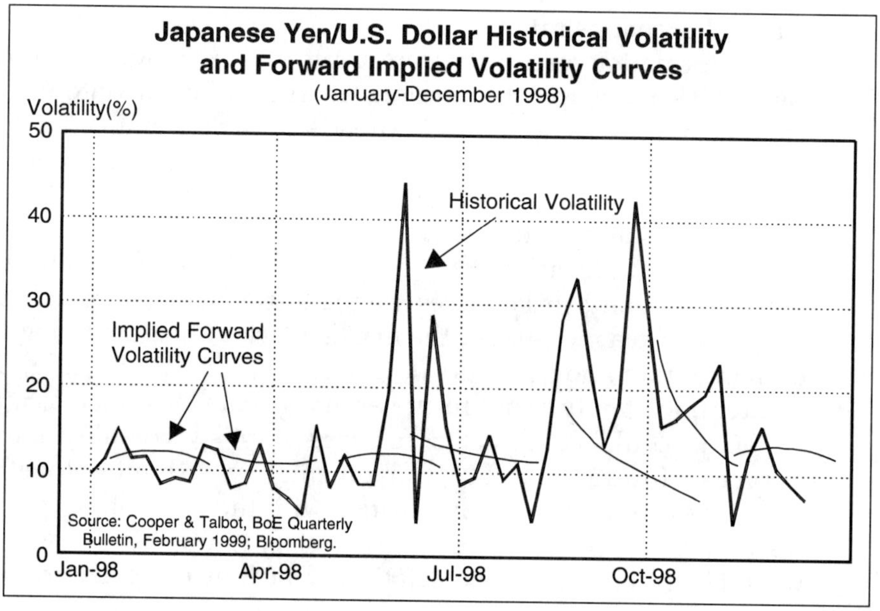

INFERRING INFORMATION ABOUT FUTURE EXCHANGE-RATE MOVEMENTS FROM CURRENCY RISK REVERSALS

FX traders often use risk reversals to glean information on whether the market might be attaching a higher probability to a large currency appreciation than to a large currency depreciation, or vice versa. A risk reversal is a currency option position that consists of the purchase of an out-of-the-money (25 *delta*) call and the simultaneous sale of an out-of-the-money (25 *delta*) put, both in equal amounts and both with the same expiration date. Risk reversals are quoted in terms of the implied volatility spread between the 25 *delta* call and 25 *delta* put. For example, if the implied volatility on the call were 2% larger than the implied volatility on the put, the risk reversal would be quoted at +2.0%. If the implied volatility on the put were 2% greater than the implied volatility on the call, the risk reversal would be quoted at −2%.

A risk reversal quoted at +2% would indicate that the market was attaching a higher probability to a large currency appreciation than to a large currency depreciation. This would indicate that the market was willing to pay more to insure against the risk that the currency will rise sharply than it was willing to pay to insure against the risk that the currency will fall sharply.

The key issue for traders and investors is whether the level or trend in currency risk reversals can be used to correctly anticipate future exchange-rate movements. The evidence indicates a high contemporaneous correlation between the trend in risk reversals and the trend in exchange rates, but no statistically significant relationship exists between lagged risk reversal data and future exchange-rate movements. Therefore, risk reversals are capable of confirming an exchange rate's trend but not predicting it (see Figure 1–17).

Nor is there evidence that overly stretched risk reversal measures can function as a consistently reliable contrary indicator. Indeed, the Bank of England's study on the unwinding of the yen carry trade in the fall of 1998 found that dollar/yen risk reversals failed to provide an early warning of the dramatic unwinding of long dollar/short yen positions that was about to occur.

FX DEALER ORDER FLOW AND THE DETERMINATION OF EXCHANGE RATES

In recent years, there has been increased interest on the part of investors and academicians in FX-dealer customer-flow data. One of the characteristics that distinguishes the FX market from the world equity market is that

FIGURE 1-17

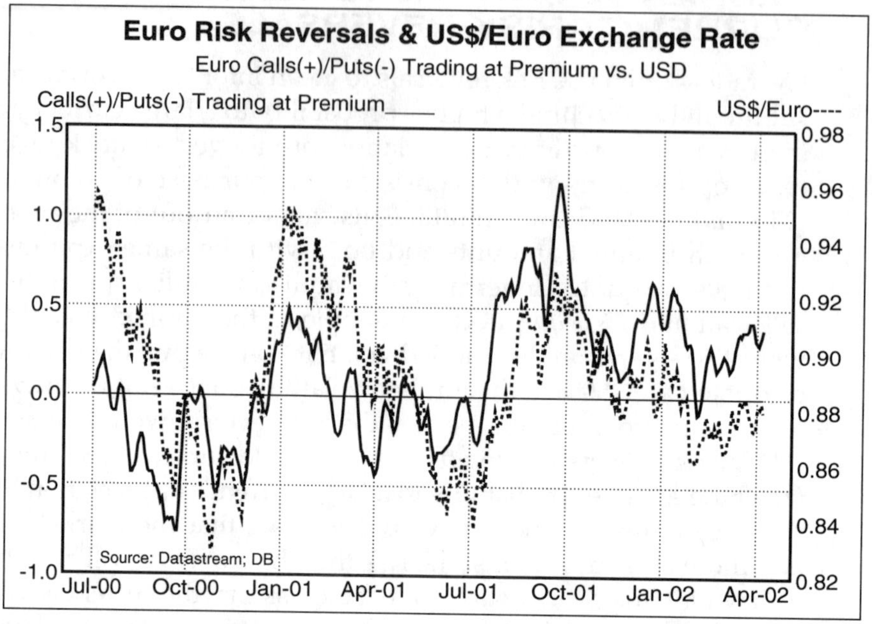

the FX market has considerably less transparency. Equity-market disclosure requirements mandate that all trades be instantly posted. Thus, volume and price data are instantly available to all parties. Not so in the FX market. No such disclosure requirements exist, which means that order-flow information is not immediately available to all parties.

Indeed, large FX dealers are in a unique position in that they are able to observe large trades that could move the market before other parties are aware of such trades. A recent survey of FX dealers indicated that most traders believe that large FX dealers have a comparative advantage over smaller dealers because they have a large customer base that gives them privileged information about customer orders.

One could envisage a marketplace where there exists both private and publicly available information. Publicly available information consists largely of macroeconomic-related data, which is available to all market participants at the same time. However, there may be microeconomic-related information that is important for exchange rates but is not publicly available. Examples of microeconomic-related information are shifts in risk appetite, liquidity needs, hedging demands, and institutional portfolio rebalancings. Such microeconomic-related FX flows give rise to buy or sell

FIGURE 1-18

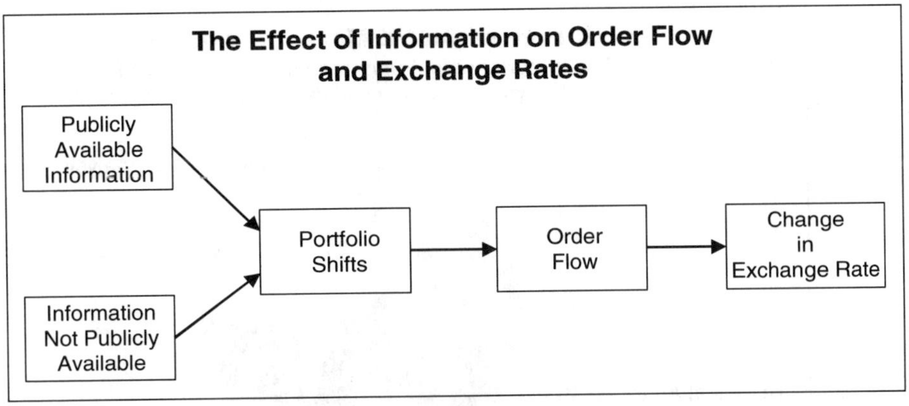

orders that influence the short-term trend in exchange rates, just as investor responses to macroeconomic-related information do. Large FX dealers can use the information gleaned from the change in their customer order flow to drive their own short-run strategies, which can then add to the upward or downward pressure on the exchange rate's value.

Viewing the impact of order flow in this manner, it is evident that order flow serves as a proximate determinant and not as the ultimate determinant of short-term exchange-rate movements. The ultimate determinant of exchange rates is the joint interplay of macroeconomic and microeconomic information underlying the change in order flow (see Figure 1–18).

Given the potential impact that order flow can have on exchange rates in the short run, a large FX dealer's order book can provide valuable information to both traders and investors who wish to keep abreast of underlying private investor shifts in portfolio behavior, whether those shifts are of a macro- or microeconomic nature.

HOW FX DEALERS AND FUND MANAGERS VIEW THE IMPORTANCE OF FLOW ANALYSIS RELATIVE TO FUNDAMENTAL AND TECHNICAL ANALYSIS

According to a recent survey of professional FX dealers and fund managers, both FX dealers and fund managers treat the analysis of foreign-exchange flows as a distinct form of analysis, independent from more traditional fundamental and technical approaches. A recent survey by Gehrig and

FIGURE 1-19

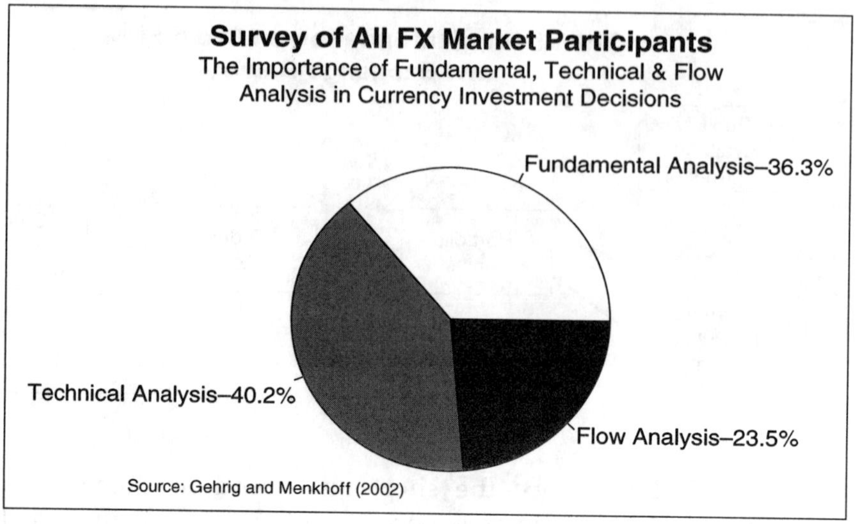

Menkhoff (2002) indicates that FX market participants in general attach the greatest weight to technical analysis (40.2%), followed by fundamental analysis (36.3%), and finally by flow analysis (23.5%) (see Figure 1–19). Among the participants surveyed, FX dealers were the ones who assigned the most weight to flow analysis, with 26.2% of them viewing it as their most important source of information. By comparison, only 16.8% of fund managers regarded flow analysis as their most important source of information, with 46.2% considering fundamental analysis as their most important source.

FX market participants generally regard the analysis of FX flows as more useful for short-term rather than long-term forecasting. As shown in the pie chart in Figure 1–20, 25.4% of all respondents believe that flow analysis provides valuable information only on an intra-day basis. Another 37.3% believe that the information provided by flow analysis can be useful up to a few days. Combined, 62.7% of all respondents believe that flow analysis should be limited to forecasting horizons up to only a few days. In terms of the longer-run usefulness of flow analysis for currency forecasting, 21.9% of FX respondents believe that flow analysis can be useful for several weeks, while only a modest 15.4% believe that flow analysis can be useful for up to several months into the future.

FIGURE 1-20

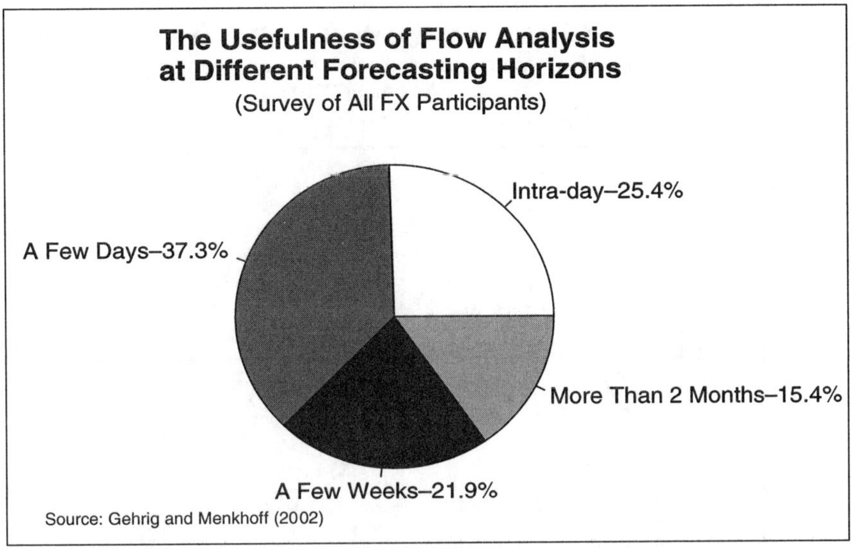

CUSTOMER ORDER FLOW AND EXCHANGE RATES—EMPIRICAL EVIDENCE

Like positioning and sentiment data, the empirical evidence suggests that FX customer order flow has a contemporaneous—rather than a predictive—relationship with exchange-rate movements. Indeed, the relationship depicted in Figure 1–21 indicates that the cumulative trends in customer-order flow and the trend in the dollar parallel one another on a contemporaneous basis. (Note that we needed to smooth out the erratic daily fluctuations in the customer-order flow data in order to discern this relationship.) There is no evidence, however, of a statistically significant relationship between lagged order flow and future exchange-rate movements, which would indicate predictive capabilities of customer order-flow on exchange-rate movements. This finding is supported by various academic studies that have investigated the importance of order flow on exchange rates.

Such findings should not come as a surprise. After all, if there are more dollar buyers than dollar sellers on a sustained basis in the FX market, both cumulative net dollar purchases and the dollar's value should rise in a parallel fashion. One should expect dollar purchases in the current period to drive the dollar higher now, not at some point in the future.

FIGURE 1-21

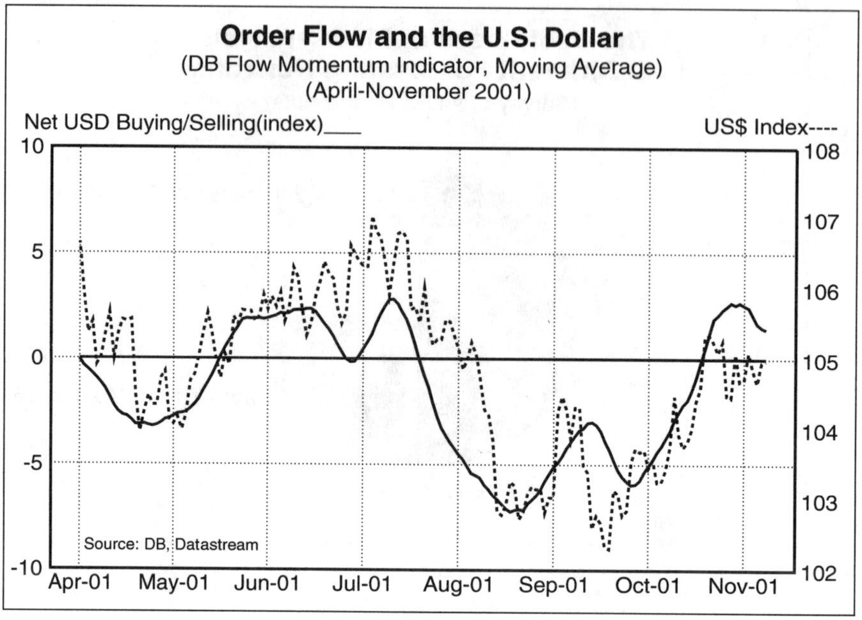

Empirical work on customer order flow's impact on exchange rates indicates that certain customers' FX orders may exert a greater impact on exchange rates than other customers' FX orders (see Figure 1–22). Research by Fan and Lyons (1999) indicates that real-money accounts (that is, unleveraged fund managers) played a more important role in driving the euro than did corporate or hedge fund players. In the case of the yen, hedge funds and corporates played a relatively more important role.

INVESTOR POSITIONING AND THE TREND IN EXCHANGE RATES

Surveys of global fund-manager positioning are another tool that FX market participants have turned to in recent years for short-term exchange-rate forecasting. The monthly Russell-Mellon survey summarizes the portfolio positions of 28 global fixed-income managers in selected currencies and bond markets, with attention normally focused on the 25th, median, and 75th percentile exposures. The trend in investor exposure to the dollar in recent years is shown in Figure 1–23.

FIGURE 1-22

The Impact of Real Money, Hedge Fund, and Corporate Customer Order Flows on Exchange Rates
(January 1993-June 1999, Monthly Data)

	Real Money (Unhedged) Flow	Leveraged (Hedged) Flow	Non-Financial Corporate Flow
Euro (R^2 = 0.27)			
Regression Coefficient	1.5	0.6	-0.2
(t-Statistic)	(4.6)	(1.6)	(-0.5)
Yen (R^2 = 0.34)			
Regression Coefficient	1.1	1.8	-2.3
(t-Statistic)	(1.9)	(4.9)	(-3.5)

*Source: Richard K. Lyons, *The Microstructure Approach to Exchange Rates*, 2001.

FIGURE 1-23

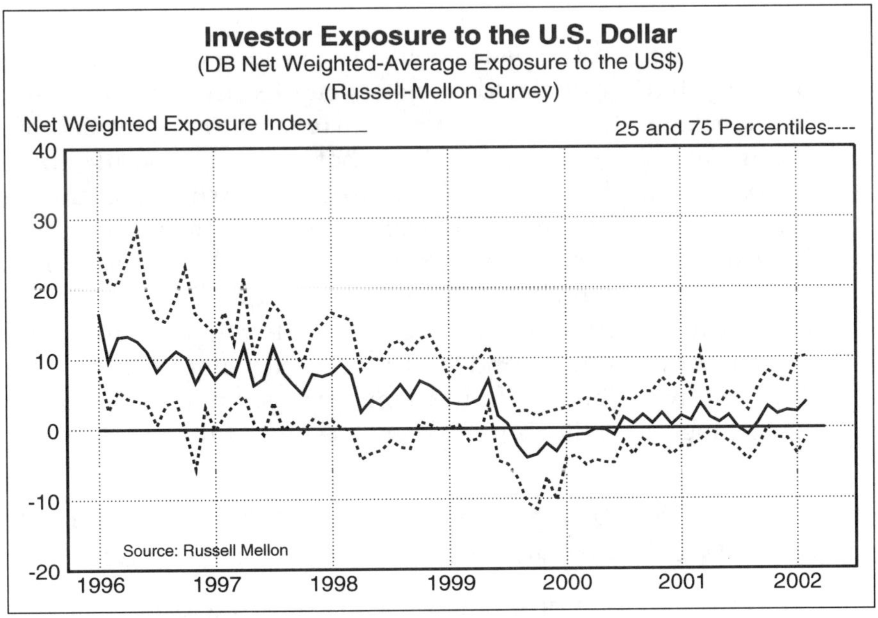

FIGURE 1-24

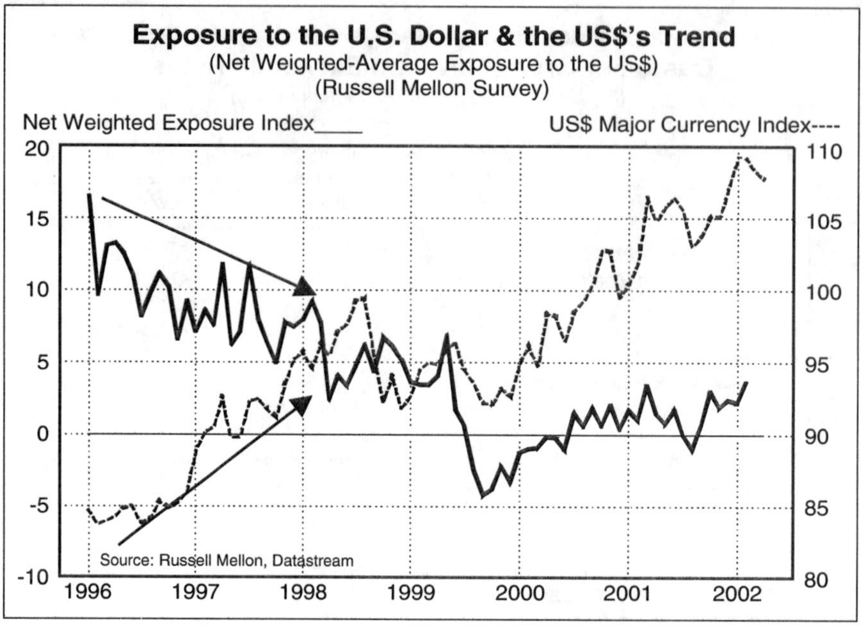

In an attempt to better detect underlying trends in currency positioning, we have calculated a net weighted-average exposure index for investor allocations to the major currencies in the Russell-Mellon survey. We make the heroic assumption that the range of all reported currency exposures can be defined by a normal distribution, and that the 25th, median, and 75th percentile exposure fit comfortably inside this normal distribution. We then calculate a net weighted-average exposure index for each currency, which can then be plotted against each of the respective currencies to determine if there is a stable relationship between the trend in investor positioning and the trend in exchange rates. As shown in Figure 1–24, the usefulness of fund-manager positioning in explaining, let alone predicting, the dollar's movements seems tenuous at best.

CURRENCY EXPOSURE AND THE DECLINE IN INVESTOR APPETITE FOR FX RISK

Surveys of investor positioning can also be used to gauge investors' appetite to take on currency risk. We have constructed a composite currency expo-

FIGURE 1-25

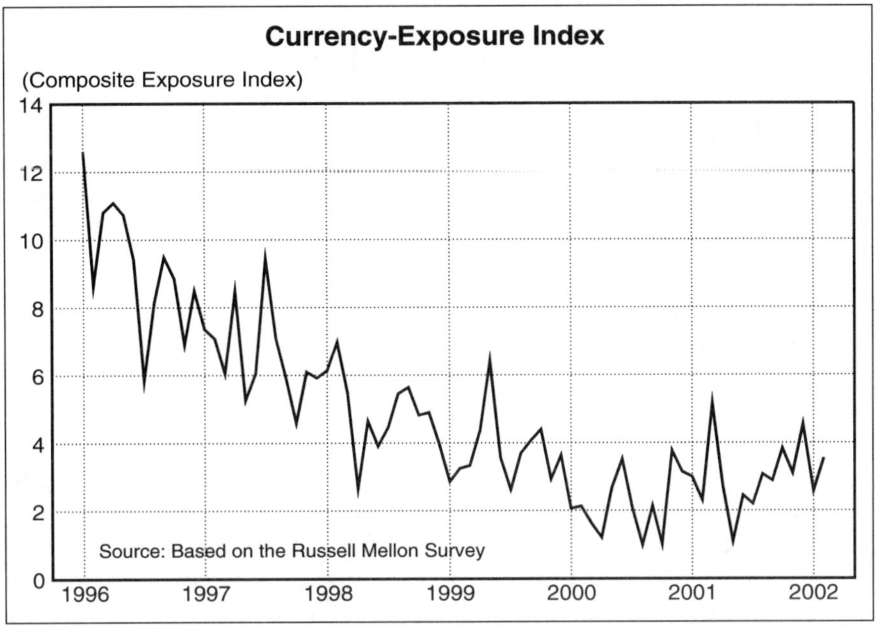

sure index using the net weighted-average exposures of the Russell-Mellon survey. The Currency-Exposure Index (see Figure 1–25) is a simple average of the absolute value of the net weighted-average overweight/underweight exposures that global fund managers maintain toward the dollar, euro, and yen. A high index value indicates that overall investor positioning is aggressive, while a low index value indicates that overall investor positioning is not aggressive.

The Currency Exposure Index reveals that investors willingly took on aggressive currency exposures in 1996–1997, with overweight and underweight positions averaging 6 to 10 percentage points above or below their benchmark weights. Over the 1997–2002 period, however, the appetite to take on greater currency exposures appears to have fallen sharply. Indeed, the average overweight and underweight currency exposures that investors were maintaining relative to their benchmark index in early 2002 amounted to just 2 or 3 percentage points relative to market norms as investors chose to position their portfolios closer to their benchmarks.

What accounts for this drop-off in investors' currency-risk appetite in the latter period? We believe that investors were caught in a bind in terms of weighting the conflicting forces of valuation and trend. For instance, investors may have felt compelled to underweight the dollar and overweight the euro, given the dollar's huge overvaluation and the euro's huge undervaluation in the late 1990s. But trend-following models were arguing that investors should have taken the opposite position. Given this conflict between valuation and trend, investors opted to take on neutral currency exposures by staying close to their benchmark weights.

RISK APPETITE SHIFTS AND CURRENCY TRENDS

Currency values can be affected by shifts in investors' overall appetite to take on risky positions. At any point in time, investors' overall appetite for risk could lean in favor of either risk taking or risk aversion. During periods of high investor confidence, investors tend to increase their exposure to risky assets. During periods of heightened risk aversion, however, investors tend to reduce their exposure to risky assets. When investors turn more risk-averse, they tend to close out positions in foreign investments and return to home base, or they tend to cut significant overweight or underweight exposures relative to their benchmarks, particularly if such exposures are leveraged.

It has been suggested that certain currencies may be more vulnerable than others during risk-averse periods. For example, countries that run large current-account deficits might see their currencies weaken if foreign capital were to exit during a period of heightened risk aversion. Likewise, high-yield currencies could be vulnerable if investors sought to unwind risky long high-yield/short low-yield carry trades in a risk-averse environment.

How does one measure investors' overall appetite for risk? A number of approaches exist, but by and large they all seek to capture increases in volatility, wider credit spreads, trends in commodity prices, and/or shifts in yield curves. We have constructed a Risk Appetite Index using the components shown in Figure 1–26.

There appears to be a strong contemporaneous relationship between the change in the dollar's value and the change in our Risk Appetite Index (see Figure 1–27). As with the other sentiment and positioning/flow measures, no leading or predictive relationship is evident, which is to be expected. After all, when investors' appetite for risk falls suddenly and sharply, it

FIGURE 1-26

Components of Risk Appetite Index

Component	Reason for Inclusion
G3 Implied Three-Month FX Volatility (average of USD/JPY, EUR/JPY and EUR/USD volatility)	Captures FX market uncertainty and risk.
VIX Index (CBOE OEX Volatility Index, expected volatility in the S&P100 index)	Captures uncertainty and risk in the U.S. and, therefore, global equity markets.
U.S. High-Yield Bond Spread	An indicator of risk in U.S. credit markets.
JP EMBI+ Composite Index	An indicator of emerging-market volatility, uncertainty, and risk.
Journal of Commerce Metals Index	Proxy for global-growth risks on the assumption that risk appetites will be higher during periods of stronger growth.
G3 Yield Curve (10-year bonds less cash rates)	Proxy for global growth risks, liquidity, and safe-haven flows into government bonds.

Construction of the RAI: The DB RAI index is a simple average of the deviation in each of the above indicators from their trend (standardized). In this way, the index overcomes problems associated with, for example, the structural widening in credit spreads in recent years. Periods spent in Risk Taking or Risk Aversion territory have been determined from the Risk Appetite Index using a standard MACD technique, designed to pick up shifts in the trend in the RAI.

should affect all markets at the same time. Implied volatility should jump upward, credit spreads should spike higher, the yield curve should immediately and perhaps dramatically alter its slope, and currency values should change at roughly the same time.

This contemporaneous relationship between exchange rates and risk aversion is evident in the way the Japanese yen/U.S. dollar exchange rate and the EMBI/U.S. Treasury yield spread (which is considered to be a measure of emerging-market risk) have behaved during recent periods of heightened risk aversion (see Figure 1–28). In the past seven years, there have been two occasions when the dollar has tumbled by 20% or more over a very short time span—January–April 1995 and August–October 1998. In both instances, the EMBI spread exploded to the upside. During both periods, the EMBI spread and the yen were responding to heightened risk aversion on a global basis as investors sought to withdraw from leveraged carry trades that had suddenly become highly vulnerable.

FIGURE 1-27

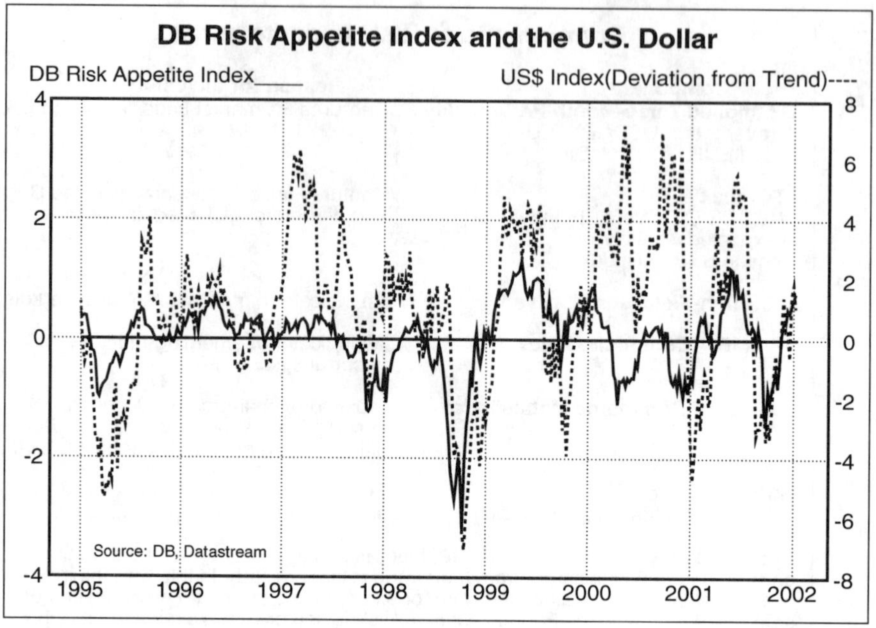

FIGURE 1-28

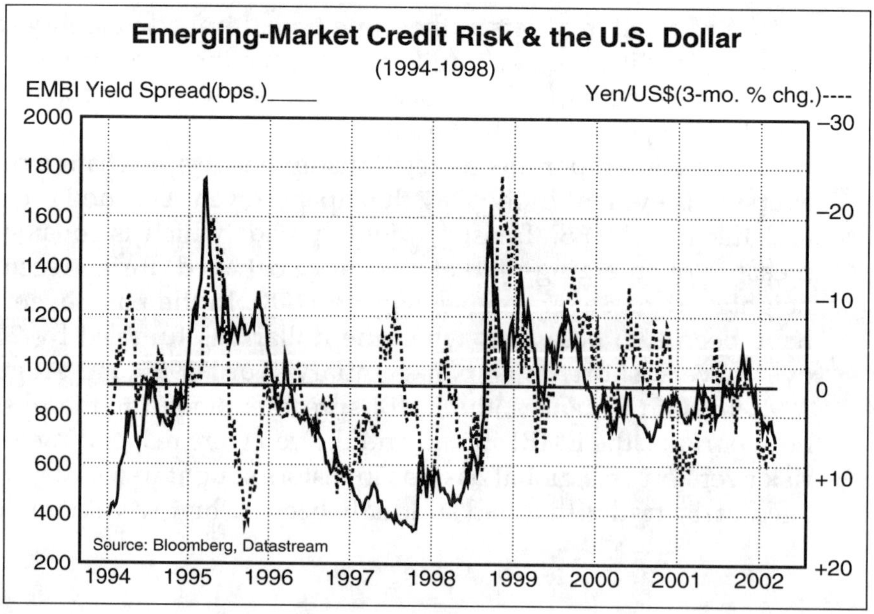

RISK APPETITE AND THE PROFITABILITY OF CARRY TRADES

Researchers have found that carry trades (long positions in high-yield currencies funded by short positions in low-yield currencies) work best in benign risk-appetite environments. That is, when investors have a strong appetite to take on risk, they are more apt to engage in riskier strategies such as carry trades, and if their level of confidence is high, they may engage in such trades on a leveraged basis. In contrast, during periods of high risk aversion, investors are more likely to cut risky positions, particularly positions that might be highly leveraged. Thus, if the inclination to take on carry trades tends to move positively with investors' appetite to take on risk, we would expect to find a close relationship between the profitability of carry trades and the trend in risk appetite indicators.

Indeed, as Figure 1–29 reveals, the rolling returns from being long the three highest yielding currencies in the industrial world and being short the three lowest yielding currencies in the industrial world closely tracks the trend in our Risk Appetite Index. Given this tight fit, fund managers who undertake carry trades on a frequent basis might find it useful to initiate carry trades when the risk appetite index is trading upward, and to cut such positions when the risk appetite index is trending downward.

FIGURE 1-29

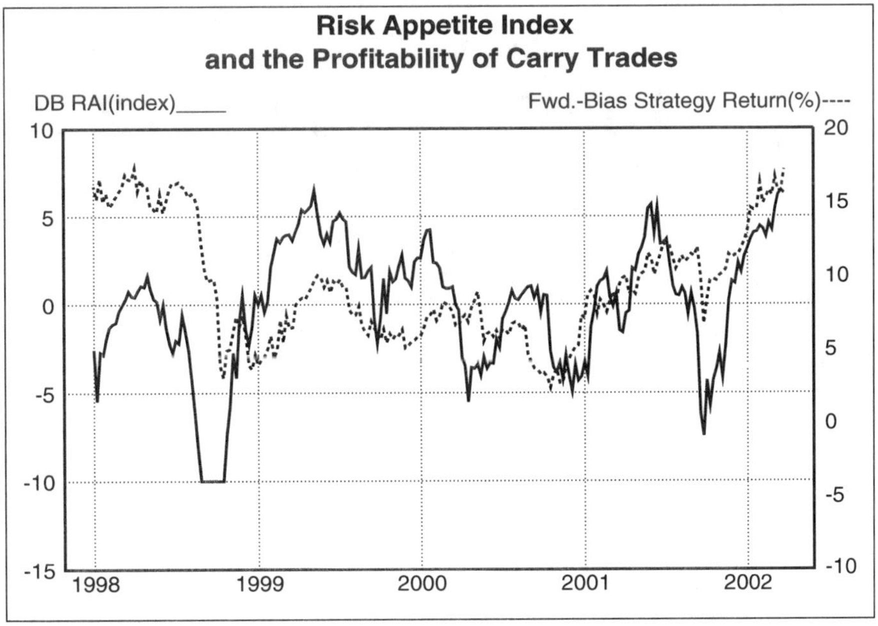

PART TWO

Exchange-Rate Determination in the Long Run

In the long run, a currency's value should gravitate toward its real long-run equilibrium value. If we were able to estimate which exchange-rate level represented long-run fair value, we would be able to identify the likely path that an exchange rate should take on a long-term basis. Unfortunately, there is no uniform agreement among economists on what exchange-rate level represents a currency's true long-run equilibrium level. The purchasing power parity (PPP) approach to assessing long-run fair value probably has the widest following among economists and strategists, but it is also broadly recognized that the PPP approach has serious limitations. That is because historically, the deviations from estimated PPP values have been both large and persistent, which suggests that fundamental forces other than relative national inflation rates have been playing an important role in driving the long-term path of exchange rates.

The failure of PPP to hold over medium-term and, in some cases, long-term horizons has led economists to consider alternative approaches to assess long-term value in the FX markets. For instance, the IMF favors the macroeconomic-balance approach to long-term exchange-rate determination, in which the long-run equilibrium exchange rate is defined as the rate that would equalize a country's normal or sustainable savings-investment balance with its underlying current-account balance. According to this approach, if there is a shift in a country's national savings, investment, or underlying current account, then the real long-run equilibrium exchange rate should adjust accordingly. This approach is quite similar to the Fundamental Equilibrium Exchange Rate (FEER) approach pioneered by John Williamson.

More recently, economists have sought to identify the long-run equilibrium path that currencies take with econometric models, by relating key economic variables to long-term trends in exchange rates. These studies have found that long-term trends in relative productivity growth, sectoral-productivity differentials, persistent trends in a country's terms of trade, the net external investment position of a country as a percentage of its GDP, and trends in national savings and investment have had some success in explaining the long-term path of exchange rates.

CHAPTER 2

Purchasing Power Parity

The absolute version of the purchasing power parity (PPP) approach to exchange-rate determination contends that the long-run equilibrium value of a currency is completely determined by the ratio of domestic prices relative to foreign prices. Absolute PPP is built on the notion of arbitrage across all tradable goods and services. Arbitrage ensures that the prices of similar goods in two countries will be equalized, when expressed in either local or foreign currency terms. For example, if the United States and Euroland produced a similar basket of goods, arbitrage should ensure that the prices of those goods would be the same in both regions. If the price of the U.S. basket suddenly rose relative to the price of the Euroland basket, the dollar would need to fall to offset the relative price change in order to keep the prices of the two baskets equalized.

The absolute evidence on PPP suggests that there are often significant and persistent departures from PPP in the short and medium run. One key reason is that arbitrage in tradable goods might be limited by transaction costs, tariffs, and entry and exit barriers. If such barriers to arbitrage were significant, a large "zone of inaction" might exist whereby firms would be unwilling to arbitrage traded-goods prices, and thus significant departures from PPP would exist over a certain range of exchange-rate movements (see Figure 2–1). Real exchange rates would fluctuate randomly inside this zone of inaction, but if the real exchange rate moved outside of the transaction bands, arbitrage would finally become profitable enough to bring the real exchange rate back inside the zone of inaction.

FIGURE 2-1

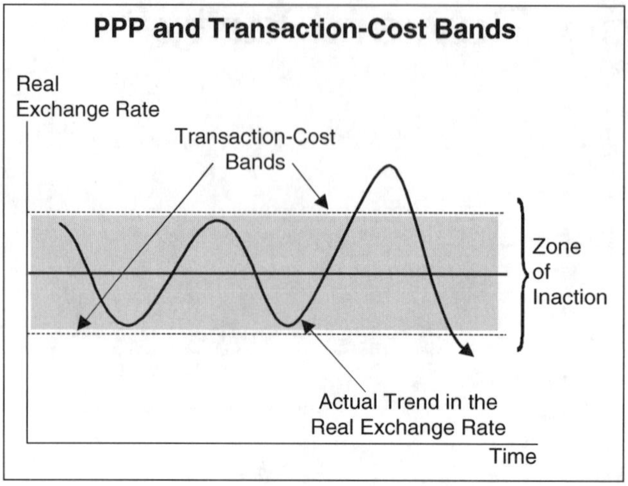

According to a recent survey, U.K.-based foreign-exchange dealers believe that PPP can be a useful tool for long-run currency forecasting but view it as a poor forecasting tool for the short and medium term (see Figure 2–2). But even for long-run forecasting, there does not appear to be overwhelming support for PPP. According to the survey, only 44.3% believed that PPP could be useful in predicting exchange-rate movements beyond 6 months, while 34.9% believed it was not useful, and 20.8% had no opinion.

PURCHASING POWER PARITY AND THE REAL EXCHANGE RATE

According to the relative version of PPP, the exchange rate over time will move to offset differences in national inflation rates. If, for example, the U.S. inflation rate averaged 5% higher than the Euroland inflation rate, the dollar would need to fall by 5% per annum versus the euro to offset the gap in relative inflation rates. Thus, if PPP held at all times, we should expect the nominal exchange-rate path to parallel the relative price level.

A country's real exchange rate can be defined as the nominal exchange rate adjusted for changes in relative inflation rates (see Figure 2–3). The dollar's real value would be unchanged if the dollar's nominal value moved exactly in line with changes in U.S./foreign inflation differentials. Thus, if the United States inflated at a rate of 5% per annum above the Euroland inflation rate, and if the dollar fell by 5% per annum versus the euro

FIGURE 2-2

Survey of U.K.-Based FX Dealers on the Validity of PPP as a Forecasting Tool

Question: Do you think PPP can be used to predict exchange-rate movements?

	Intra-Day	Medium Run (within 6 months)	Long Run (over 6 months)
Yes	4.8	16.4	44.3
No	87.4	67.3	34.9
No Opinion	7.8	16.3	20.8

Source: Cheung, Chinn and Marsh, NBER Working Paper 7524, Feb. 2000.

FIGURE 2-3

Real Exchange Rate Determination

$$\dot{q} = \dot{e} - (\dot{p}^* - \dot{p})$$

where:

$\dot{q}$ = change in the real exchange rate

$\dot{e}$ = change in the nominal exchange rate

$(\dot{p}^* - \dot{p})$ = change in relative price levels

at the same time, the dollar's real value versus the euro would be unchanged over time. Indeed, if PPP holds over time, then the real exchange rate would be constant over time as well.

Many analysts use the trend in real exchange rates as a gauge to assess a country's long-run competitiveness. If a country inflated at a rapid rate relative to its trading partners, and if its currency failed to decline in tandem, the currency's real value would, as a consequence, rise. The rise in the real exchange rate could be viewed as a measure of the loss in that country's competitiveness versus its trading partners. If, instead, the nominal exchange rate declined to exactly offset the difference in relative inflation rates, then the real exchange rate would have been constant and there would have been no change in price competitiveness (see Figure 2–4).

FIGURE 2-4

Relative Price Levels and Nominal and Real Exchange Rates

If PPP held at all times, then nominal exchange rates would be expected to track changes in relative prices...

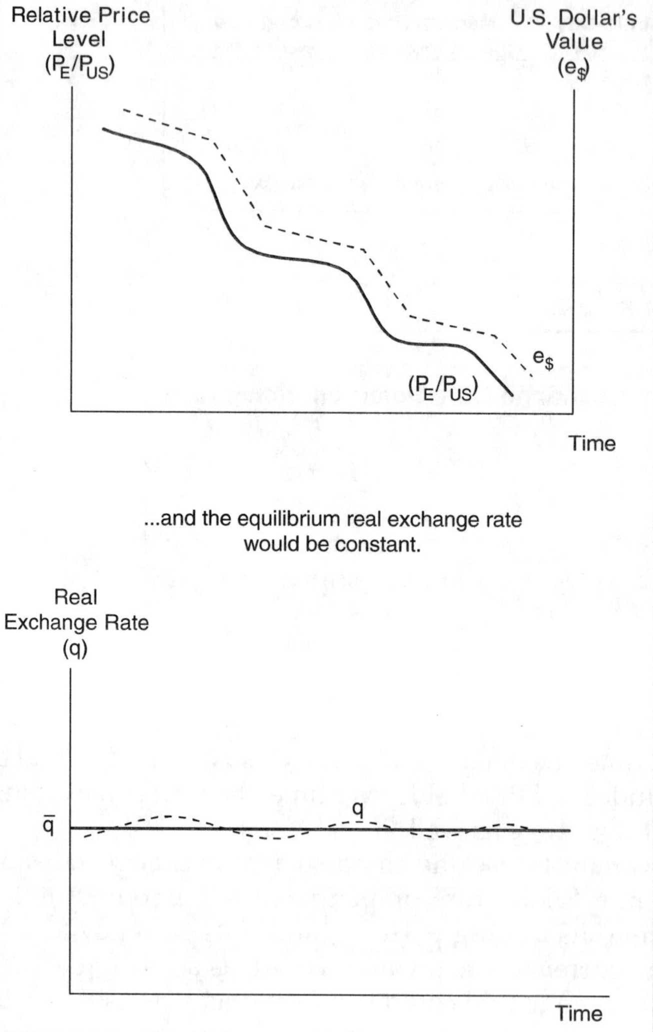

REAL APPRECIATIONS AND EXCHANGE-RATE MISALIGNMENTS

PPP misalignments occur when nominal exchange rates fail to move in line with relative inflation rates. Consider what would happen if the U.S. inflation rate averaged 5% per annum faster than Euroland's inflation rate but the U.S. dollar/euro exchange rate was fixed. By preventing a decline in the dollar's nominal value that would offset the relatively higher Unied States inflation rate, the dollar's real value

$$\dot{q}_\$ = \bar{\dot{e}}_\$ - (\dot{p}_E - \dot{p}_{US})$$

would be pushed steadily higher as the gap between the fixed nominal value for the dollar, $\bar{\dot{e}}_\$$, and a falling inflation differential, $(\dot{p}_E - \dot{p}_{US})$, steadily widened. The more the United States inflates relative to Euroland, with no offsetting dollar depreciation, the less competitive the United States would be (see Figure 2–5).

PPP misalignments can also occur if the nominal exchange rate rises or falls by large amounts relative to modestly changing or unchanging inflation differentials. For example, if the United States and Euroland inflated at similar rates, but the dollar's nominal value nevertheless soared versus the euro, then the dollar's real value

$$\dot{q}_\$ = \dot{e}_\$ - \overline{(\dot{p}_E - \dot{p}_{US})}$$

would rise as the gap between a rising dollar, $\dot{e}_\$$, and an unchanged inflation differential, $\overline{(\dot{p}_E - \dot{p}_{US})}$, steadily widened (see Figure 2–6). The consequences of a steadily rising real value for the dollar would be a long-run decline in U.S. competitiveness.

PPP MISALIGNMENTS AND THEIR EVENTUAL CORRECTIONS

Evidence for both developed and developing countries suggests that PPP misalignments tend to build up gradually over time. A key reason why this pattern tends to recur so often is that in the early years of an overly appreciated currency, firms and households find a way to adjust, and this, at least temporarily, works to temper the harsh effects of real currency appreciation on the domestic economy. For example, firms may try to maintain market share by cutting their profit margins, while households may attempt to maintain their spending by running down their savings. Because of these and other adjustments, real growth might not show any

FIGURE 2-5

The Response of Real Exchange Rates to Changes in Relative Prices When Nominal Exchange Rates Are Fixed

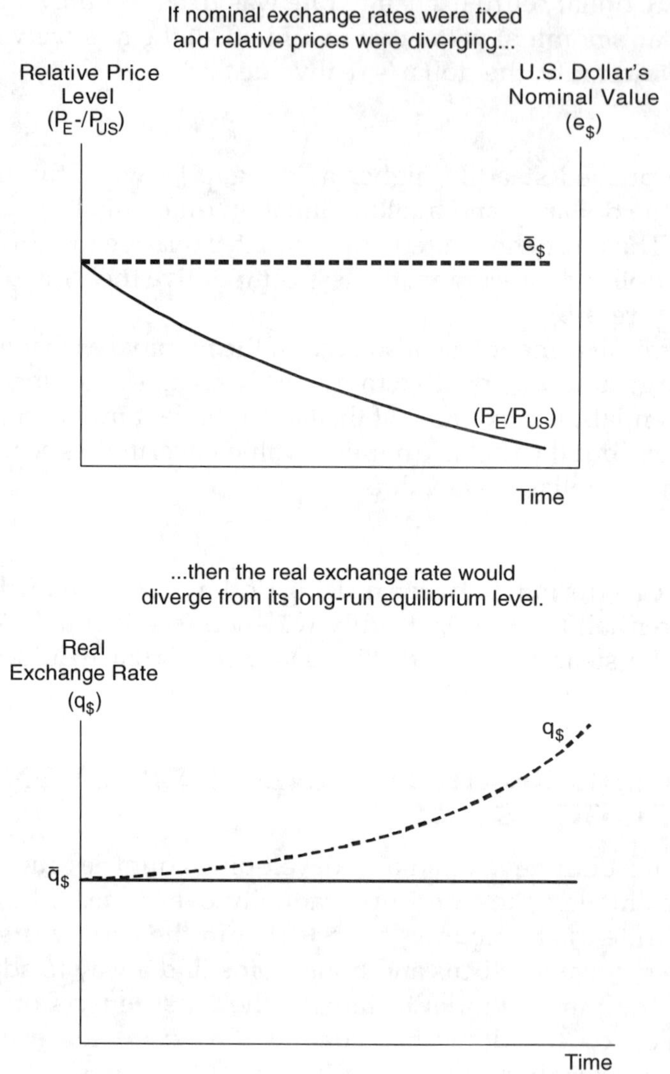

FIGURE 2-6

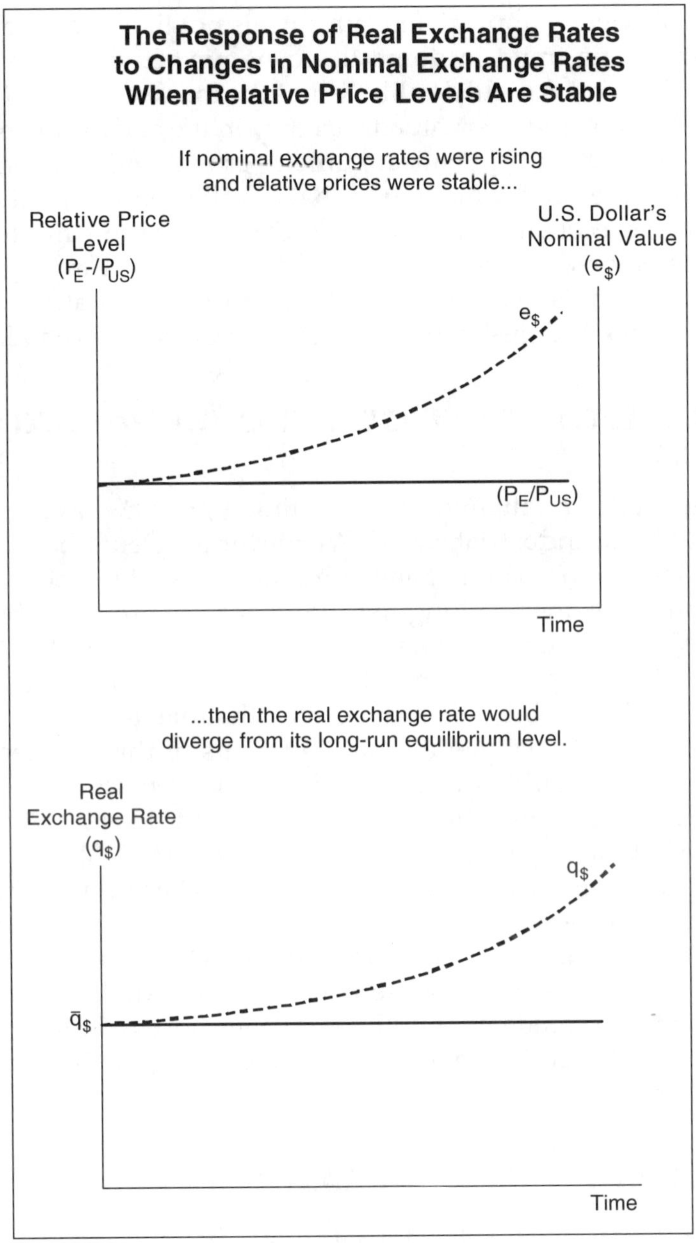
The Response of Real Exchange Rates
to Changes in Nominal Exchange Rates
When Relative Price Levels Are Stable
If nominal exchange rates were rising
and relative prices were stable...
Relative Price
Level
(PE-/PUS)
U.S. Dollar's
Nominal Value
(e$)
e$
(PE/PUS)
Time
...then the real exchange rate would
diverge from its long-run equilibrium level.
Real
Exchange Rate
(q$)
q$
q̄$
Time

visible signs of weakness and the current-account balance might not deteriorate significantly in the early years of a misaligned exchange rate.

Since an overly appreciated currency is not likely to give rise initially to a deteriorating trend in domestic economic activity or in the current-account balance, it is highly unlikely that the market will feel compelled to wage an attack on the overvalued currency in the early years of real appreciation. The larger a PPP misalignment grows and the longer it lasts, however, the greater the likelihood that it will eventually lead to a visible deterioration in economic fundamentals. Only when economic fundamentals deteriorate beyond a certain threshold level (point *A* in Figure 2–7) will market participants become emboldened to wage an attack on the misaligned currency and push it back toward its real long-run equilibrium level.

PPP CASE STUDY: DOLLAR OVERVALUATION IN 2001–20

Historically, PPP misalignments exceeding +/− 20% have been rare and short-lived in the industrial world. Whenever the Deutschemark/U.S. dollar exchange rate has risen or fallen by more than 20% relative to its PPP equilibrium level, the resulting misalignment has proven to be transitory.

In 2000–2001, the dollar was overvalued by 25% to 30%. This was the largest PPP misalignment that the dollar had experienced since the 1984–1985 dollar bubble, which suggested that the dollar was in an upside overshoot. Since exchange-rate misalignments of this size tend not to be sustainable, one should have expected that the Deutschemark/U.S. dollar exchange rate would eventually move back inside its +/− 20% PPP band, which is what indeed happened in 2002 (see Figure 2–8).

There are signs that the overvalued dollar has been taking its toll on U.S. competitiveness since 2000. A recent survey conducted by the Federal Reserve Bank of Philadelphia suggests that over 45% of U.S. firms were negatively affected in some manner by the dollar's overvaluation. Further evidence could be found in the rising chorus of complaints by U.S. industry, as reflected in the letter, reprinted in Figure 2–10, from leading manufacturing associations to the U.S. Treasury Secretary.

U.S. DOLLAR PPP ESTIMATES IN 2002

Different approaches to calculating PPP are likely to yield different estimates of the dollar's PPP fair value. We favor a long-run averaging approach that allows us to circumvent the "base period" problem, in which

FIGURE 2-7

PPP Cycle of Exchange-Rate Misalignment and Correction

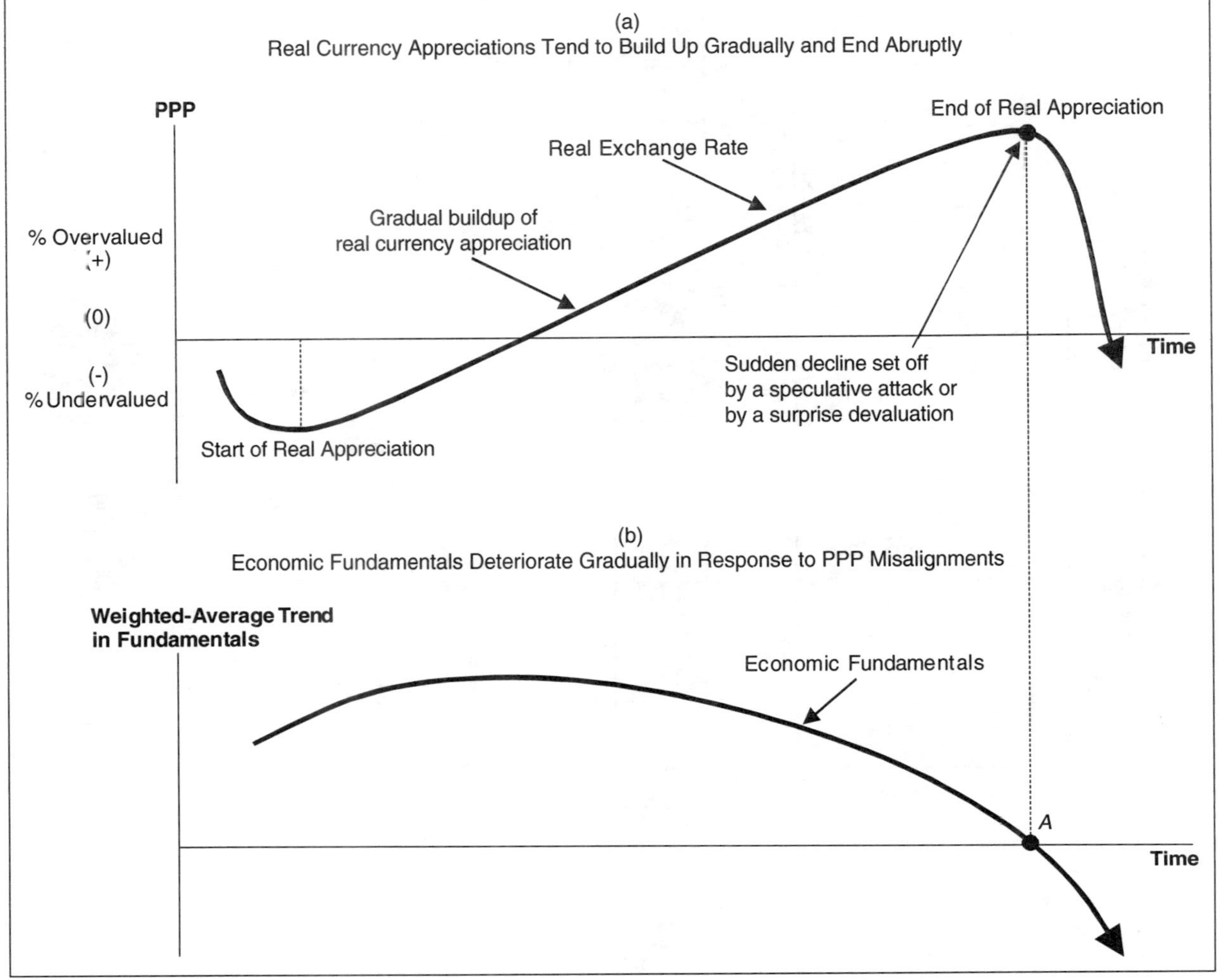

FIGURE 2-8

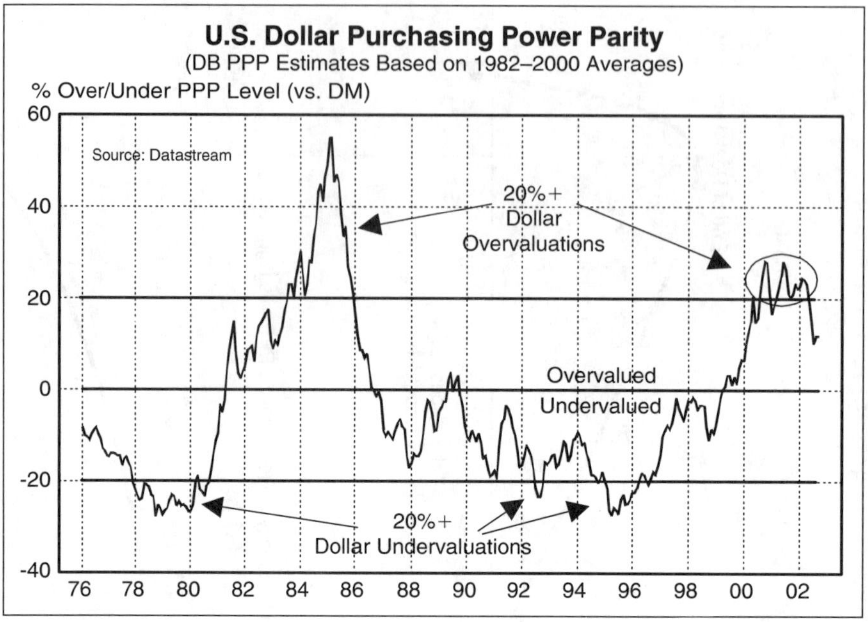

FIGURE 2-9

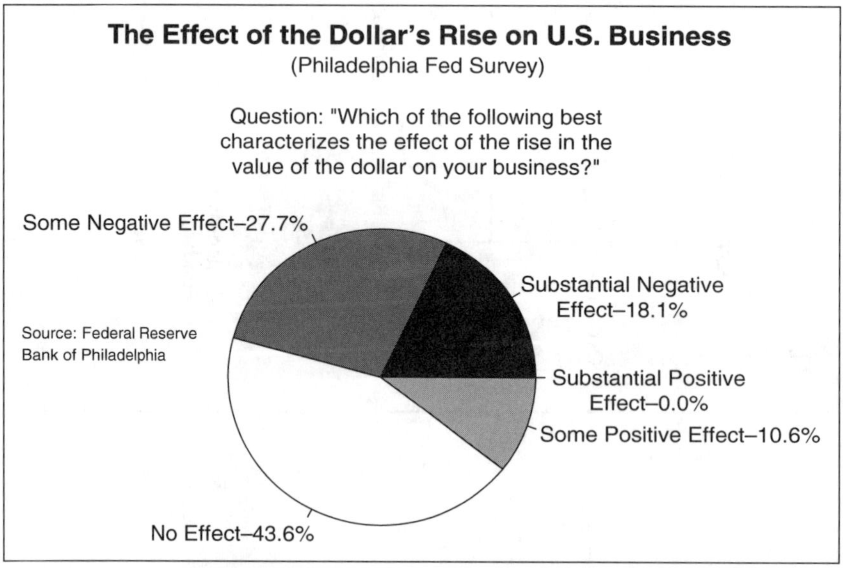

FIGURE 2-10

The Honorable Paul O'Neill
Secretary of the Treasury
Washington DC 20220
June 4, 2001

Dear Mr. Secretary:

We are writing to tell you that at current levels the exchange value of the dollar is having a strong negative impact on manufacturing exports, production, and employment. A growing number of American factory workers are now being laid off principally because the dollar is pricing our products out of markets—both at home and abroad. Small firms are being affected as well as large ones. As you balance your responsibilities for international monetary stability and domestic economic growth, we ask that you take into account the growing burden an overvalued dollar is imposing on U.S. manufacturing.

Since early 1997 the dollar has appreciated by 27 percent. Industries such as aircraft, automobiles and parts, paper and forest products, machine tools, medical equipment, steel, and other capital goods—as well as consumer goods producers—are being affected very significantly. No amount of cost cutting can offset a nearly 30 percent dollar markup.

The total effect on the U.S. economy is staggering. These output losses are particularly serious at this time, as they coincide with a general economic slowdown. The economic fundamentals have changed dramatically in the last six months. Production and profitability are down, and manufacturing employment has fallen by more than a half million jobs since mid-2000. Yet, in the face of slowing economic growth, declining interest rates, and rising manufacturing unemployment, the dollar has remained high.

In our view, a clarification of Treasury policy is in order, to be certain that it is not seen as endorsing an ever stronger dollar irrespective of the economic fundamentals. We urge the Treasury to make it clear that the value of the dollar should be consistent with economic reality and market conditions. This policy should be buttressed by a commitment to further reductions in interest rates and to cooperating in exchange markets as appropriate. Moreover, it is vital that the Treasury not condone currency manipulation by trading partners seeking to make their exports more competitive.

Mr. Secretary, 18 million workers and their families depend directly on the continued strength and competitiveness of American manufacturing. Many more Americans rely on stockholding in our companies for their retirement income. We would like to meet with you to describe more fully the effects the value of the dollar is having on us. We hope you will be able to accommodate our request.

Respectfully,

Jerry J. Jasinowski, President
National Association of Manufacturers

John W. Douglass, President and CEO
Aerospace Industries Association

W. Henson Moore, President and CEO
American Forest and Paper Association

Don Carlson, President
AMT—The Association for Manufacturing Technology

Stephen Collins, President
Automotive Trade Policy Council

Christopher M. Bates, President & CEO
Motor Equipment Manufacturers Association

PPP estimates can be distorted upward or downward if a particular year is chosen as the base period. In early 2002, we found the dollar to be significantly overvalued—by over 20% versus the euro—using either relative consumer or producer price inflation rates to generate long-run average PPP estimates (see Figures 2–11 and 2–12).

The Economist magazine's Big Mac Index estimated that the dollar was only 10% overvalued versus the euro in 2002. The price of a McDonald's Big Mac hamburger in Germany and France is roughly equal to the price of the Big Mac in the United States, but in Italy and Spain, Big Macs are 20% cheaper than in the United States (see Figure 2–13).

PURCHASING POWER PARITY AND THE YEN

PPP estimates are often better guides to medium- and long-run exchange-rate movements when traded-goods price indices are used to derive PPP estimates rather than when nontradable goods price indices are used. For example, the yen tends to move much more in line with the trend in Japanese/U.S. relative export prices than it does with the trend in relative consumer prices (see Figures 2–14 and 2–15).

Since PPP operates on the principle of arbitrage, international trade should ensure that tradable-goods prices in different countries are broadly similar when measured in a single national currency.

FIGURE 2-11

CPI-Based Purchasing Power Parity (PPP) Estimates

Currency (vs. US$)	March 15, 2002 Spot Rate	PPP Estimate	% Over/ Undervalued
Swedish Krona	10.32	7.02	-47.0
Canadian Dollar	1.59	1.24	-27.7
Australian Dollar	0.53	0.72	-27.5
N.Z. Dollar	0.44	0.60	-27.2
Euro	0.88	1.18	-25.4
Norwegian Krone	8.78	7.11	-23.5
Deutschemark	2.21	1.80	-22.9
Danish Krone	8.41	7.07	-18.9
Swiss Franc	1.66	1.45	-14.5
Japanese Yen	129.06	117.32	-10.0
British Pound	1.43	1.55	-8.0
US$ Index	117.18	96.32	21.7

FIGURE 2-12

PPI-Based Purchasing Power Parity (PPP) Estimates

Currency (vs. US$)	March 15, 2002 Spot Rate	PPP Estimate	% Over/ Undervalued
Swedish Krona	10.32	7.73	-33.4
Euro	0.88	1.14	-22.7
Australian Dollar	0.53	0.67	-22.1
Swiss Franc	1.66	1.38	-20.0
Deutschemark	2.21	1.85	-19.8
N.Z. Dollar	0.44	0.52	-15.9
Norwegian Krone	8.78	7.75	-13.3
Danish Krone	8.41	7.46	-12.8
Canadian Dollar	1.59	1.43	-11.2
Japanese Yen	129.06	117.36	-10.0
British Pound	1.43	1.46	-2.6
US$ Index	117.18	104.22	12.4

FIGURE 2-13

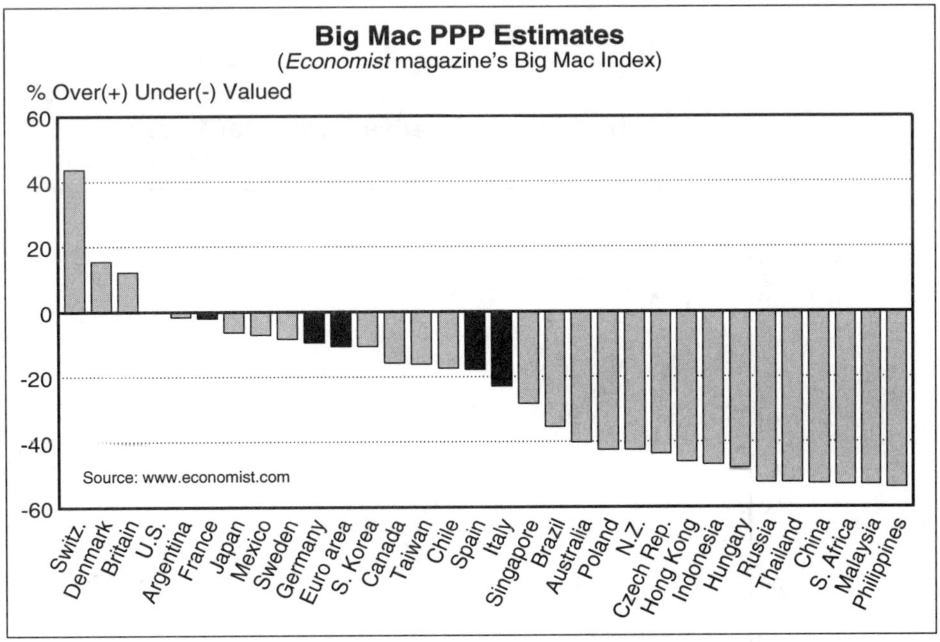

FIGURE 2-14

FIGURE 2-15

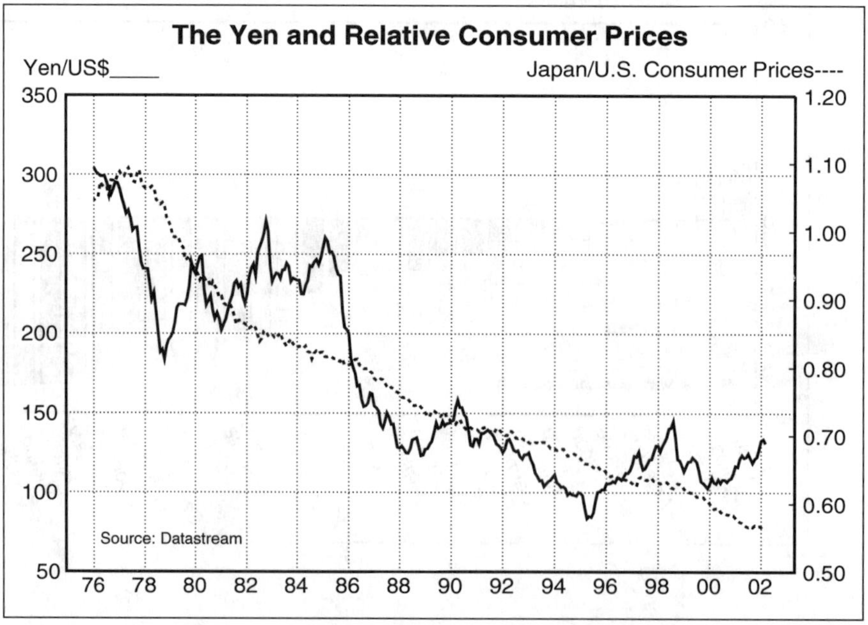

EMPIRICAL EVIDENCE ON PPP

There exists a huge volume of empirical work on whether or not PPP represents a valid tool for forecasting purposes. The weight of evidence suggests that although there are often significant and persistent departures from PPP in both the short and medium term, exchange rates do exhibit a tendency to gravitate toward their PPP values in the long run.

The consensus among academic researchers is that the speed of convergence to PPP is quite slow—PPP deviations appear to dampen at a rate of roughly 15% per year. This places the half-life of PPP deviations at around 4½ years for exchange rates in industrial nations. In other words, for any given deviation of an exchange rate from its estimated PPP value, roughly half of that deviation should be removed in 4½ years' time. As the charts in Figure 2–16 show, there is no positive relationship between changes in exchange rates and changes in relative inflation rates on a 1-year basis. However, as the time horizon is lengthened, to 6 years and beyond, a strong positive relationship becomes apparent.

PPP AND INVESTMENT STRATEGY

Since many empirical studies find that exchange rates exhibit a tendency to gravitate toward their PPP levels in the long run, long-term investors and issuers would stand to benefit by positioning themselves for an eventual correction of a large PPP misalignment. If investors could count on a rapid return to PPP, they could purchase undervalued currencies in the hope that the undervaluation would soon be corrected via an appreciation of the currency. Similarly, they would look to sell overvalued currencies.

For instance, the euro's gross PPP undervaluations versus both the dollar and the yen in 2002 did not appear to be sustainable, given the long-run track record of these two crossrates (see Figures 2–17 and 2–18). Yet long-dated euro/dollar and euro/yen forward exchange rates in 2002 did not anticipate a significant correction in the euro's PPP misalignment over the next 5 years. With conventional PPP analysis arguing for a long-term appreciation of the euro versus both the dollar and the yen, this seemed to present an opportunity for investors and issuers to exploit the divergent trends in PPP and long-dated forward rates.

Because the deviations from PPP can be large and persistent over short- and medium-term horizons, it can be dangerous to pursue strategies that are based solely on an expected rapid return of exchange rates to their estimated PPP values. The major risk to such strategies is that the deviations from PPP may widen further instead of narrowing. Investors who embrace a PPP approach to investment strategy would have to have

FIGURE 2-16

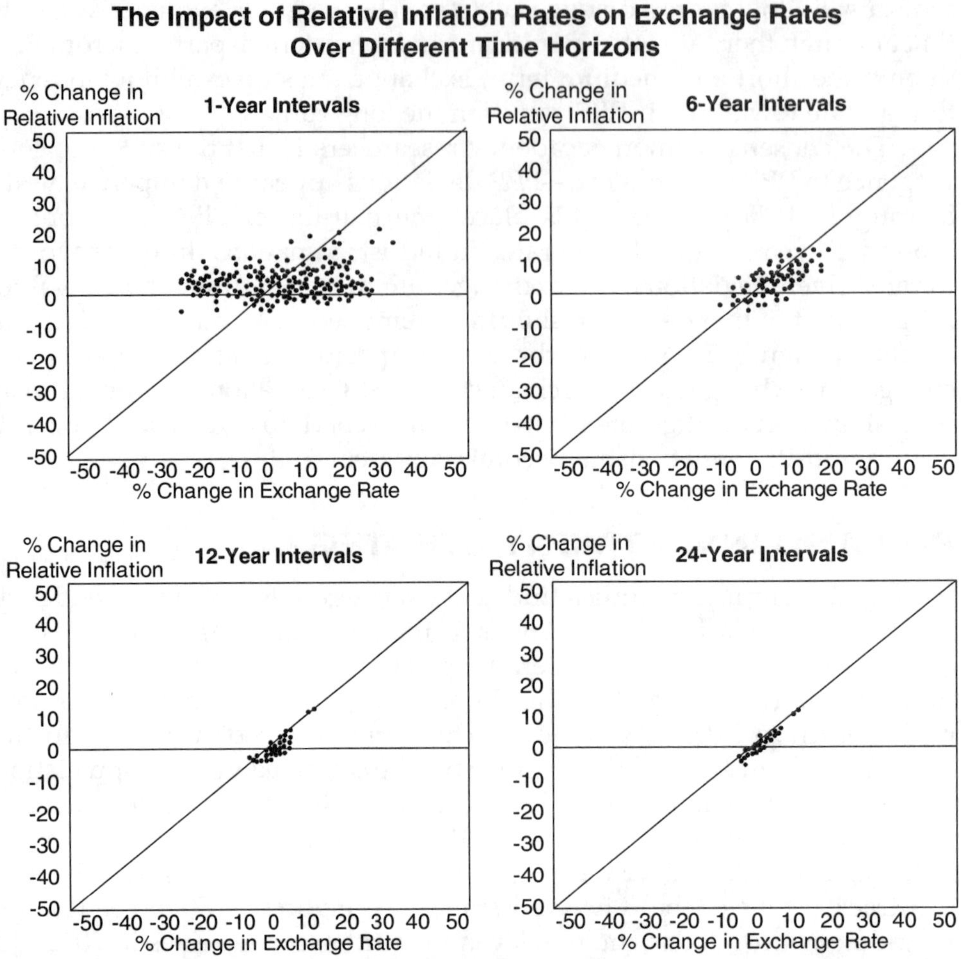

Adapted from Peter Isard, Hamid Faruqee, G. Russell Kincaid, and Marin Fetherston, "Methodology for Current Account and Exchange Rate Assessments," IMF Occasional Paper 209, 2001.

substantial risk capital on hand to absorb losses that could be incurred if the departures from PPP proved to be sizable and persistent.

One way to manage FX risk using a PPP approach to investment strategy would be to gradually take on long positions in undervalued currencies (or short positions in overvalued currencies) as misalignments build. Modest positions would be undertaken when the misalignments are small, and as the deviations from PPP grow and persist, more aggressive positions could then be undertaken.

FIGURE 2-17

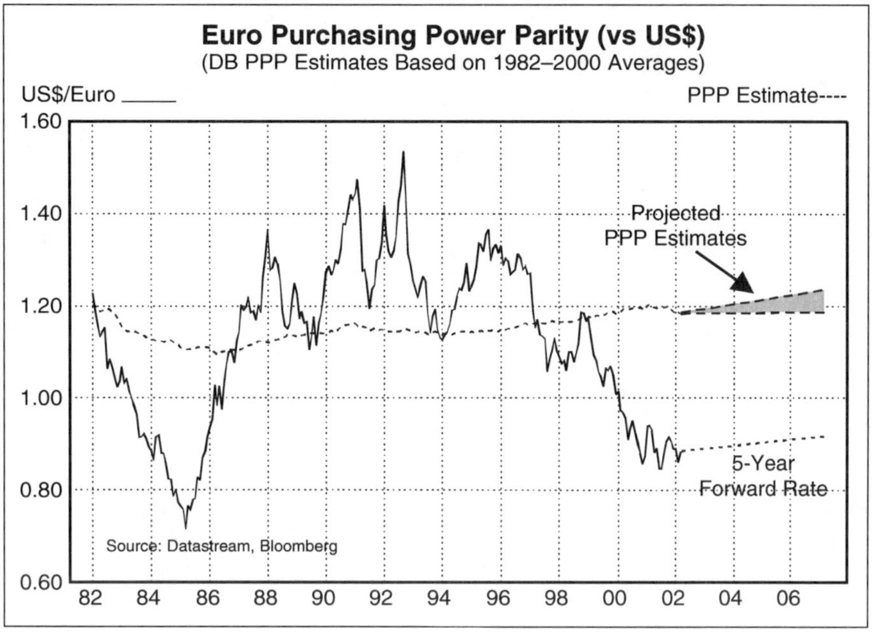

FIGURE 2-18

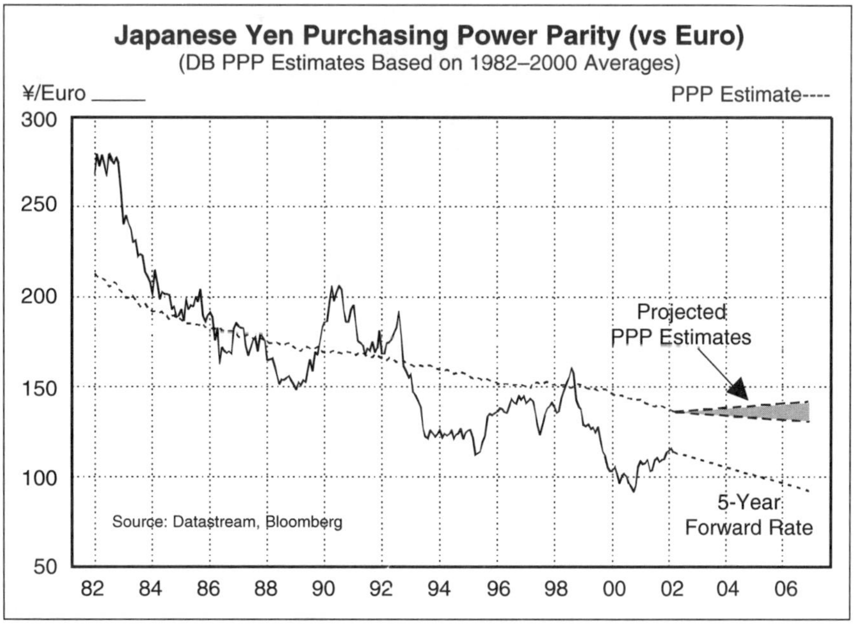

CHAPTER 3

The Macroeconomic-Balance Approach to Long-Run Exchange-Rate Determination

According to the macroeconomic-balance approach to long-run exchange-rate determination, a currency's real long-run equilibrium value is defined as that rate that equalizes a country's normal or sustainable savings-investment balance with its underlying current-account balance. The IMF uses the macroeconomic-balance approach to derive quantitative estimates of long-run fair value for all industrial-country currencies. The IMF's approach follows a three-step procedure.

1. The IMF first estimates a trade-equation model to calculate a country's underlying current-account position.
2. The IMF then estimates a national income model to determine the normal or sustainable savings-investment imbalance that would prevail over the medium run if that country were operating at its full-employment potential.
3. Finally, the IMF estimates the equilibrium exchange rate that would equate the underlying current-account imbalance with the sustainable savings-investment gap.

The IMF's framework can be visualized graphically using Figures 3–1 through 3–3. As illustrated in Figure 3–1, a country's underlying current-account balance tends to move inversely with the real exchange rate. That is, a country's current account would tend to improve as the currency's real value moved lower and its tradable goods became more competitive. Hence, the underlying current-account balance, CAB, is shown to be negatively related to the real exchange rate in Figure 3–1.

FIGURE 3-1

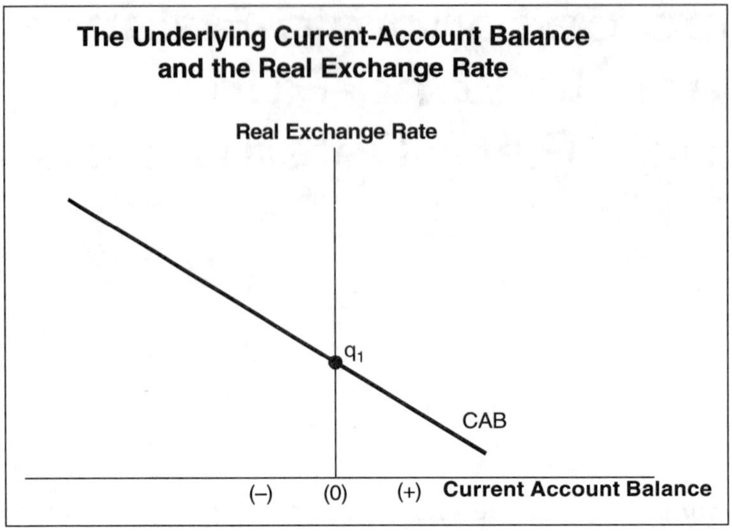

A country's savings-investment gap typically moves positively with the real exchange rate. Although the overall level of national savings does not typically respond to changes in the exchange rate, investment spending tends to move inversely with changes in the real exchange rate. This is because a rising real exchange rate lowers competitiveness and profitability, which in turn discourages investment spending. Thus, as the real exchange rate rises, investment spending should fall, and the gap between savings and investment should therefore rise. Hence, the savings-investment (S-I) gap is shown in Figure 3–2 to move positively with the real exchange rate.

A currency's real long-run equilibrium value is determined at the point where a country's savings-investment imbalance just matches its underlying current-account imbalance. The equilibrium exchange rate is shown to be $\bar{q}_0$ in Figure 3–3 where the S-I and CAB schedules intersect at point *E*.

EQUILIBRIUM EXCHANGE RATE: CONSTANT OR VARIABLE?

If a currency's real long-run equilibrium value is determined by the interaction of savings, investment, and external-balance considerations, its value would be constant over time only if there were no structural changes on the savings, investment, or external-balance fronts over the relevant time period (see Figure 3–4).

FIGURE 3-2

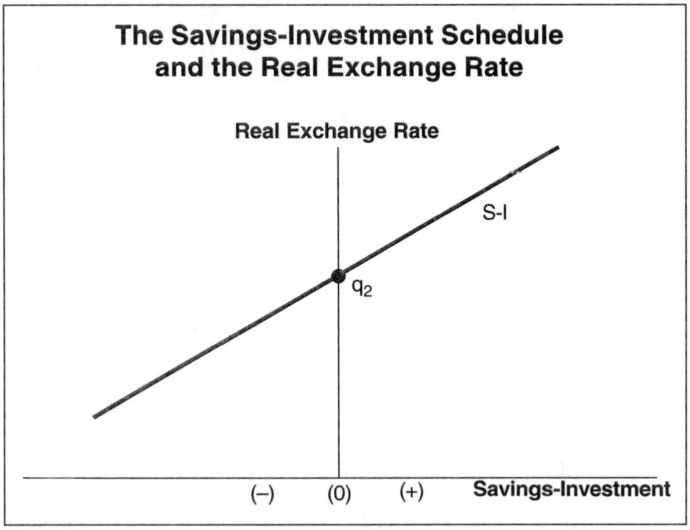

FIGURE 3-3

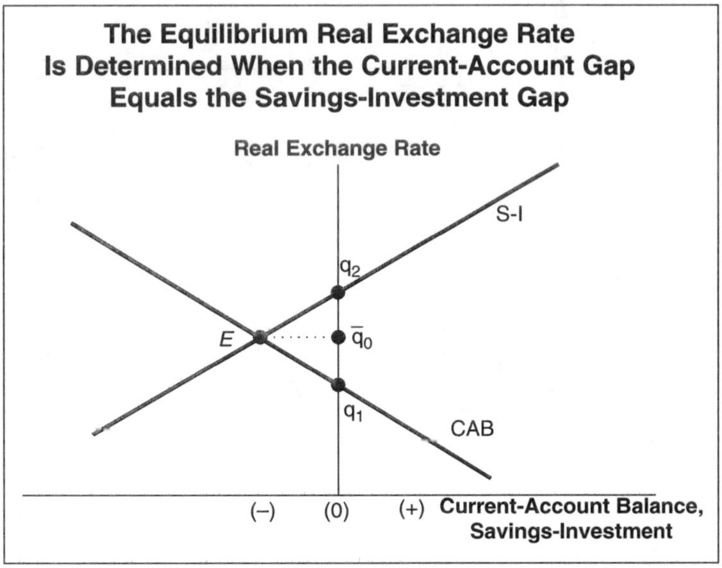

FIGURE 3-4

Stable Real Long-Run Equilibrium Exchange Rate

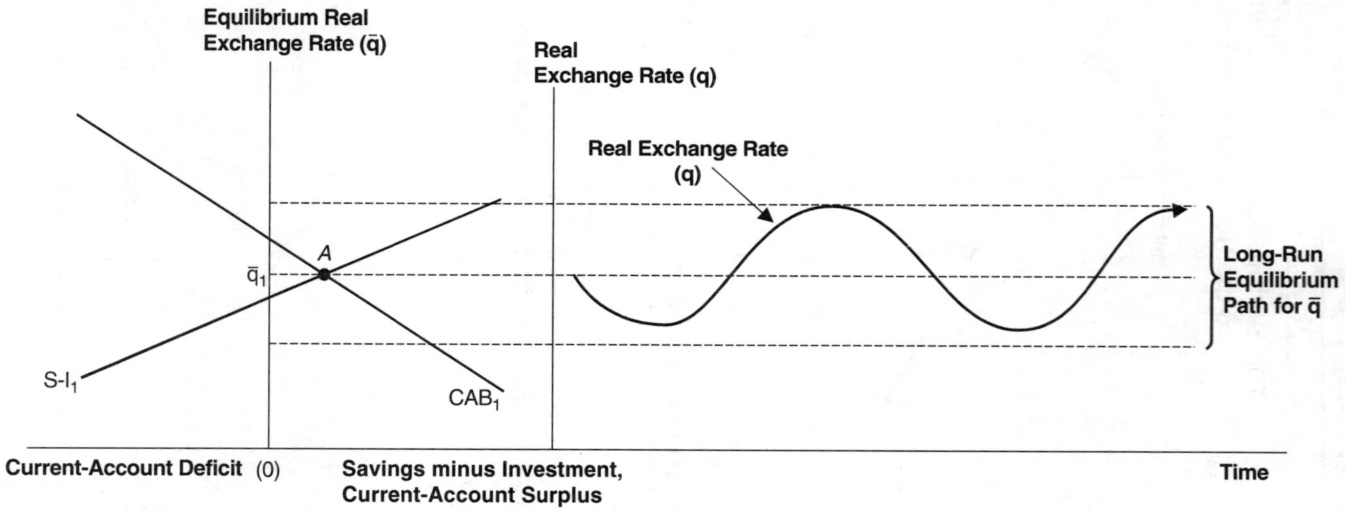

When structural changes on those three fronts occur, however, the real long-run equilibrium exchange rate will either rise or fall in response to those changes. A structural rise in investment spending, a sustained move toward fiscal stimulus, or a persistent decline in private savings should give rise to a trend increase in the real long-run equilibrium exchange rate over time, as shown in Figure 3–5. The opposite would give rise to a trend decline in the real long-run equilibrium exchange rate.

CHANGES IN REAL LONG-RUN EQUILIBRIUM EXCHANGE RATES

Structural changes on a country's *internal-balance front* can exert a powerful influence on the trend in exchange rates over time. When a country enjoys a major investment boom, such as the United States experienced in the second half of the 1990s, it will give rise to an upward shift in the S-I schedule and to a rise in the equilibrium exchange rate over time. Similarly, a major move toward fiscal stimulus, as the United States experienced in the first half of the 1980s, would shift the S-I curve upward and push the currency's real long-run equilibrium value higher, as shown in Figure 3–6.

Structural changes on a country's *external-balance front* can also exert a powerful influence on the trend in exchange rates over time. Productivity changes and technological innovations in a country's traded-goods sector can give rise to a sustained improvement in a country's current-account balance and thereby contribute to a trend rise in the real exchange rate over time, as shown in Figure 3–7. Japan's large and persistent current-account surpluses played a key role in driving the yen's real value higher in the 1980s and early 1990s.

During certain periods, structural changes might be occurring on both the internal and external-balance fronts at the same time. The net impact of those changes will determine whether the exchange rate will rise or fall. For example, in the case of Japan in 2000–2001, both internal and external-balance forces were working jointly to lower the yen's real long-run equilibrium value. Japan's fiscal stance was tightening, investment spending was declining, and, at the same time, Japan's current-account surplus was undergoing a structural deterioration as competition from Asia intensified. As illustrated in Figure 3–8 those forces combined to cause the yen's equilibrium value to decline from $\bar{q}_1$ to $\bar{q}_2$.

FIGURE 3-5

Trending Real Long-Run Equilibrium Exchange Rate

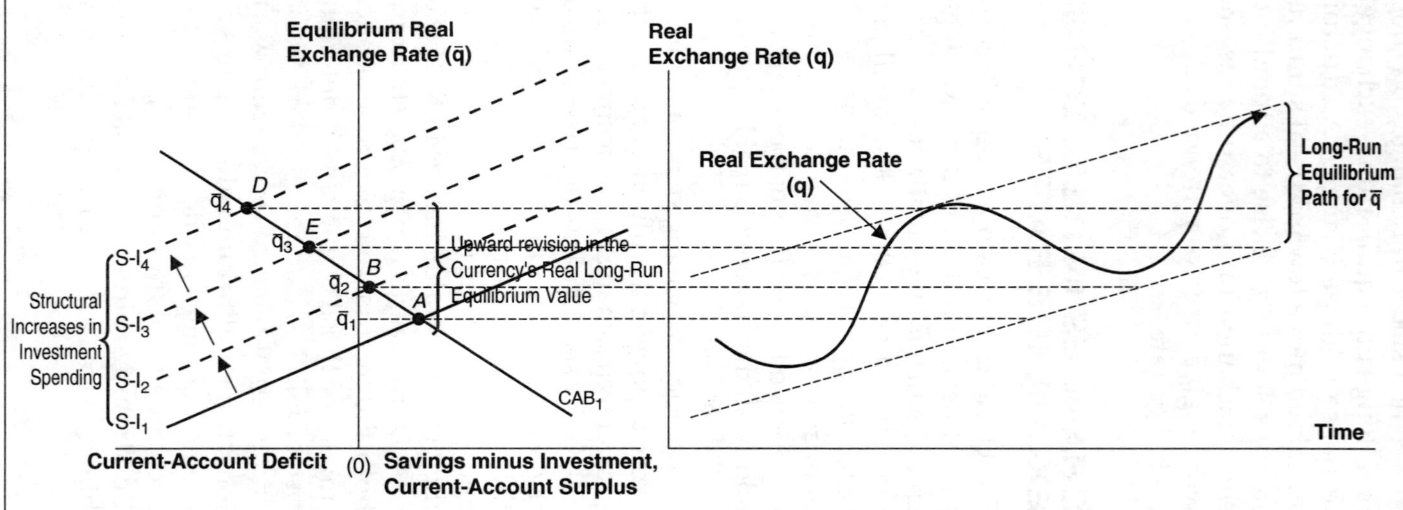

FIGURE 3-6

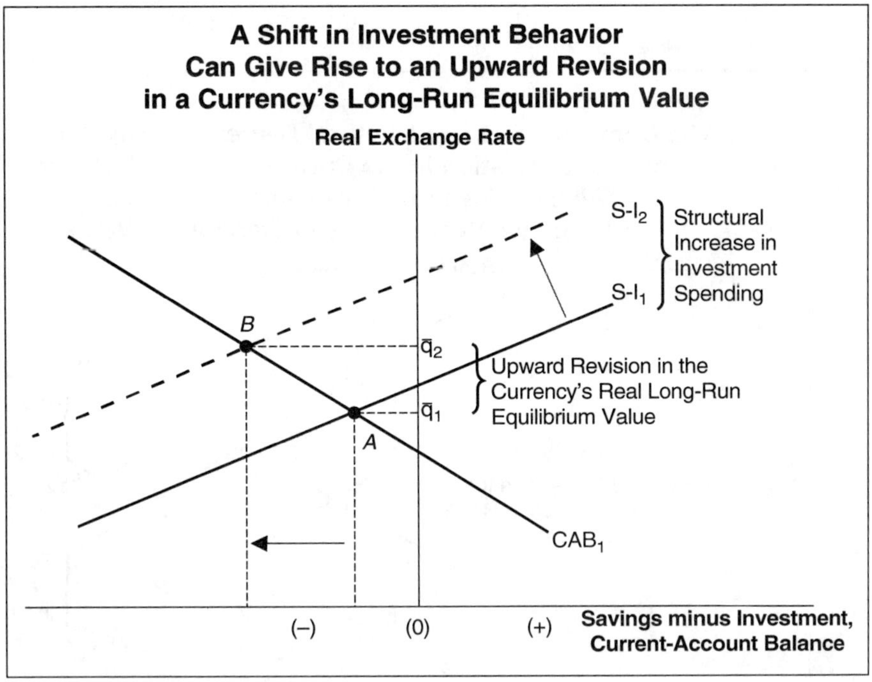

FIGURE 3-7

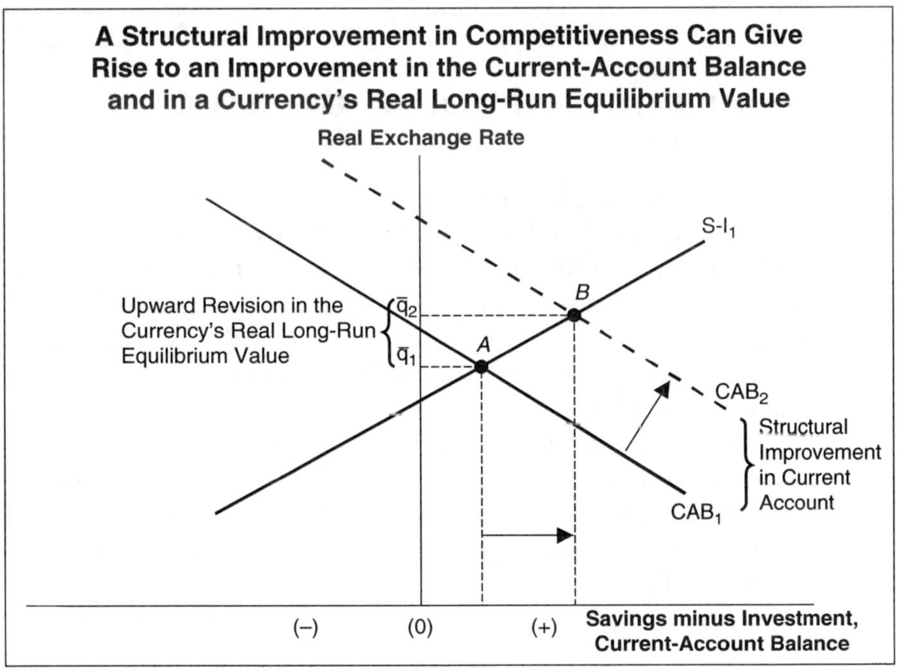

FIGURE 3-8

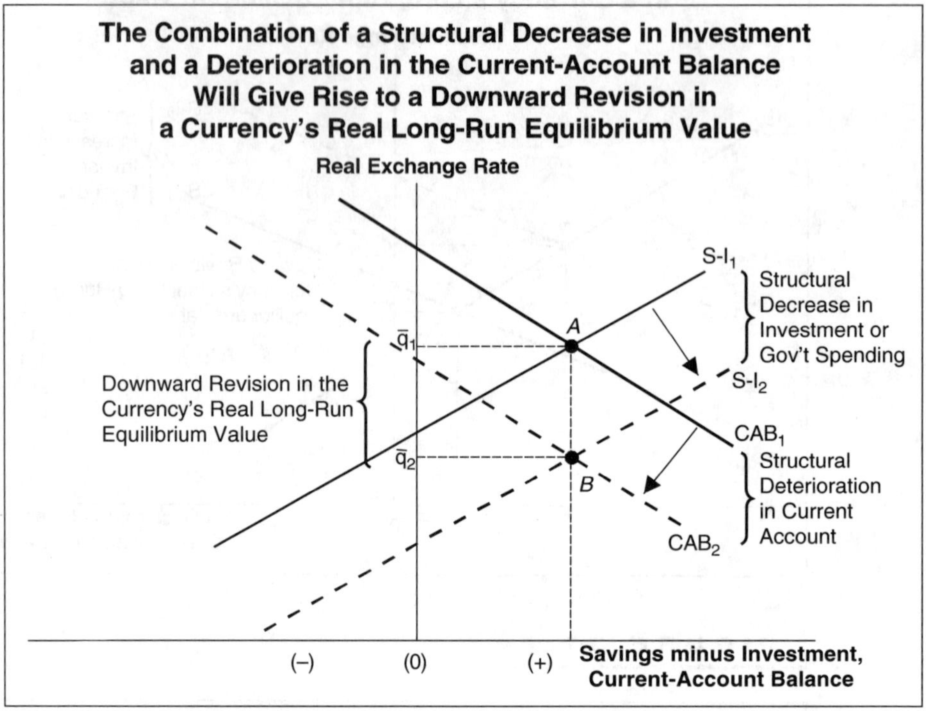

EQUILIBRIUM EXCHANGE-RATE ESTIMATES

The problem for currency forecasters and investment strategists is how to precisely quantify what exchange-rate level truly represents a currency's real long-run equilibrium level. Estimates of the equilibrium exchange rate are often sensitive to the assumptions that a macroeconometric modeler might make. Indeed, it is quite possible that a wide range of equilibrium exchange-rate estimates are plausible, with each estimate dependent on the underlying assumptions made.

Estimates of the dollar's equilibrium value by the Institute for International Economics show the dollar to be significantly overvalued versus the yen and euro by 25% to 30% (see Figure 3–9). A recent report by the OECD surveyed a broad range of econometric studies that constructed estimates for the euro's long-run equilibrium value. Although the estimates vary widely, they tend to center around the U.S. dollar/euro 1.10–1.20

FIGURE 3-9

Fundamental Equilibrium Exchange-Rate Estimates
(Estimates of U.S. Dollar FEERs for 2000)

	Euro	Japanese Yen
Range	1.135-1.387	77.3-94.5
Midpoint	1.26	86.0

Source: Simon Wren-Lewis and Rebecca Driver, *Exchange Rates for the Year 2000*, Institute for International Economics, 1998.

range, suggesting that the euro was significantly undervalued versus the U.S. dollar in 2000–2002 (see Figure 3–10).

PRODUCTIVITY TRENDS AND EXCHANGE RATES

Many economists cite the rise in U.S. productivity growth relative to productivity growth overseas beginning in the second half of the 1990s as one of the key variables that drove the dollar sharply higher versus most major currencies. Clearly, the gains in productivity growth were a uniquely U.S. phenomenon. A recent Federal Reserve Board Study found that multifactor productivity growth in the United States surged in the second half of the 1990s, while it decelerated in Japan and was broadly unchanged in Euroland (see Figure 3–11).

Fed Chairman Alan Greenspan has been a strong advocate of the thesis that the dollar's 7-year uptrend was productivity-related. According to Mr. Greenspan, "The evident strengthened demand for the dollar, relative to the euro, has reflected a market expectation that productivity growth in the United States is likely to be greater than in continental Europe in the years ahead."

The importance of relative productivity growth as a key determinant of the dollar's value versus the euro can be gleaned from Figures 3–12 and 3–13. As shown in Figure 3–12, U.S. labor productivity growth was weaker than Euroland labor productivity growth in the 1980s and early 1990s. But beginning in 1995, U.S. productivity growth surged relative to the trend in Euroland. Indeed, the trend in long-term Euroland/U.S. relative productivity growth appears to explain a large portion of the 1995–2000 slide in the euro's value versus the U.S. dollar.

FIGURE 3-10

Selected Estimates of the Euro's Medium/Long-Run "Equilibrium" Value

Study	Key Explanatory Variables/Models	Equilibrium Exchange-Rate Estimate (US$/e)
Wren-Lewis & Driver (1998)	FEER Model	1.19-1.45
Borowski and Couharde (2000)	FEER Model	1.23-1.31
Alberola et al. (1999)	Ratio of Nontraded/Traded Goods Prices, Net Foreign Assets	1.26
Chinn and Alquist (2000)	M1, GDP, Short-Term Interest Rates, CPI, Ratio of Nontraded/Traded Goods Prices	1.19-1.28
Lorenzen and Thygessen (2000)	Net Foreign Assets, R&D Spending Demographics, Ratio of Nontraded/Traded Goods Prices	1.17-1.24
Duval (2001)	Consumption, Multi-Factor Productivity, Real Long-Term Yield Spread, Ratio of Nontraded/Traded Goods Prices	1.15
Clostermann and Schnatz (2000)	Real Long-Term Yield Spread, Oil Price, Government Spending, Ratio of Nontraded/Traded Goods Prices	1.13
Teiletche (2000)	Productivity, Government Spending, Real Long-Term Yield Spread, M1 Industrial Production	1.09
OECD	GDP PPP	1.09
Gern et al.	Short-Term Real Interest-Rate Differential	1.03
Schulmeister	PPP for Tradables	0.87
Deutsche Bank	PPP (Long-Run Average)	1.20

Source: OECD Working Paper Number 298, June 2001 (for other than Deutsche Bank).

U.S. PRODUCTIVITY GROWTH SURGE AND THE DOLLAR: A MEDIUM OR LONG-TERM PHENOMENON?

There has been a great deal of debate among economists over what contributed to the recent stellar gains in U.S. productivity growth and whether those gains will prove sustainable in the long term. A number of researchers

FIGURE 3-11

Productivity Growth Rates
(Percentage Changes in Multifactor Productivity)

	1990-95 (%)	1996-99 (%)
U.S.	0.79	**1.47**
Canada	0.26	0.27
France	0.89	1.12
Germany	1.02	**1.07**
Italy	1.32	-0.14
Japan	1.31	**0.85**
U.K.	1.21	0.95
Australia	1.15	2.11
Denmark	2.37	0.31
Norway	2.48	1.13
Switzerland	-0.57	0.84

Source: Gust, C. and Marquez, J., "Productivity Developments Abroad," *Federal Reserve Bulletin*, October 2000.

FIGURE 3-12

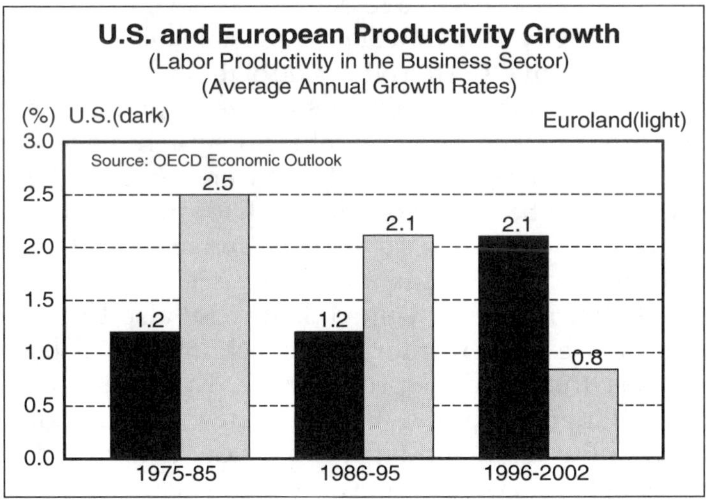

FIGURE 3-13

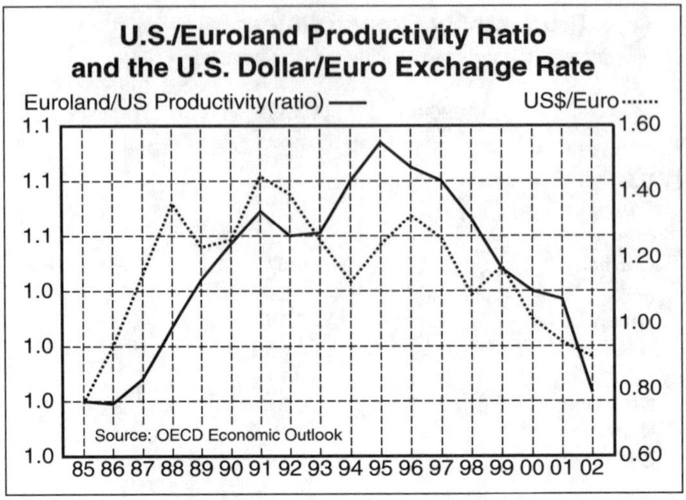

believe that the absolute gains in U.S. productivity growth were largely an information technology (IT) phenomenon, and since the IT boom was largely a U.S. story, the relative gains in U.S. productivity could be explained by IT as well. Many of those same researchers believe that the recent gains in U.S. labor productivity growth will prove sustainable in the long run, which would be dollar positive. On the other side of the argument, some researchers are not convinced that the United States enjoyed a productivity miracle, contending instead that favorable cyclical factors might have exaggerated the rise in reported productivity gains. If that were the case, then U.S. productivity growth should be expected to fall back toward its long-term trend.

A recent Conference Board report demonstrates that the relatively robust U.S. productivity gains were due not only to the comparative advantage of IT firms in the United States, but also to the ability of U.S. non-IT firms to use the new information technologies developed by the IT sector to boost their overall productivity. This was made possible by U.S. firms' willingness to invest in these new technologies. In contrast, non-IT firms in Euroland and Japan were slow to invest in new technologies, even though such technologies were as available to them as they were to non-IT firms in the United States. The net result is that productivity gains in the non-IT sector of the United States were several times greater than the productivity gains by comparable firms in Euroland and Japan (see Figures 3–14 and 3–15).

FIGURE 3-14

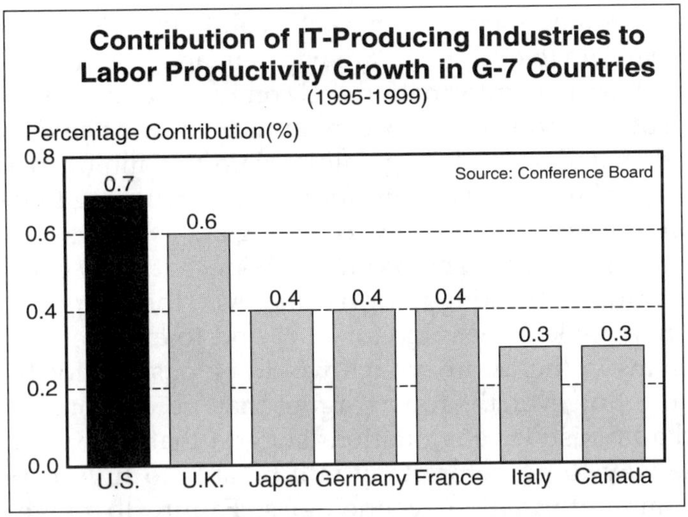

FIGURE 3-15

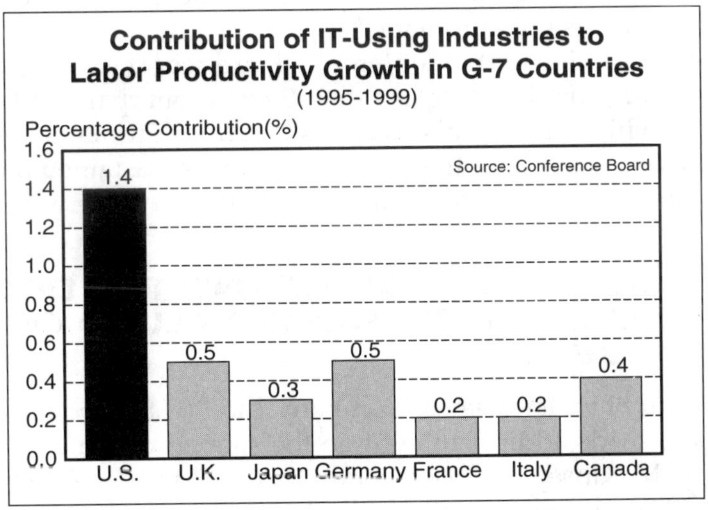

According to the Conference Board report, the failure of Euroland firms to embrace the new technologies "can be traced to insufficient liberalization and impediments to market evolution." The report adds that Euroland "barriers to change . . . are widespread . . . and opportunities are still restricted in many information and communications technology-using industries, such as transportation, communication and banking." The report emphasized that Euroland "regulatory rigidities inhibit reallocations of labor and capital to their most productive uses, reducing the benefits to be obtained from investment in new technologies."

The Conference Board holds out the hope that "new competitive rules in communications, banking reforms, and even the adoption of the single currency" may make it possible for Euroland to experience stronger productivity gains in the future, which would be positive for the euro. On a negative note, however, the report argues that "recent compilations of economic and administrative regulations suggest that Europe and Japan still have some way to go before they will be able to fully exploit the new computer and information technologies. Failure to move forward on regulatory liberalization and the reduction of impediments to market evolution would perpetuate the present underinvestment in information and communications technology." The report then wryly concludes that "realizing the potential growth effects from information and communications technology is not automatic."

One implication of the Conference Board report is that U.S. firms may enjoy stronger productivity gains than their counterparts in Euroland and Japan for a while longer. This suggests that until Euroland begins to close the productivity gap with the United States on a sustained basis, the euro may encounter difficulty in making significant headway versus the dollar.

U.S. PRODUCTIVITY GAINS AND THE DOLLAR: IS THE DOLLAR NOW FAIRLY VALUED OR OVERVALUED?

A recent study by McKinsey & Company, Inc. ("U.S. Productivity Growth: 1995-2000") sheds additional light on the sources of the U.S. productivity surge. The McKinsey study contends that U.S. productivity increased in the 1995–2000 period for both cyclical and structural reasons. The study finds that U.S. labor productivity growth rose from an average 1.4% per annum over the 1987–1995 period to an average 2.5% per annum over the 1995-2000 period, with about one-half of the incremental gains projected to be long-lasting (see Figure 3–16).

FIGURE 3-16

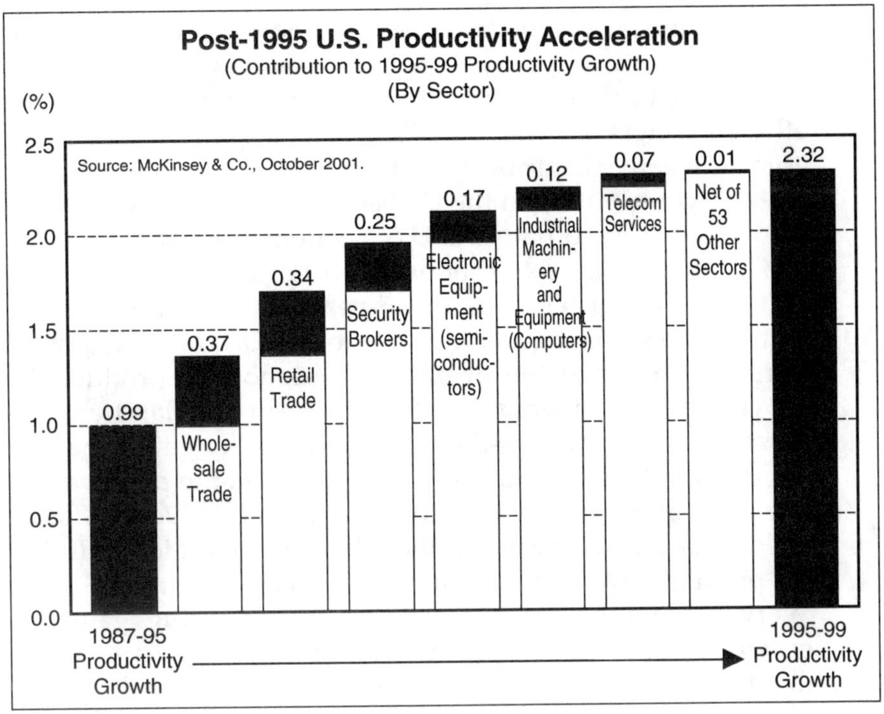

The McKinsey study projects that U.S. labor productivity growth will ease a bit toward an average 2.0% per annum pace over the next 5 years as the influence of shorter-run cyclical factors washes out. While this would represent a slowdown from the 1995–2000 pace, it would nevertheless exceed the pace of productivity growth in 1987–1995.

A 0.5% per annum increase in labor productivity growth might not seem like a lot, but if such a gain were sustained over a 10-year period, it could contribute up to $1.2 trillion in additional surpluses on the U.S. federal government budget balance. It could also cut the cost of a 50-year fix to Social Security in half.

The McKinsey study finds that the gain in U.S. labor productivity growth over the 1995–2000 period was more than just an IT story. The study contends that regulatory changes, strong competition, better management, and favorable cyclical factors all played a positive role in boosting U.S. productivity growth. Interestingly, the study finds that of the 59 sectors of the U.S. economy that were investigated, only six sectors, representing 28% of the economy, contributed meaningfully to the 1995–2000 productivity gains. The six sectors that made substantial contributions to U.S. productivity growth were (1) wholesale trade, (2) retail trade, (3) security and commodity brokers, (4) electronic equipment/semiconductor firms, (5) industrial equipment/computer firms, and (6) telecom services. The other 53 sectors, representing 72% of the economy, made either small positive or negative contributions that effectively washed each other out for a net-zero contribution to the U.S. economy's total productivity gains.

Of concern to both the U.S. economy and the dollar is the fact that 72% of the overall U.S. economy did not fully participate in the productivity gains registered in the 5-year period. The dollar rose strongly because the gains registered by the other 28% were so powerful that they were able to boost the overall U.S. economy's productivity growth far above the pace of productivity growth in Euroland and elsewhere. For those sectors that enjoyed strong productivity gains, the dollar's rise has not dented their overall competitiveness, as the positive effects of a relative rise in productivity growth have effectively offset the negative effects of a rising dollar. But the other 72% that did not fully participate in the productivity surge have been left to compete in world markets with an overvalued exchange rate without an offsetting gain in productivity growth. That is why a large number of U.S. firms have begun to complain that the dollar's strength is negatively affecting their long-run competitiveness.

PRODUCTIVITY GROWTH IN THE TRADED-GOODS SECTOR AND THE DETERMINATION OF EXCHANGE RATES

Productivity gains will tend to exert a greater impact on exchange rates if those productivity gains are concentrated in the traded-goods sector of an economy. A recent Federal Reserve Bank of New York study ("To What Extent Does Productivity Drive the Dollar?", *Current Issues in Economics and Finance*, Volume 7, Number 8, August 2001) finds that most of the gains in U.S. productivity in the 1990s were concentrated in the U.S. traded-goods sector.

Looking at sectoral productivity gaps (the difference between traded-goods productivity and non-traded-goods productivity) in the United States, Japan, and Euroland, one finds that the U.S. sectoral productivity gap has risen in the past 30 years as the gap between U.S. traded and non-traded productivity growth has widened (see Figure 3–17). In contrast,

FIGURE 3-17

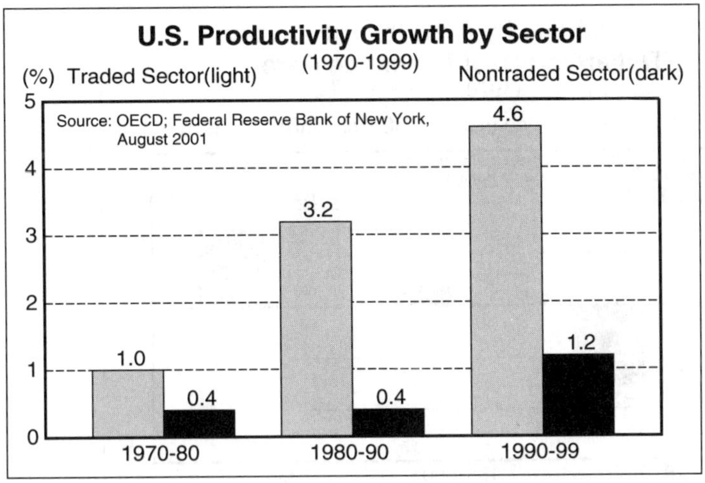

the sectoral productivity gap has fallen in Japan and has been steady in Euroland. The New York Fed's findings reveal that relative sectoral productivity gaps explain more than two-thirds of the movement in the yen and euro versus the dollar in the past decade (see Figures 3–18 and 3–19).

TERMS OF TRADE CHANGES AND EXCHANGE RATES

Changes in a country's terms of trade can, at times, exert a strong influence on the direction that exchange rates take. For instance, in commodity-oriented industrial economies such as Australia, New Zealand, and Canada, where commodity exports make up a large part of GDP (relative to the rather small shares in the G3 economies), one finds a strong positive relationship between the trend in relevant commodity-price indices and the trend in the Australian dollar, the New Zealand dollar, and the Canadian dollar, respectively (see Figures 3–20 and 3–21).

In the case of the euro, the price of oil has been found to be an important explanatory variable, with higher oil prices contributing to a weaker euro, and vice versa (see Figure 3–22). A recent Bank of Canada study found that a similar relationship held between energy prices and the Canadian dollar, with higher energy prices bearish for the Canadian dollar and lower energy prices bullish for the Canadian dollar.

FIGURE 3-18

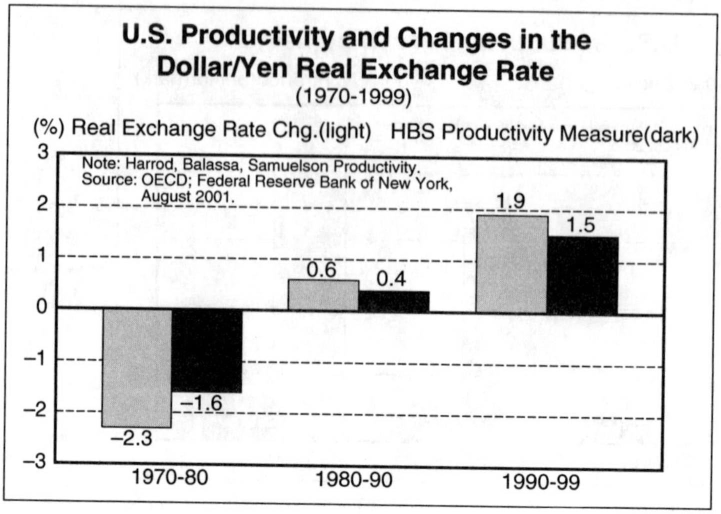

FIGURE 3-19

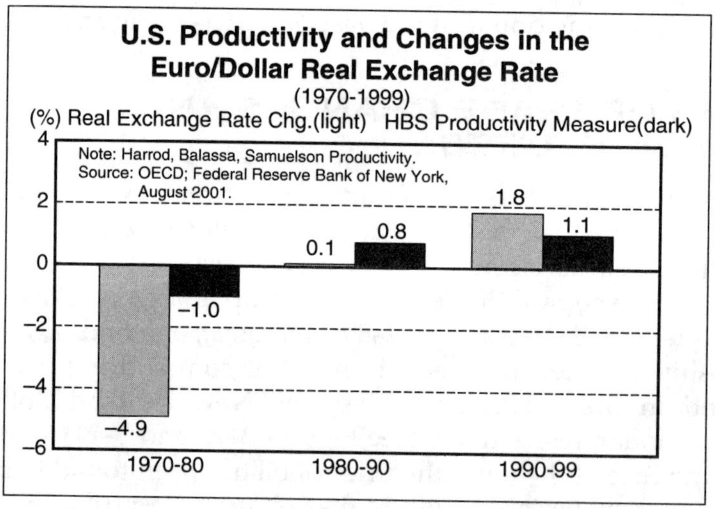

FIGURE 3-20

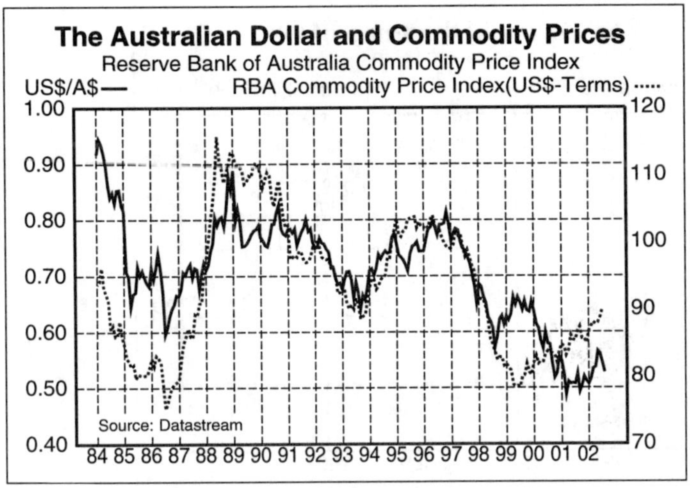

FIGURE 3-21

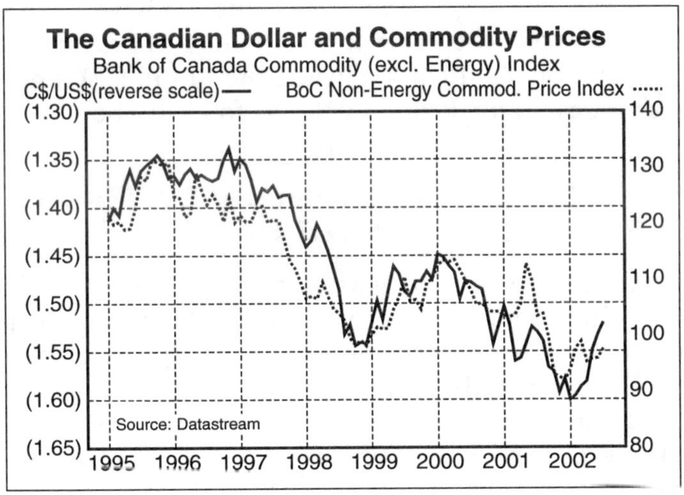

FIGURE 3-22

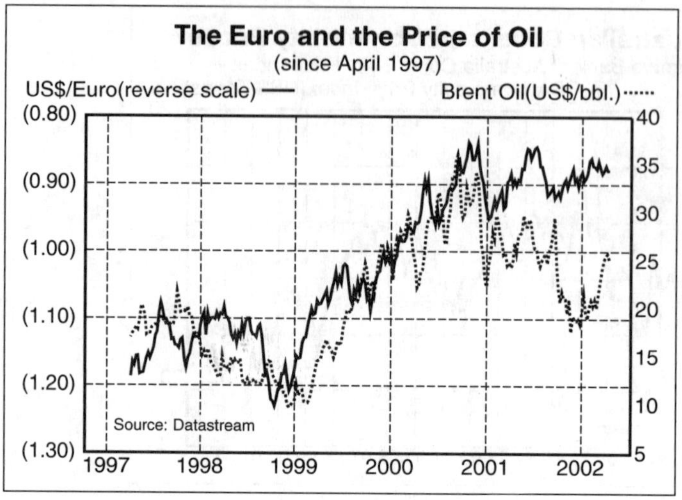

A recent study by the central bank of Norway (Norges Bank) finds that there exists a nonlinear relationship between oil prices and the Norwegian krone. A change in oil prices tends to have a larger impact on the krone's value when the price of oil is below $14 a barrel or above $20 a barrel. When oil prices fluctuate inside the $14 to $20 range, the impact of oil price changes on the krone's value is found to be insignificant.

NET INTERNATIONAL INVESTMENT AND THE EQUILIBRIUM EXCHANGE RATE

Several researchers have noted that there exists a positive long-run relationship between a country's net international investment position as a percentage of GDP and its real effective exchange rate. There are several reasons why this relationship tends to hold.

First, exchange rates typically do not adjust to equilibrate the current-account balance in each and every period. The reason for this is that a deficit country may be able to attract sufficient capital inflows to finance its deficit for a considerable time. Indeed, if those inflows are considerable, the deficit country's currency might, in fact, rise even as the current-account deficit widens. Witness what happened in the United States in 1981 to 1985 and again in 1995 to 2001.

If a country's current-account deficit rises persistently over time, however, there is likely to come a point when it can no longer be easily financed. When that point is reached, a currency's real value could then come under considerable downward pressure. Hence, although the exchange rate and the current-account imbalance may not appear to be positively related on a monthly or quarterly basis, cumulative trends in current-account imbalances and exchange rates tend to be more closely aligned.

A second reason for the positive relationship between the trend in net international investment positions and the trend in real exchange rates is the effect of the transfer of wealth implied by cumulative external imbalances. The cumulative trend in current-account imbalances gives rise to shifts in the residence of wealth from deficit to surplus countries, and such wealth transfers give rise to portfolio adjustments that put upward pressure on surplus-country currencies and downward pressure on deficit-country currencies over time.

Given that most investors prefer to keep the bulk of their wealth in domestic and not foreign-currency assets—the so-called home-country bias—investors in surplus countries will find themselves accumulating more foreign-currency assets than they desire relative to their domestic holdings. Over time, surplus country investors will attempt to rebalance their portfolios in favor of domestic-currency assets. As they do, the surplus country's currency will tend to rise relative to the deficit country's currency. The Japanese yen and the Deutschemark, to a lesser degree, underwent long-term appreciations from the 1980s until the mid-1990s as their cumulative current-account surpluses rose (see Figures 3–23 and 3–24).

A final reason why the trends in net international investment positions and real exchange rates are positively related is that heavily indebted nations need to service their net external debts, and that can only be done if the debtor country runs a trade surplus to generate the income to service those debts. In order for the debtor country to run a trade surplus consistently over time, the real exchange rate of a debtor country would need to decline. Similarly, a country with a large cumulative current-account surplus would need to see its currency's real value rise over time to insure that the surplus and the associated net foreign asset position did not continue rising to unsustainably high levels.

Although the United States has seen its net international investment position deteriorate sharply in the past decade (see Figure 3–25), the dollar has nevertheless remained extraordinarily resilient. One explanation for this is that, although U.S. external liabilities exceed U.S. external assets by

FIGURE 3-23

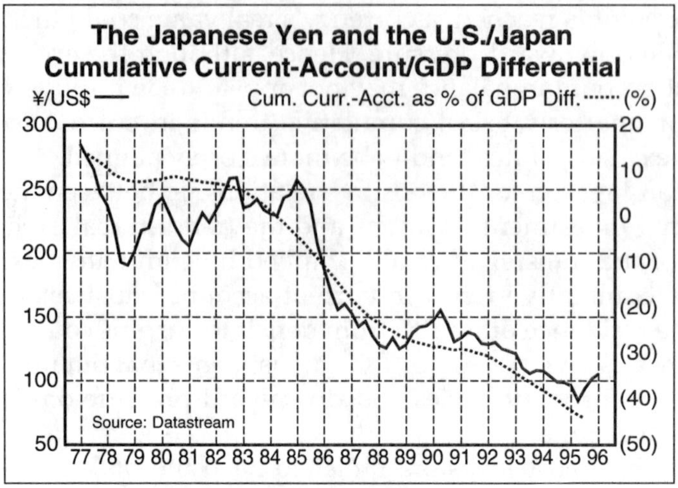

FIGURE 3-24

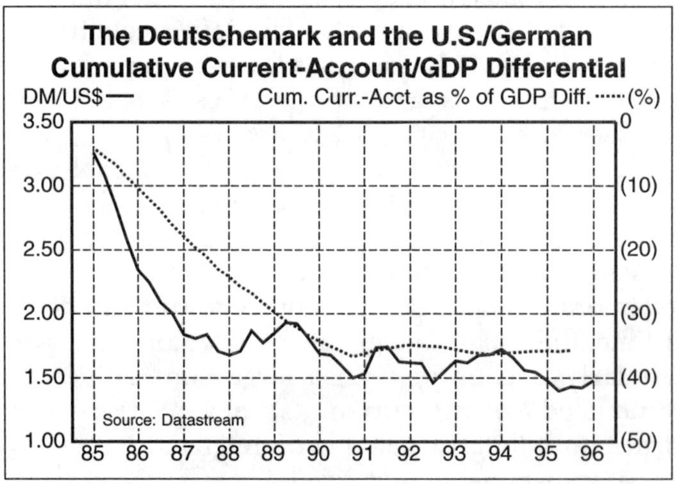

FIGURE 3-25

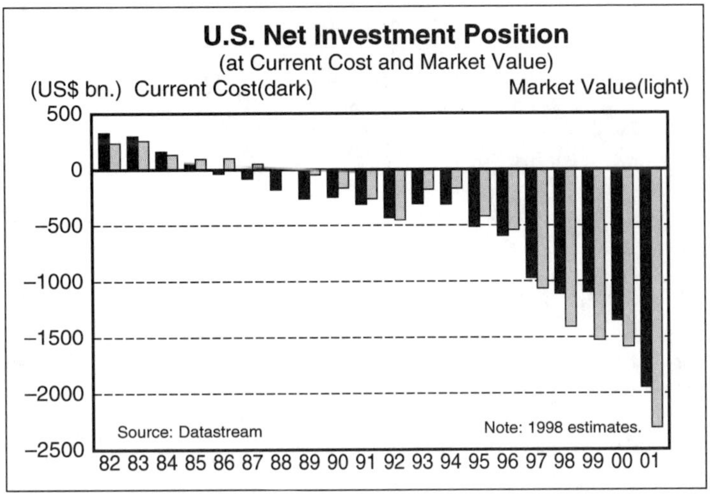

a wide margin, the United States has tended to earn a higher return on its external assets than it has paid out on its external liabilities. The result has been that net investment income flows, until recently, posted a modest surplus. While U.S. net investment income flows have recently swung into a modest deficit position, the deficit does not appear to be sizeable enough at this stage to seriously damage the dollar's long-run prospects.

CHAPTER 4

Long-Term Cycles in Exchange Rates

The dollar has exhibited a tendency to both rise and fall over long-term cycles (see Figures 4–1 and 4–2), with each of the dollar cycles since the beginning of floating exchange rates in 1973 sharing a number of common features.

First, the magnitude of the dollar's exchange-rate movements in each cycle has generally been large, often far exceeding the forecasts of portfolio managers, market pundits, and forward-exchange rates.

Second, the length of each dollar cycle has tended to be long, often surpassing by a wide margin the typical length of U.S. and foreign business cycles. In most cases, dollar cycles have lasted for 5 years or even longer (see Figure 4–3). That would suggest that cyclical factors alone cannot account for the tendency of the dollar to move in large and protracted swings.

Third, at the end of each major cycle, the dollar has tended to overshoot its long-run equilibrium level, often in a climactic fashion (see Figure 4–4).

Finally, when the dollar has overshot its fair value at the end of a long cycle, the deviation in the dollar's value from its estimated PPP value has often given rise to serious imbalances on either the internal- or external-balance fronts in the United States, Europe, or Japan. When those imbalances reached a critical level, it often set market forces in motion to bring the overshoot to an end, and to plant the seeds for a 180-degree shift in the dollar's long-term trend.

FIGURE 4-1

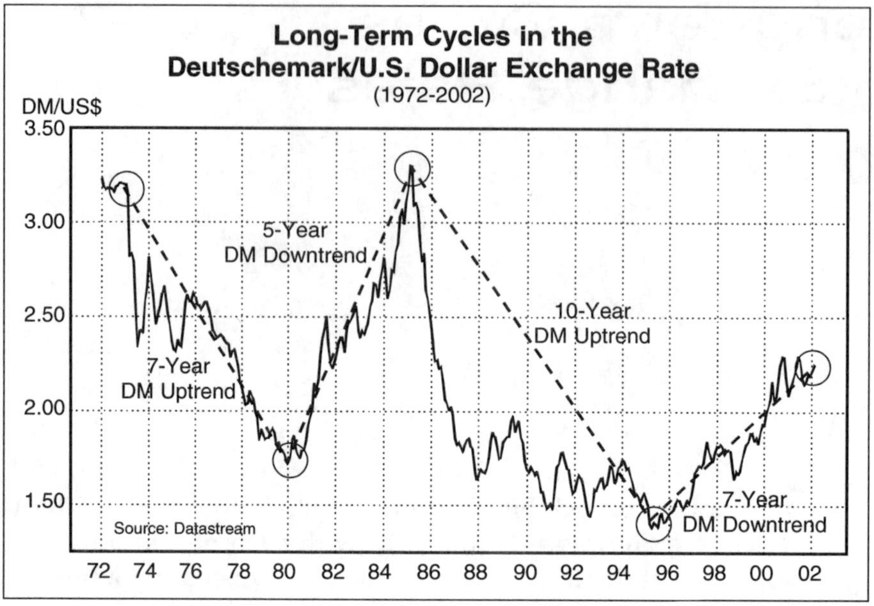

FIGURE 4-2

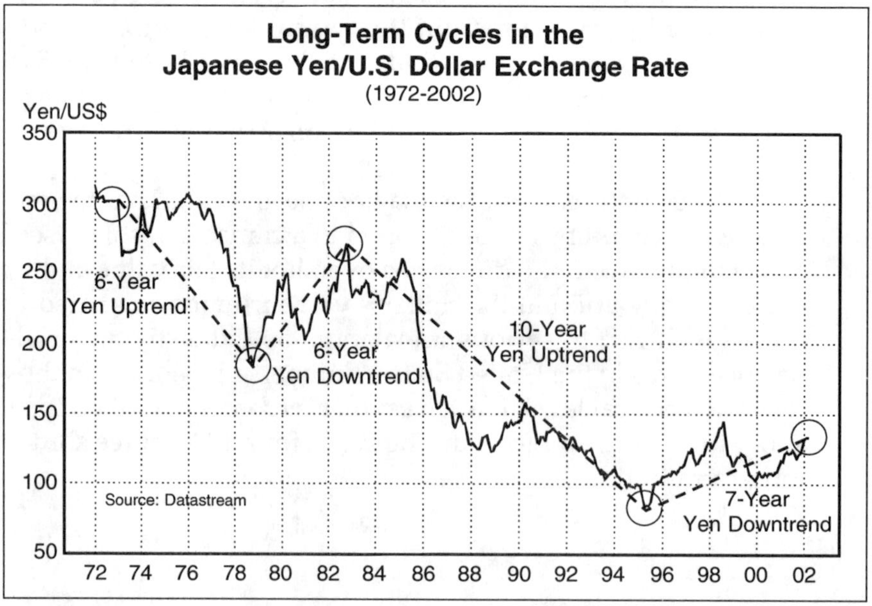

FIGURE 4-3

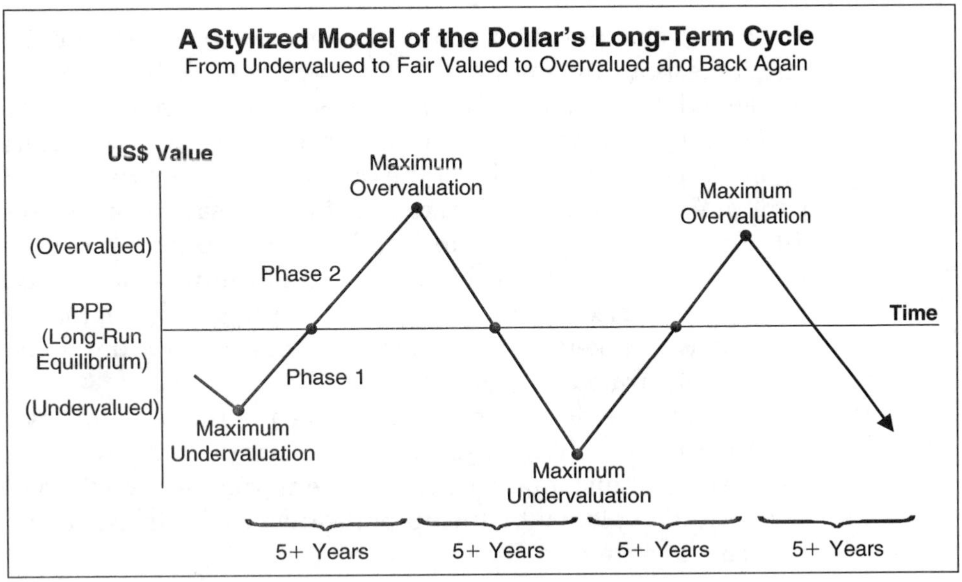

FIGURE 4-4

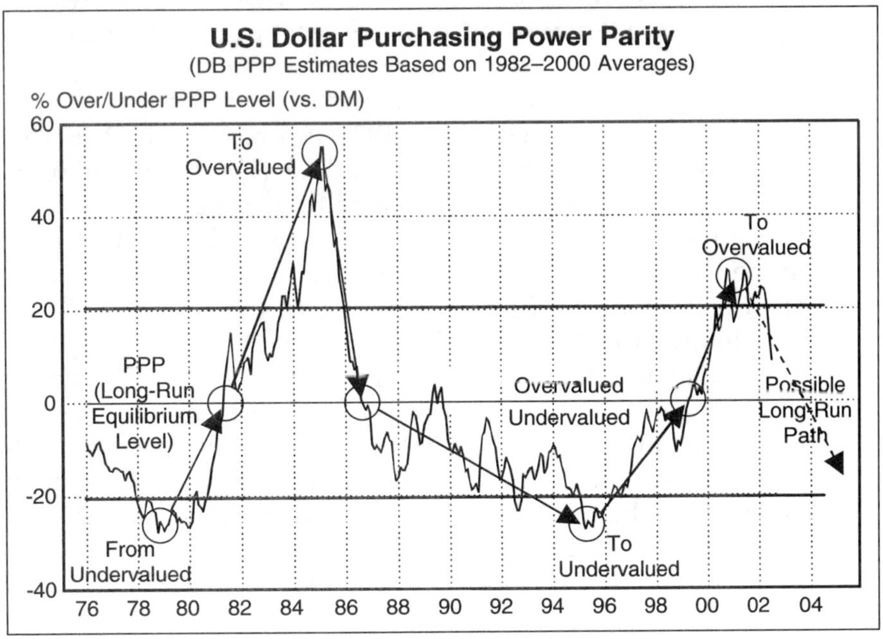

FACTORS CONTRIBUTING TO LONG-TERM CYCLES

Structural changes on a country's internal- or external-balance front are largely responsible for the long-term cycles in exchange rates that we have witnessed. For instance, the U.S. investment boom of the second half of the 1990s and the structural rise in U.S. productivity growth during that period are largely responsible for the dollar's persistent rise over the 1995–2002 period. As illustrated in Figure 4–5, the U.S. savings-investment schedule, S-I, gradually shifted upward and to the left, giving rise to a persistent uptrend in the dollar's real long-run equilibrium value over time. Likewise, the persistent rise in Japan's current-account surplus in the 1980s and early 1990s played a key role in lifting the yen's equilibrium value higher over time, as illustrated in Figure 4–6.

In both the dollar's and the yen's case, the upward revisions in their real long-run equilibrium exchange rates appear to have taken place gradually, and not instantaneously, as several theories would have suggested. This would explain why the up-and-down cycles in exchange rates endure for years at a time.

LONG-TERM CYCLES IN EXCHANGE RATES: THE DOLLAR AND EURO IN THE 1990S

Most long-term exchange-rate cycles are driven, not by a single shock to the internal- or external-balance schedules, but rather by a series of separate, yet related shocks that reinforce one another in driving an exchange rate higher or lower over time. For instance, the dollar's long-term uptrend versus the euro between April 1995 and November 2000 reflected a combination of favorable factors including (1) "New Economy" forces that helped propel U.S. investment spending and productivity growth higher, (2) a structural shift in capital flows from emerging markets and Euroland to the United States, (3) higher oil prices, and (4) relatively tight U.S. monetary and credit conditions up until 2001 (see Figure 4–7).

In the case of the euro, its long-term decline since the early 1990s also reflected a multitude of problems including (1) pervasive structural rigidities in European labor and product markets, (2) an adverse fiscal/monetary policy mix in Euroland, (3) higher oil prices, (4) an adverse structural shift in Euroland capital flows, and (5) excessive pessimism regarding the potential problems associated with the launch of the new euro notes and coins in early 2002 (see Figure 4–8).

FIGURE 4-5

The Positive Effects over Time of Structural Increases in Investment on a Currency's Long-Run Equilibrium Value

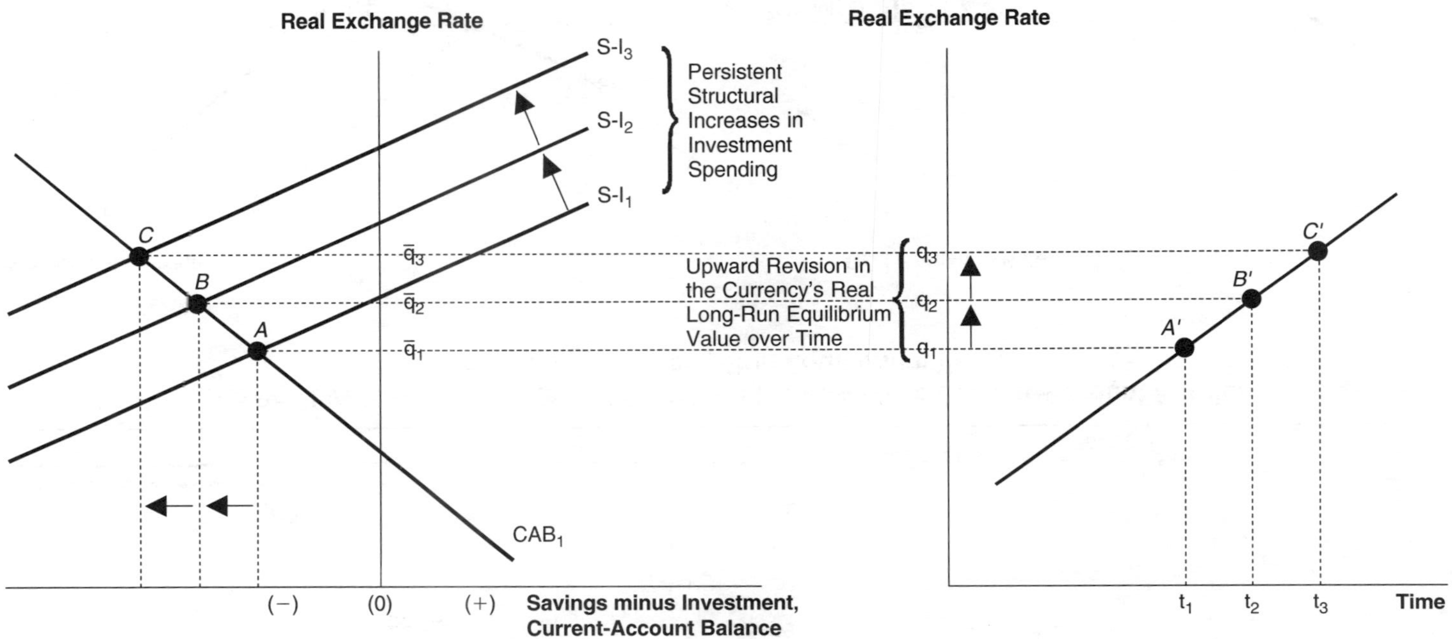

FIGURE 4-6

The Positive Effects over Time of Structural Increases in a Current-Account Surplus on a Currency's Long-Run Equilibrium Value

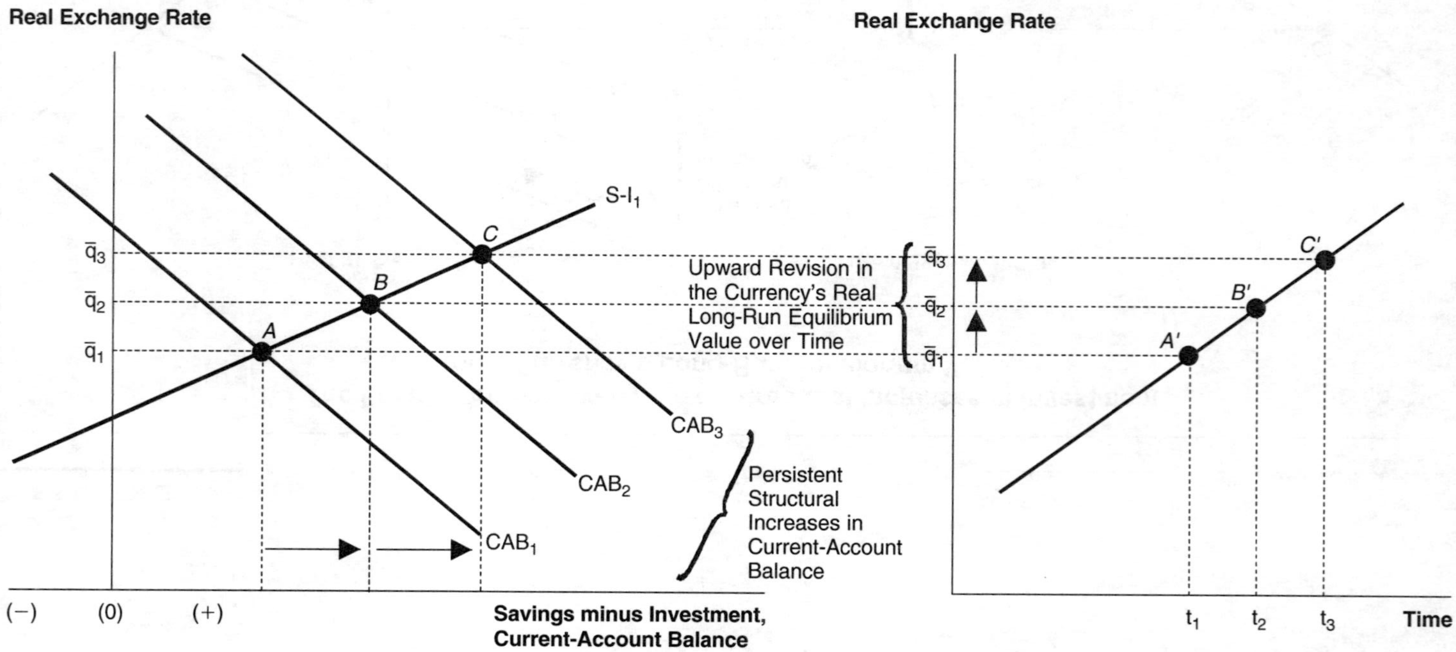

FIGURE 4-7

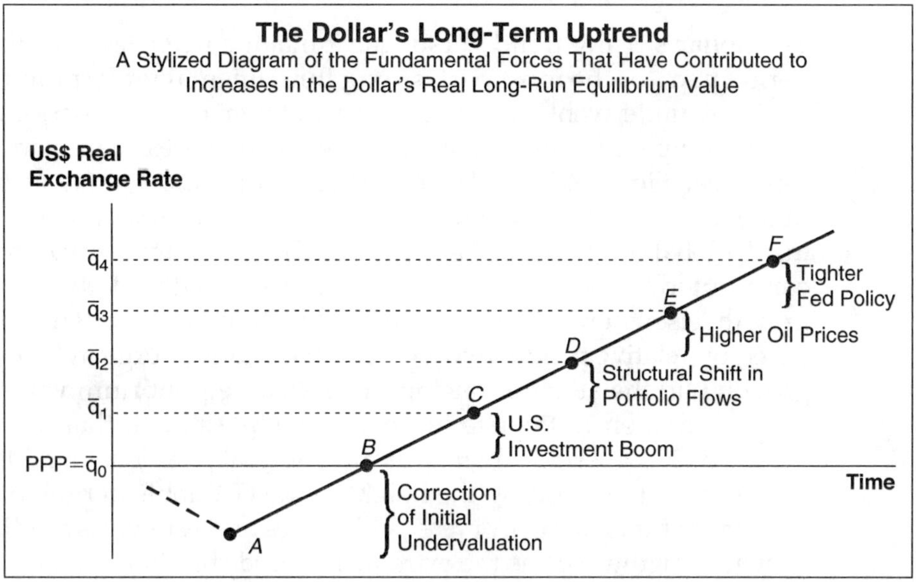

FIGURE 4-8

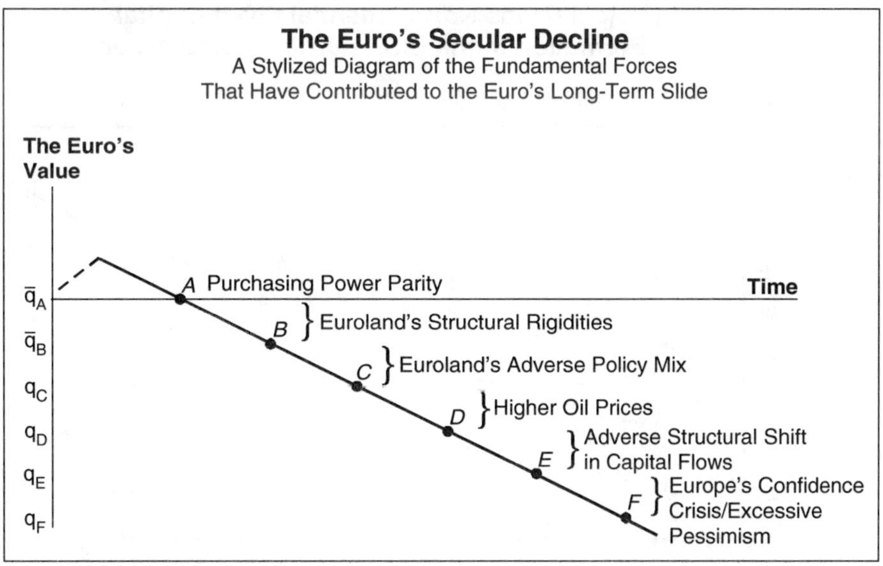

THE 1990S U.S. INVESTMENT BOOM AND THE DOLLAR

The dollar's rising trend versus most major currencies over the 1995–2002 period had, for the most part, strong fundamental underpinnings. The U.S. economy underwent a major investment boom over this period, particularly when compared with the weak investment performance in Europe and Japan (see Figure 4–9). A large portion of the U.S. boom was concentrated in the information technology (IT) arena, where U.S. industry held a dominant, global position (see Figure 4–10). The IT-led investment boom, in turn, contributed to a surge in U.S. productivity growth relative to productivity growth elsewhere. Since exchange-rate trends are often strongly influenced by relative productivity trends, the relative surge in U.S. productivity growth had the effect of raising the dollar's equilibrium value.

In addition to the rise in productive investment that occurred during the 1995–2000 period, there was probably also a considerable amount of excess investment during the height of the IT bubble period, particularly in the Internet and telecom areas. This excess investment spending, which is shown in Figure 4–11 as the extreme leftward shift in the savings-investment

FIGURE 4-9

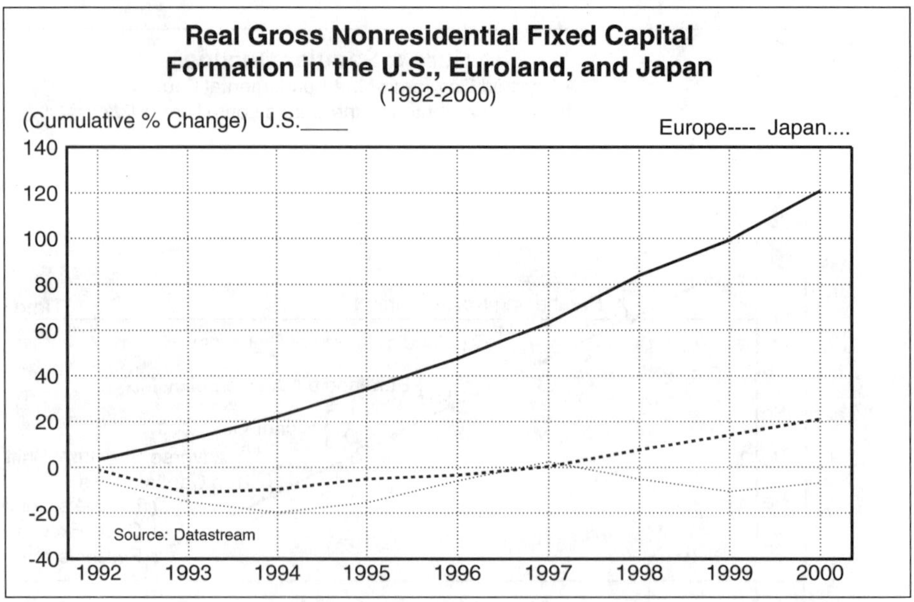

FIGURE 4-10

schedule to $S\text{-}I_3$, actually began to unwind in 2001–2002 (see Figure 4–11). This suggests that the S-I curve has begun to shift back down to perhaps $S\text{-}I_2$, and in the process the dollar's value has started to shift downward as well.

THE DOLLAR'S DRAMATIC RISE IN 1999-2000 MAY HAVE BEEN DRIVEN BY A SUDDEN UPWARD REVISION IN THE DOLLAR'S REAL LONG-RUN EQUILIBRIUM LEVEL

The dollar's dramatic surge between the fall of 1999 and the fall of 2000 may have been propelled by a sudden and dramatic upward revision in the market's expectations regarding the U.S. economy's long-run growth prospects. This shift in long-run growth expectations might have contributed to an equally dramatic upward revision in the marketplace's notion of the dollar's real long-run equilibrium value.

The U.S. economy had been growing faster than the Euroland economy for much of the 1990s, but it wasn't until late in the decade that observers

FIGURE 4-11

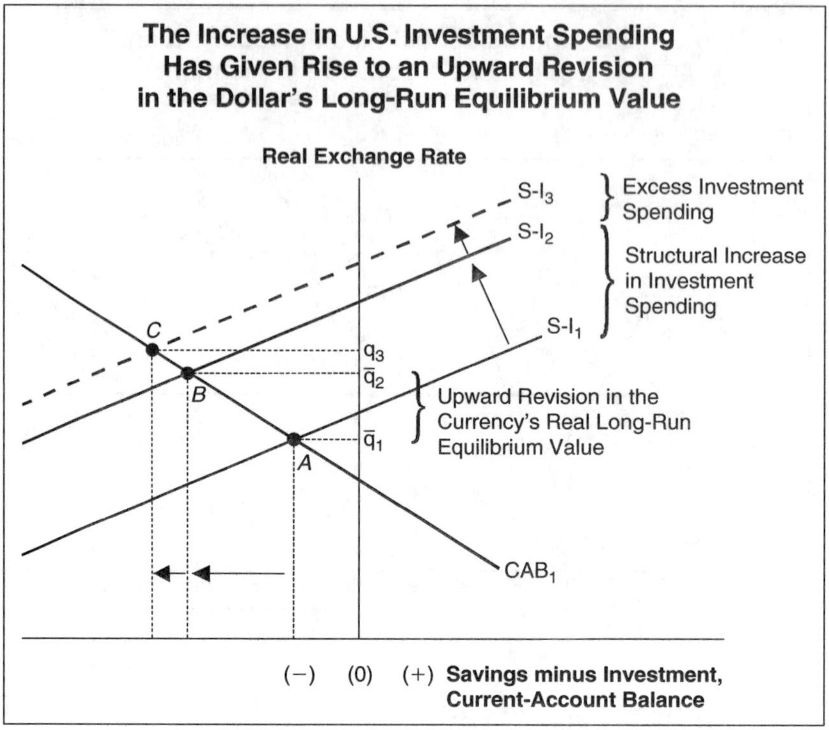

began to take notice that "something special" was taking place that was distancing the United States from the rest of the world. As Figures 4–12 and 4–13 show, in annual surveys from 1992 to 1999, professional economists had been projecting a relatively bland long-term U.S. economic outlook, with real GDP growth expected to average 2.5% per annum and productivity growth expected to rise by a modest 1.5% per annum over each ensuing 10-year period.

Normally, one would think that shifts in expectations regarding the U.S. long-term growth outlook would take place gradually over a number of years. But between 1999 and 2000, expectations seemed to change overnight. In the 2000 and 2001 surveys, professional economists' long-term projections were pushed up sharply. Economists were now forecasting long-term U.S. real GDP growth of 3.3% and U.S. productivity growth of 2.5% per annum.

It was as if economists suddenly embraced the notion that the U.S. was now enjoying a productivity miracle, brought about by "New Economy" forces, and that the gains in productivity growth would be permanent. Quite

FIGURE 4-12

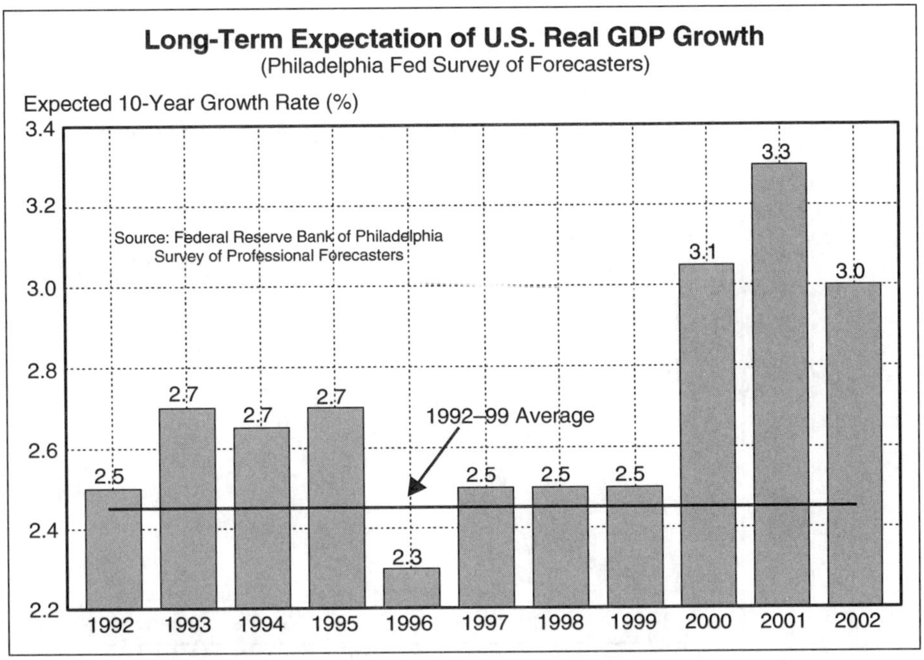

FIGURE 4-13

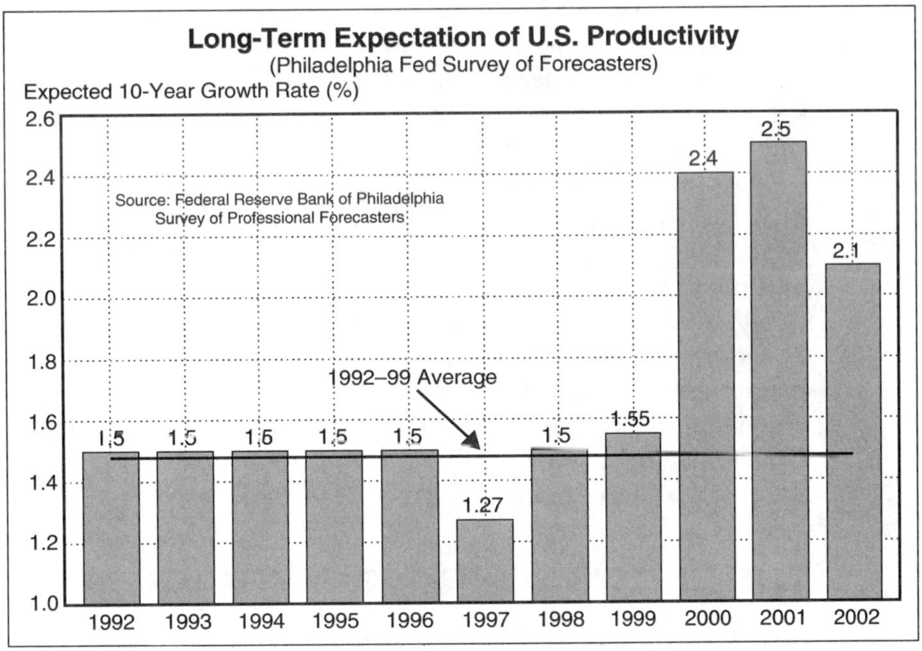

FIGURE 4-14

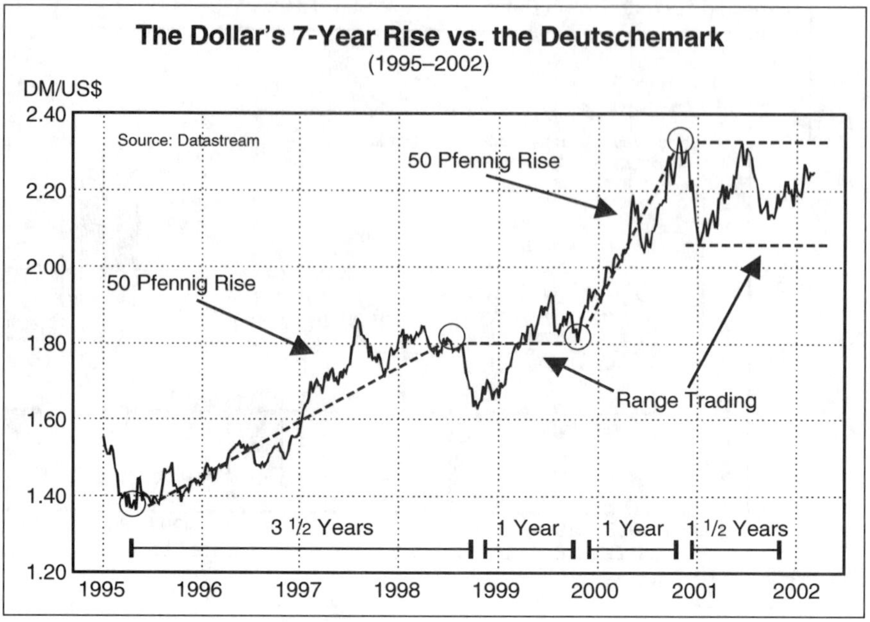

likely, a literature search would show a quantum leap in the number of academic articles that appeared with the term *New Economy* in the title beginning in 1999. (For a discussion of the New Economy's impact on the FX market, see Liesbeth Van de Craen and Peter Vanden Haute, *The New Economy and the Foreign Exchange Market*.)

Assuming the marketplace embraced the same long-term views of the U.S. economy as those held by professional forecasters, it is not hard to explain why the dollar rose 50 pfennigs versus the Deutschemark between autumn 1999 and autumn 2000 (see Figure 4–14). We believe that the suddenly improved long-term growth outlook for the U.S. economy compelled market participants to revise up sharply their notion of the dollar's real long-run equilibrium value. Indeed, the dollar's rise from the autumn of 1999 to the autumn of 2000, which followed the upward revision in the U.S. long-term growth outlook, roughly matched, in terms of magnitude, the rise that occurred in the prior 3½ years.

THE EURO'S LONG-TERM STRUGGLE

The "synthetic" euro's real trade-weighted value had been declining on a trend basis for much of the decade heading into its 1999 launch date. Yet

FIGURE 4-15

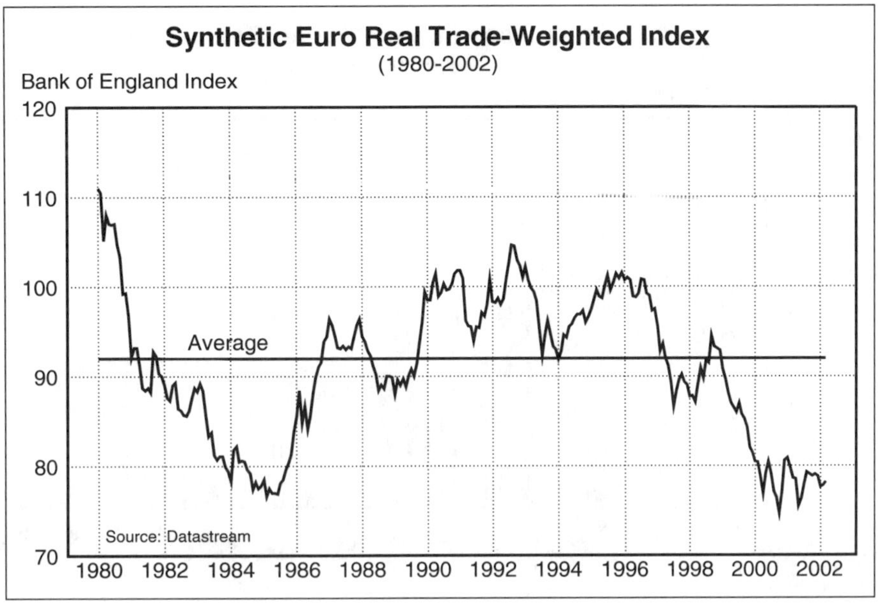

many pundits expected that the new single currency would be strong, believing that the euro would embrace all of the hard-currency attributes of the Deutschemark and would discard all of the soft-currency attributes of its depreciation-prone ERM members. This did not happen. By the fall of 2000, the euro had plummeted to a 20-year low versus the yen and British pound, and—except for the 1985 dollar bubble—the euro was trading close to a record low versus the U.S. dollar (see Figure 4–15).

Perhaps those pundits failed to recognize that the euro's long-term behavior, being a weighted average of all EMU member currencies, resembled that of a soft and not a hard currency. In fact, its persistent decline versus a wide range of currencies suggests that negative fundamental developments intrinsic to Euroland probably played a large role in the euro's long-term slide.

EUROLAND'S STRUCTURAL RIGIDITIES AND THE EURO'S REAL LONG-RUN EQUILIBRIUM VALUE

Structural rigidities in Europe's labor and product markets undoubtedly have adversely affected Europe's long-term growth potential and thus

FIGURE 4-16

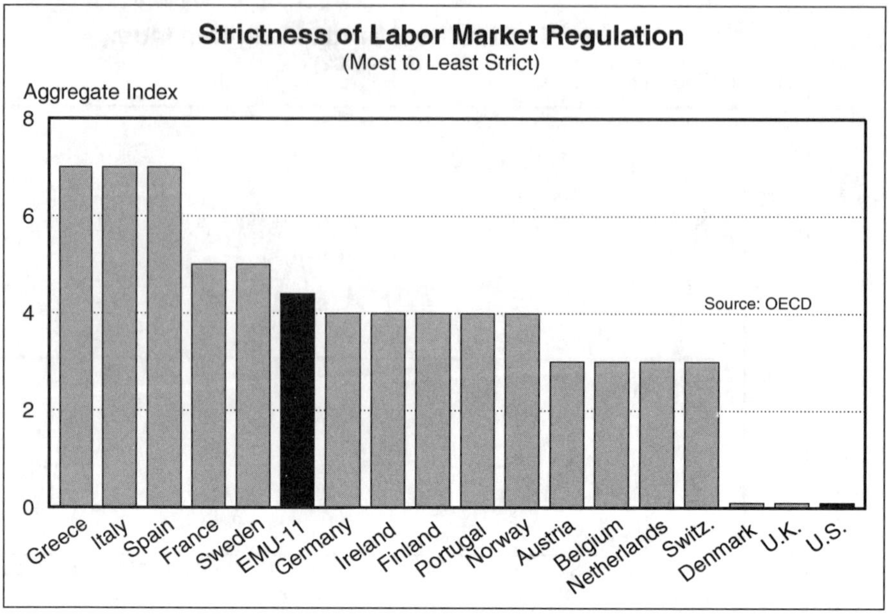

probably contributed to a downward revision in the market's assessment of the euro's real long-run equilibrium value as well. Structural rigidities in Europe's labor market include job protection legislation, working time regulations, overly generous early retirement schemes, unemployment insurance and welfare benefits, and barriers to hiring skilled labor from abroad.

On the product front, structural rigidities include the sluggishness of firms to adopt a culture of risk taking, the high cost of telecommunications, and the unwillingness of many European governments to allow market forces to operate unfettered. Figures 4–16 to 4–18 show that European labor markets are far more regulated than U.S. ones, unemployment benefits are far more generous in Europe than they are in the United States, while European taxes and real labor costs are higher than they are in the United States as well.

OVERSHOOTING EXCHANGE RATES

Since the beginning of floating exchange rates, there have been a number of occasions when exchange rates have significantly overshot their long-run

FIGURE 4-17

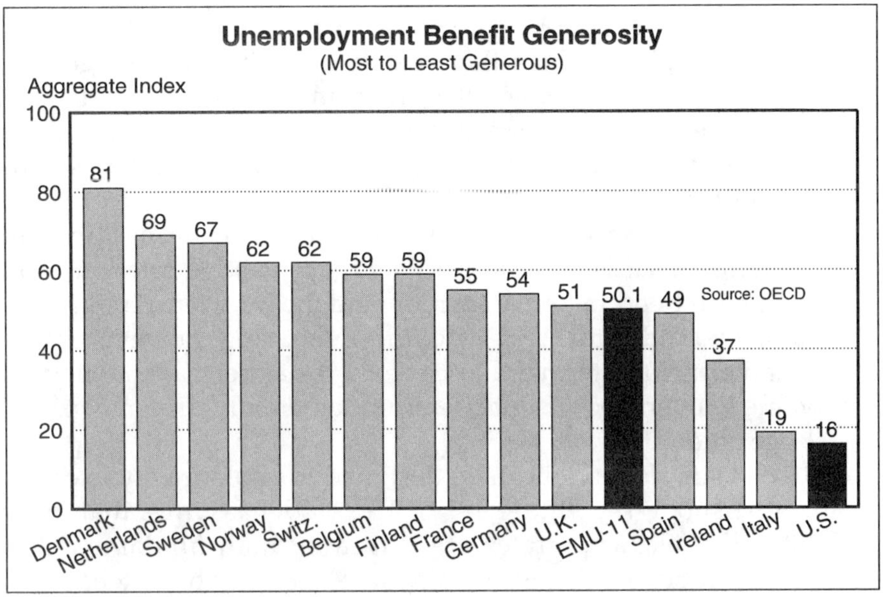

FIGURE 4-18

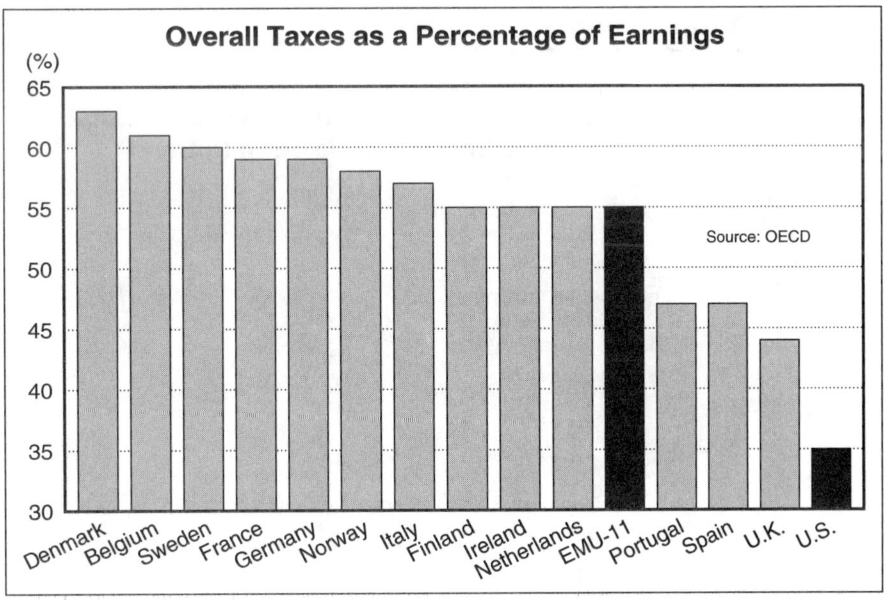

equilibrium path, either on the upside or the downside. We define an exchange-rate overshoot episode as one in which an exchange rate deviates by more than +20% or −20% from its long-run purchasing power parity path and/or where there exists a significant divergence between the actual trend in exchange rates and some long-term key determinant—such as the trend in real interest-rate differentials in the case of the Deutschemark, or the trend in relative monetary-base growth rates in the case of the Japanese yen.

For the most part, long-term cycles have strong fundamental underpinnings. That is, we can find a strong positive relationship between the long-term trend in exchange rates and the long-term trend in some key fundamental indicator. What we find interesting, however, is that at the end of a typical long-term dollar cycle there has been a tendency for the dollar's value to overshoot its long-run fundamentally driven equilibrium path by large amounts.

A simple model can be designed to explain why exchange rates tend to overshoot (see Figure 4–19). The model assumes that investors' expectations of exchange rates are driven by both fundamental and technical considerations. Mathematically, let's assume that exchange-rate expectations, e_t^e, in time period t are driven by fundamental forces, fund_t, and by the past pattern of exchange-rate movements, e_{t-1}.

FIGURE 4-19

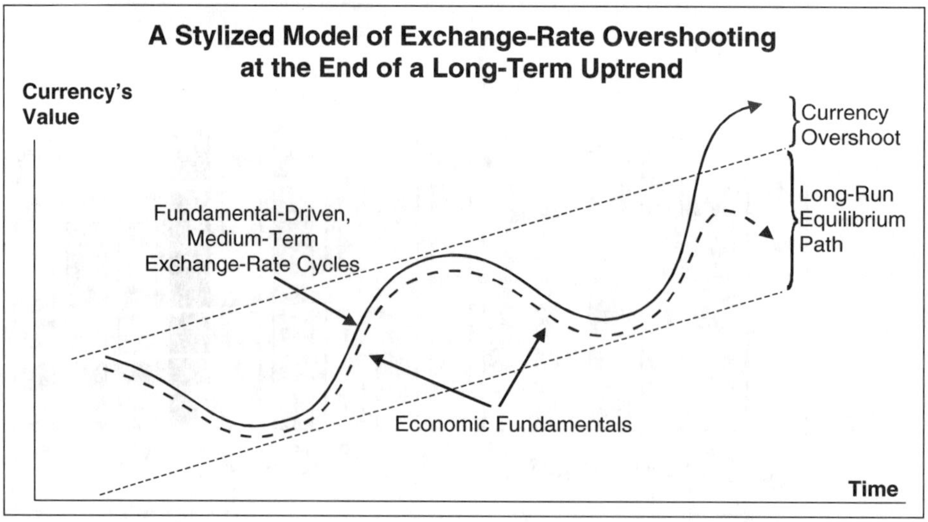

Let's further assume that the market will attach specific weights to the current trend in fundamental forces, w, and to the past pattern of exchange-rate movements, $1 - w$, in formulating its overall exchange-rate expectations. Those weights are assumed to vary over time, with the market assigning more weight to fundamentals and less weight to technicals, and vice versa, as fundamental and technical forces vary in terms of influencing the path that currencies take. Exchange-rate expectations can therefore be expressed as

$$e_t^e = w(\text{fund}_t) + (1 - w)e_{t-1}$$

Typically, in the early and middle stages of an extended exchange-rate cycle, the market tends to attach greater weight to the trend in economic fundamentals (that is, w rises). This is because the trend in exchange rates and the trend in key fundamental variables parallel each other quite closely in the early phases of most exchange-rate cycles. In the latter stages of an extended exchange-rate cycle, however, there often occurs some disconnect between the trend in the exchange rate and the trend in key fundamental variables.

What causes this disconnect to occur is the tendency of the market at the end of a long cycle to assign less weight to fundamental forces and more weight to the prevailing trend in exchange rates (that is, $1 - w$ rises). For instance, after a long cycle of currency appreciation, the market gets accustomed to being long the appreciating currency and tends to shrug off any adverse underlying fundamental developments as being just a temporary phenomenon. Hence, the market will begin to attach less weight to the deteriorating trend in fundamentals (that is, w will gradually fall) and more weight to the past favorable trend in the exchange rate (that is, $1 - w$ will gradually rise) (see Figure 4–20).

By attaching greater weight to expectations that the prevailing trend will remain strong and less weight to the deterioration of fundamental forces, the trend in exchange rates and the trend in fundamentals becomes disconnected. Eventually, a point will be reached when the market finally recognizes that the deterioration in fundamentals is a permanent phenomenon, not just a temporary one. At that point, market expectations will shift, resulting in greater weight being assigned to deteriorating fundamental forces and less weight to the prospect that the exchange-rate overshoot will persist. At this stage the unwinding of long speculative positions gives rise to a rapid, and at times violent, correction of the exchange-rate overshoot.

There have been several extraordinary episodes of major currency

FIGURE 4-20

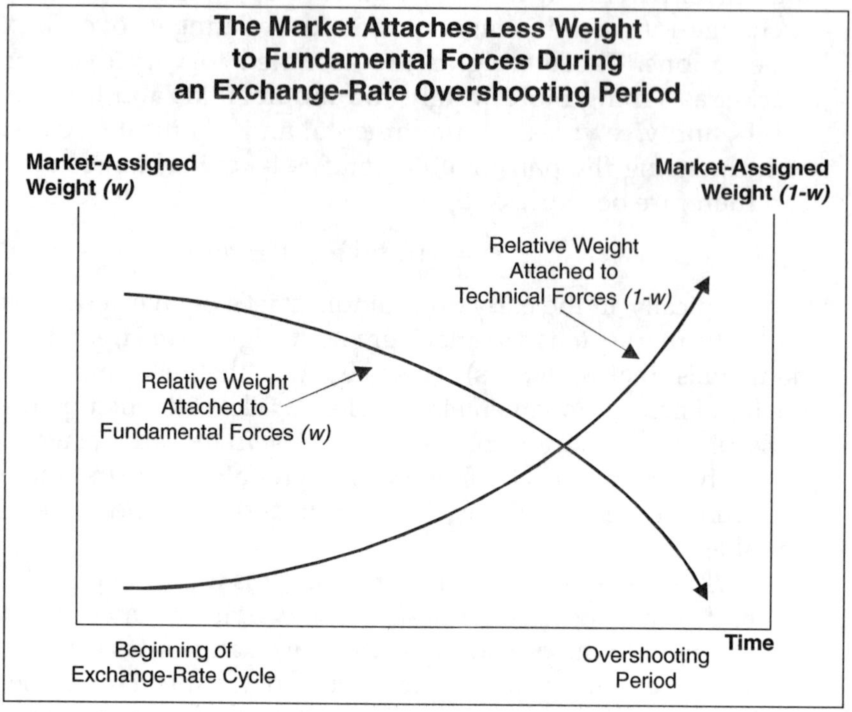

overshooting since the beginning of floating exchange rates—the Deutschemark/dollar exchange rate in the mid-1980s, the yen/dollar exchange rate in 1995 and 1998, and the euro/dollar exchange rate in 2000. In the case of the Deutschemark/dollar exchange rate in the mid-1980s, there was a significant disconnect between the trend in U.S.–German real long-term interest-rate differentials and the Deutschemark/U.S. dollar exchange rate toward the end of the dollar's remarkable run upward during the 1984–1985 dollar bubble period. There was simply no way to explain the dollar's surge in 1984–1985 on the basis of real yield spreads, and this overshoot in the dollar's value was eventually corrected in 1985–1987.

In the case of the yen/dollar exchange rate, there was a similar disconnect between the trend in U.S. and Japanese relative monetary-base growth and the trend in the yen's value versus the dollar in 1995 and again in 1998. The dollar overshot to the downside in 1995 and overshot to the upside in 1998, and in both cases the overshoots were subsequently corrected.

HOW A SHORTAGE OF STABILIZING SPECULATIVE CAPITAL CAN GIVE RISE TO EXCHANGE-RATE OVERSHOOTING

It is widely recognized that financial markets need stabilizing speculators to ensure that financial market prices do not wander too far from fair value. By buying at price levels that are perceived to be low and selling at price levels that are perceived to be high, speculators will ensure that asset prices do not become too stretched relative to fair value. If there is a fairly elastic supply of speculative capital in the foreign-exchange market, a sig-

FIGURE 4-21

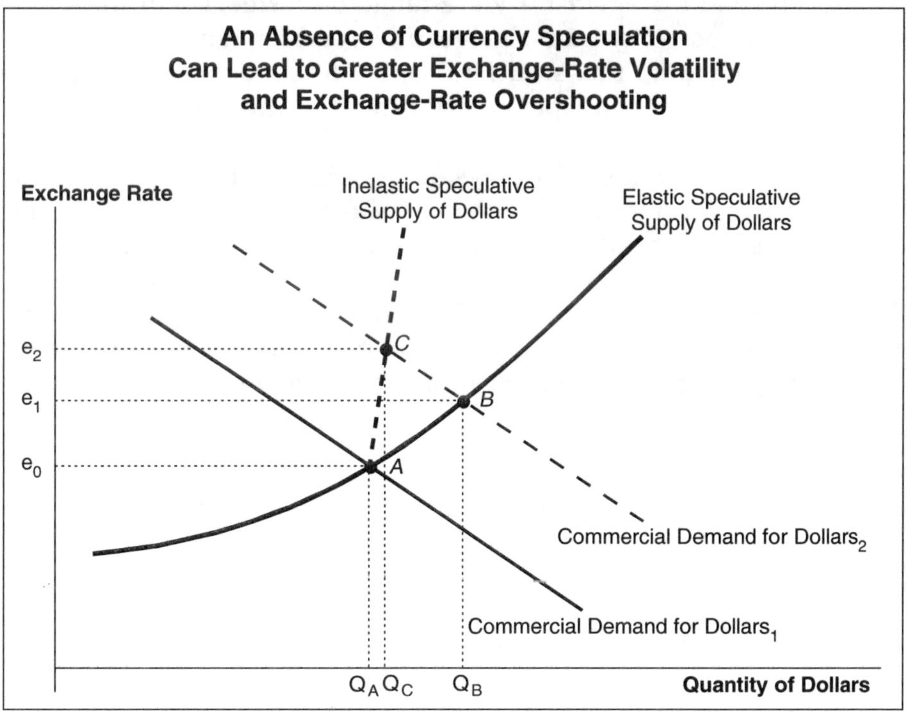

nificant increase in commercial demand for dollars (perhaps generated by a foreign acquisition of a U.S. firm) need not give rise to a dramatic rise in the dollar's value. Instead, the increased commercial demand for dollars may give rise to only a modest increase in the dollar's value from e_0 to e_1, as shown in Figure 4–21.

However, consider a situation in which there is an absence or a shortage of stabilizing speculative capital. This might occur if hedge funds, investors, and foreign-exchange traders are unwilling or unable to commit relatively large sums of capital for speculative purposes. In such a case, the supply of speculative capital in the foreign-exchange market would appear to be relatively inelastic. In that environment, it may only take a modest increase in the commercial demand for dollars to push the dollar's value sharply higher from e_0 to e_2. In other words, when there is a shortage of stabilizing speculative capital, exchange rates are likely to be more volatile and prone to overshooting, even amid modest changes in the commercial demand for dollars.

Such behavior might explain why the dollar remained significantly overvalued against a wide range of currencies in the 1999–2002 period. With many investors, hedge funds, and foreign-exchange traders unwilling or unable to risk sufficient capital to bet against the dollar, there simply was not enough speculative capital in the market to reverse the dollar's overshoot.

The tendency of speculative capital to dry up when market prices move far out of line with fair value is not unique to the foreign-exchange market. Indeed, most speculative bubbles, particularly at their peaks, are not fed by excessive speculation but instead are driven by an absence of stabilizing speculation. When an absence of stabilizing speculative capital causes exchange rates to overshoot their long-run equilibrium value, central banks often must intervene and take on the role of a stabilizing speculator.

PART THREE

Exchange-Rate Determination in the Medium Run

Exchange rates are simultaneously determined by long-term structural, medium-term cyclical, and short-term speculative forces. Since long-term structural forces often change at a glacial pace, they are likely to exert a greater influence on a currency's long-run equilibrium path than on a currency's short- or medium-term path. A variety of structural forces operate jointly to influence a currency's long-run equilibrium path. These include the long-term trend in national inflation rates, relative productivity growth, long-term trends in net foreign asset and liability positions, persistent trends in a country's terms of trade, and long-term trends in national savings and investment.

Medium-term cyclical forces often cause a currency to either rise or fall relative to its long-run equilibrium path. In many cases the medium-term deviations from the long-run equilibrium path can be quite sizeable, and in some instances they can be quite persistent. In the long run, these medium-term cyclical forces tend to wash out, and once they do, there is a tendency for the exchange rate to return to its long-run equilibrium path.

Nevertheless, in the interim, fund managers must find a way to adjust their portfolios to account for these deviations from long-run equilibrium levels or else risk serious underperformance over medium-term horizons. Since investment performance is often evaluated over relatively short time spans today, it is important for fund managers to channel their energies toward getting the direction that exchange rates take over short- and medium-term horizons right.

Medium-term trends in exchange rates tend to be influenced by the direction of macroeconomic variables. The key medium-term determinants

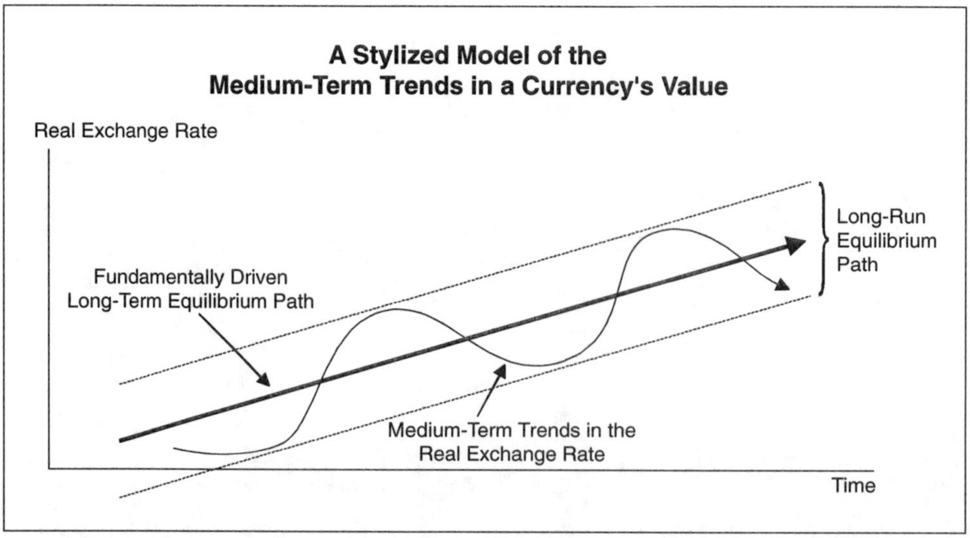

of exchange rates include trends in real interest-rate differentials, current and capital account trends, relative monetary and fiscal policies, relative economic growth, and portfolio-balance considerations. The success that these variables have had in explaining the medium-term trends that exchange rates have taken in the past is at best mixed. In many cases, one can find evidence of a strong correlation between one or more of these variables and the trend in exchange rates over several cycles. But something often happens to break this tight cyclical linkage. When it does, the subsequent usefulness of that variable as an explanatory variable becomes seriously undermined.

Overall, we find that shifts in fiscal and monetary policies play the most important role in driving a currency's value on a medium-term basis, with many of the major exchange-rate cycles in the 1990s attributable to shifts in fiscal/monetary policy mixes of individual countries. We find that the trend in the ratio of Japan's monetary base to the U.S. monetary base has done the best job of explaining the Japanese yen/U.S. dollar exchange rate's medium-term cyclical path over the past 12 years. In the case of the Deutschemark (and now the euro), the trend in the U.S./German (Euroland) real long-term yield spread has done the best job of explaining the medium-term cyclical paths that the Deutschemark (euro)/U.S. dollar exchange rate has taken over the past 25 years.

CHAPTER 5

International Parity Conditions

International parity conditions are financial arbitrage conditions that would exist in an ideal world. The key international parity conditions are (1) purchasing power parity, (2) covered interest-rate parity, (3) uncovered interest-rate parity, (4) the Fisher effect, which focuses on inflation as the key determinant of nominal interest rates, and (5) the forward exchange rate as an unbiased predictor of the future spot rate. Parity conditions show how inflation differentials, interest-rate differentials, forward exchange rates, and expected changes in exchange rates are linked internationally. Parity conditions tell us that high (low)-inflation countries should see their currencies depreciate (appreciate) over time, and that forward exchange rates should function as unbiased predictors of future spot rates. These international parity conditions form the building blocks of many of the major macro models of exchange-rate determination.

Empirical evidence indicates that most of the key international parity conditions rarely hold in either the short or medium term. There are often significant departures from purchasing power parity, interest-rate differentials often fail to explain future exchange-rate changes, and the forward exchange rate has been found to be a poor predictor of the future spot exchange rate. Why study international parity conditions if they fail to hold? Actually, if international parity conditions held at all times, there would be no profitable arbitrage opportunities available for international investors to exploit by moving capital from one market to another. It is only when international parity conditions fail to hold that profit opportunities from cross-border investments become available.

The following international parity conditions form the building blocks of modern exchange-rate analysis:

Ex Ante Purchasing Power Parity

According to ex ante purchasing power parity (PPP), the expected change in the spot exchange rate should equal the difference in expected national inflation rates (see Figure 5–1). Ex ante PPP tells us that a high-inflation country should see its currency depreciate and that a low-inflation country should see its currency appreciate over time.

FIGURE 5-1

$$\dot{e}^e = \dot{p}_F{}^e - \dot{p}_D{}^e$$

Expected Change in Exchange Rate = Foreign-Domestic Expected Inflation Differential

Covered Interest-Rate Parity

According to the covered interest-rate parity condition, an investment in a foreign-currency deposit completely hedged against exchange-rate risk should yield exactly the same return as a comparable domestic-currency deposit. Since a hedged foreign-currency investment will have the same risk characteristics as a domestic-currency investment, we should expect the yield on the domestic investment, i_D, to equal the foreign interest rate, i_F, less the forward discount, FD (see Figure 5–2). Indeed, arbitrage should insure that this would always be the case. The empirical evidence in support of covered interest-rate parity is quite robust.

FIGURE 5-2

$$i_F - i_D = FD$$

Foreign-Domestic Interest-Rate Differential = Forward Discount

Uncovered Interest-Rate Parity

According to the uncovered interest-rate parity (UIP) condition, the expected return on an uncovered foreign-currency investment should equal the expected return on a comparable domestic-currency investment (see Figure 5–3). The expected return on a domestic-currency investment, i_D, is known with certainty, while the expected return on an uncovered foreign-currency investment, $i_F - \dot{e}^e_F$, is not known with certainty because the actual change in the exchange rate, $\dot{e}$, may turn out to be different from the expected change in the exchange rate, $\dot{e}^e$. The UIP condition implies that investors do not need to be compensated—in the form of a risk premium—for taking on the risk that their expectations may prove to be wrong. In the absence of a risk premium, the yield spread between foreign and domestic currency deposits, $i_F - i_D$, should adjust to equal the expected change in the exchange rate, $\dot{e}^e$. The empirical evidence is not highly supportive of UIP in either the short or medium run.

FIGURE 5-3

$$\dot{e}^e = i_F - i_D$$

Expected Change in Exchange Rate	=	Foreign-Domestic Interest-Rate Differential

Fisher Effect

According to the Fisher effect, the nominal interest rate, i, in a given country will equal the real interest rate, r, plus the expected inflation rate, $\dot{p}^e$. If the real interest rate in the foreign country is equal to the domestic real interest rate, $r_F = r_D$, then the yield spread between two countries, $i_F - i_D$, should equal the expected inflation differential between the two countries, $\dot{p}^e_F - \dot{p}^e_D$ (see Figure 5–4). Empirical evidence suggests that real interest rates often differ among countries. Thus, nominal yield spreads will not necessarily reflect differences in national inflation rates.

FIGURE 5-4

$$i_F - i_D = \dot{p}_F{}^e - \dot{p}_D{}^e$$

Foreign-Domestic Interest-Rate Differential	=	Foreign-Domestic Expected Inflation Differential

Forward Rate as an Unbiased Predictor of the Future Spot Rate

If covered interest-rate parity holds such that $i_F - i_D = \text{FD}$, and uncovered interest-rate parity holds such that $\dot{e}^e = i_F - i_D$, then the forward discount, FD, will equal the expected change in the spot exchange rate, $\dot{e}^e$ (see Figure 5–5). Empirical evidence suggests, however, that the forward exchange rate is a poor and biased predictor of the future spot exchange rate.

FIGURE 5-5

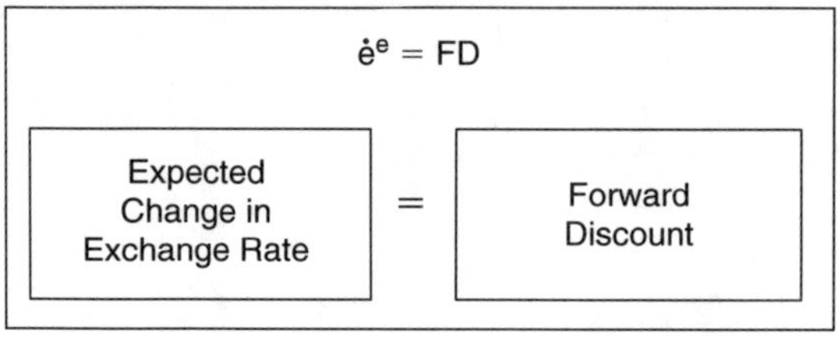

International Parity Conditions: How Spot Exchange Rates, Forward Exchange Rates, and Interest Rates Are Linked Internationally

If all of the key international parity conditions held at all times, the expected change in the spot exchange rate would equal (1) the forward discount, (2) the interest-rate differential, and (3) the expected inflation differential (see Figure 5–6). These conditions will hold only in an ideal world. Empirical studies actually reject most of the parity conditions (covered interest-rate parity being the exception). There are often large and persistent deviations from PPP and UIP, and the forward exchange rate has been found to be both a poor and a biased predictor of the future spot rate. When these parity conditions fail to hold, profitable investment opportunities become available.

THE REAL INTEREST-RATE DIFFERENTIAL MODEL OF EXCHANGE-RATE DETERMINATION

International capital flows have become increasingly mobile in the past 20 years as barriers to cross-border movements of capital have been gradually lifted in most markets. As cross-border capital flows have risen in importance, interest-rate differentials have come to play a more important role in the determination of exchange rates. Indeed, empirical evidence has shown that relative current-account trends have become less important in explain-

FIGURE 5-6

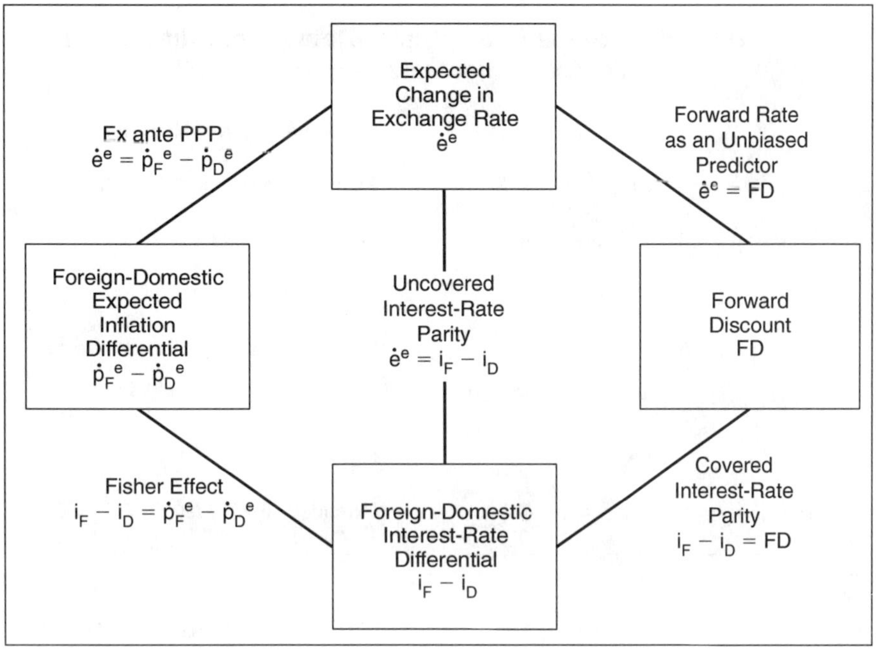

ing exchange-rate movements in the past two decades, while interest-rate differentials have become more important.

To analyze the role that interest-rate differentials play in the determination of exchange rates, many international economists use the real interest-rate differential (RID) model as their principal analytical tool. The RID model is a formal model that links the trend in real exchange rates to the trend in real interest-rate differentials (see Figure 5–7).

The RID model is fairly simple to derive. If it is assumed that both uncovered interest-rate parity (equation 1) and ex ante purchasing power parity (equation 2) hold in the long run, then the expected long-run change in the dollar's real value will equal the real long-term yield spread (equations 3 and 4). If it is assumed that the expected change in the dollar's real value in the long run equals the difference between the dollar's actual real value and its real long-run equilibrium level (equation 5), it can then be shown in equation 7 that the dollar's actual real value, $q_\$$, can be expressed as a function of two key variables—the dollar's real long-run equilibrium value, $\bar{q}_\$$, and the real long-term interest-rate differential, $r_{US} - r_F$. According to this model, the dollar's real value would rise if there were an upward revision in the market's assessment of the dollar's real long-run equilibrium value and/or if there were a rise in the U.S./foreign real long-term interest-rate differential.

FIGURE 5-7

Derivation of the Real Interest-Rate Differential Model of Exchange-Rate Determination

(1)	$\dot{e}^e_\$ = i_F - i_{US}$	Uncovered Interest-Rate Parity
(2)	$\dot{e}^e_\$ = \dot{q}^e_\$ + (\dot{p}^e_F - \dot{p}^e_{US})$	Ex Ante Purchasing Power Parity
(3)	$\dot{q}^e_\$ = (i_F - \dot{p}^e_F) - (i_{US} - \dot{p}^e_{US})$	(1) minus (2)
(4)	$\dot{q}^e_\$ = r_F - r_{US}$	Real Interest-Rate Parity
(5)	$\dot{q}^e_\$ = \bar{q}_\$ - q_\$$	Long-Run Exchange-Rate Adjustment
(6)	$\bar{q}_\$ - q_\$ = r_F - r_{US}$	Combine (4) and (5)
(7)	$q_\$ = \bar{q}_\$ + (r_{US} - r_F)$	RID Model
(8)	$q_\$ = \bar{q}_\$ + (r_{US} - r_F) - (\phi_{US} - \phi_F)$	Extended RID Model

The RID model can be extended to incorporate shifts in risk premiums on U.S., ϕ_{US}, and foreign assets, ϕ_F. The extended model is shown in equation 8, where a rise in the risk premium on U.S. assets tends to exert downward pressure on the dollar's value, while a rise in the risk premium on foreign assets tends to exert upward pressure on the dollar's value.

THE REAL INTEREST-RATE DIFFERENTIAL MODEL: THEORY

Empirical studies have found that the trend in real long-term yield spreads does a better job of explaining exchange-rate movements than the trend in nominal short-term yield spreads. There are two reasons for this. First, real yields—rather than nominal yields—better reflect structural shifts in savings and investment and the easing/tightening moves by central banks. Second, changes in long-term interest rates are likely to have a more profound impact on exchange rates than changes in short-term rates because changes in short-term rates alone can be and often are transitory, while changes in long-term rates often reflect expectations of sustained movements of short-term interest rates in the future. Taking both of these factors together, the historical evidence supports a stronger linkage between exchange rates and real long-term yield spreads than between exchange rates and nominal short-term yield spreads.

Figure 5–8 shows that the magnitude of an exchange-rate response to a given change in real interest-rate spreads is far greater when real long-term yield spreads change (from q_0 to q_5) than when real short-term yield spreads change (from q_0 to q_1). That is because exchange rates tend to respond more vigorously to changes in real interest-rate spreads that are expected to persist. Figure 5–8 also suggests that large changes in exchange rates may result from fairly modest changes in real long-term interest-rate differentials. The diagram illustrates as well that in the long run, the response of an exchange rate to a change in real yield spreads will only be transitory.

In theory, the rise in the real exchange rate in response to the change in real yield spreads should be instantaneous, followed by a gradual decline in the real exchange rate back to its real long-run equilibrium value as real yield spreads return to their normal levels. In practice, both the change in real yield spreads and the change in exchange rates tend to be much more gradual than the diagram depicts. It is this more gradual response that gives rise to the tight graphical relationship that one finds when comparing the trend in the dollar's value with the trend in U.S./foreign real long-term yield spreads.

THE REAL INTEREST-RATE DIFFERENTIAL MODEL: EVIDENCE

The trend in real long-term interest-rate differentials has played a pivotal role in driving the dollar's value versus the Deutschemark in the past few decades (as shown in Figures 5–9 to 5–11, which chart the various periods).

FIGURE 5-8

Real Exchange-Rate Response to a Rise in Real Short- and Long-Term Interest-Rate Differentials

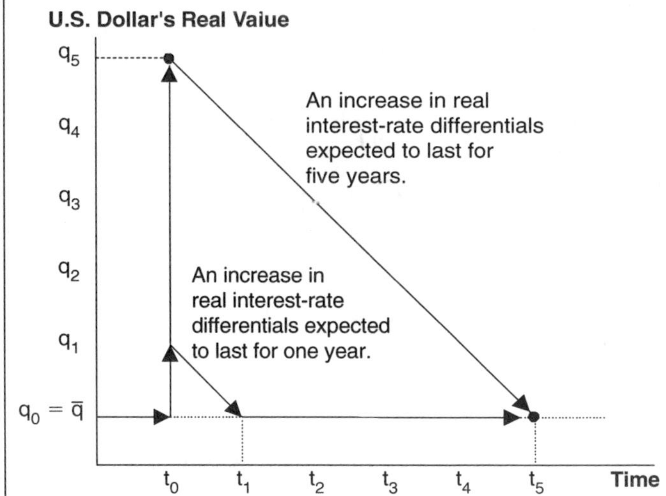

Source: Adapted from Clark *et al.* (1994).

FIGURE 5-9

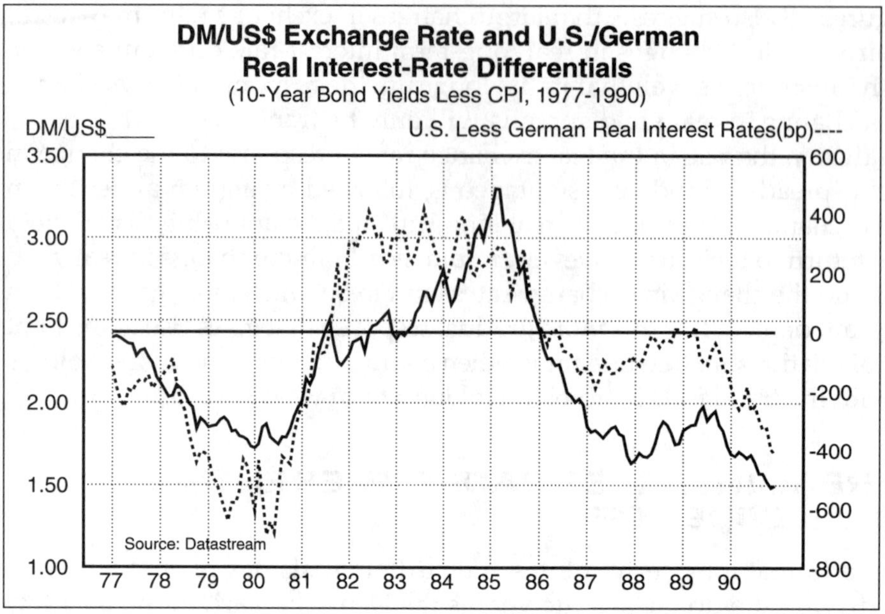

FIGURE 5-10

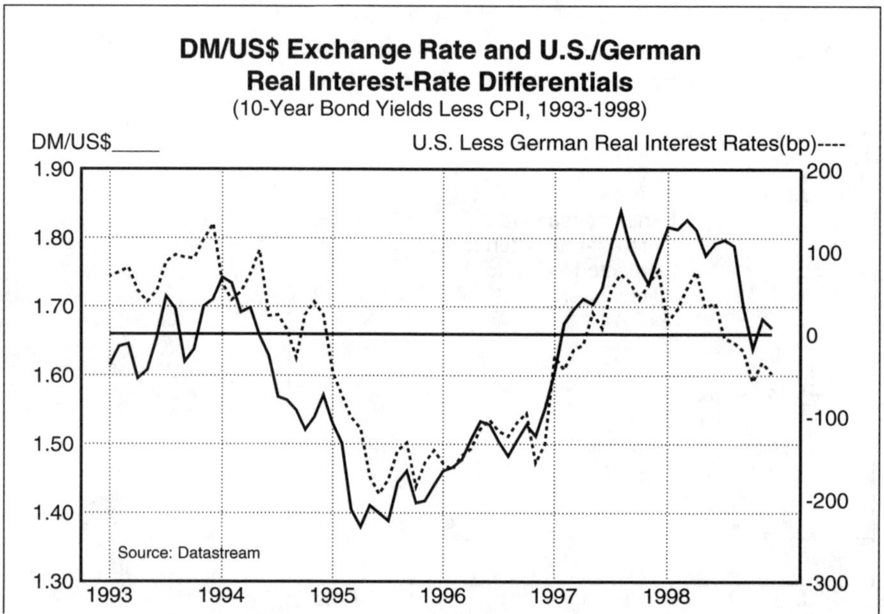

FIGURE 5-11

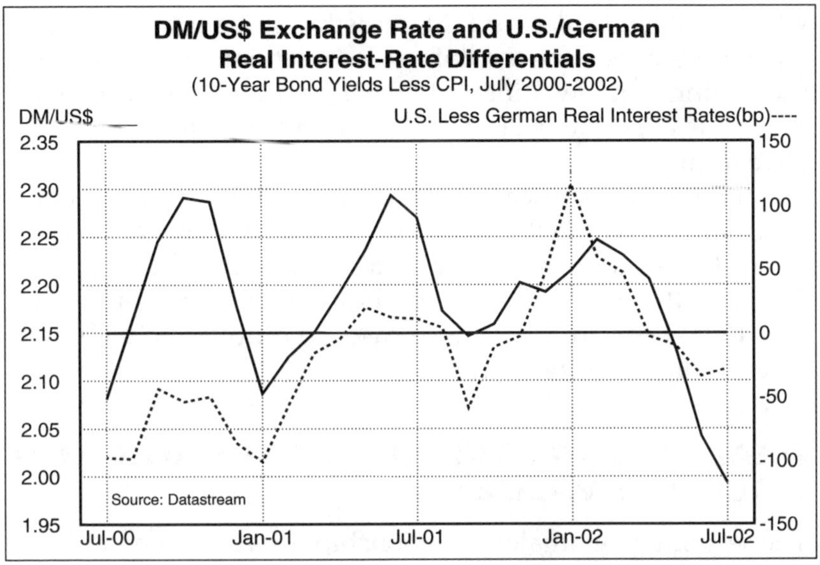

The decline of the dollar in the late 1970s, the rise of the dollar in the first half of the 1980s, and the dollar's decline after 1985 can be attributed to changes in U.S./German real long-term yield spreads.

Over the 1993–1998 period, an adverse shift in real yield spreads led to the dollar's decline in 1994–1995, while the dollar's rise in 1995–1998 can be attributed to a shift in the U.S./German real yield spread that was favorable to the dollar.

Beginning in the fall of 1999, however, the relationship broke down for a year when the trend in Deutschemark (now the euro) completely diverged from the trend in the U.S./German (now the U.S./European) real long-term yield spread. Although real yield spreads moved against the United States, the dollar nevertheless surged against the euro. The dollar's gains were likely attributable to a rise in the dollar's real long-run equilibrium level, $\bar{q}_{\$}$, which more than offset the decline in the real yield spread.

The breakdown in the real yield spread/exchange rate linkage in 1999–2000 appears to have been only a temporary phenomenon. The indications are that the real-interest-rate-spread/exchange-rate linkage was re-established in 2001–2002.

NOMINAL SHORT-TERM YIELDS AND THE DOLLAR'S VALUE

To many FX market participants, 2001 was a highly unusual year. The Federal Reserve cut short-term interest rates from 6.5% to 1.75% and

U.S./foreign short-term yield spreads narrowed dramatically, yet the dollar remained remarkably resilient. This has led some observers to question whether the old rules for FX forecasting still apply. Indeed, some observers have tried to redefine the linkage between interest rates and exchange rates by arguing that lower interest rates may, in fact, be positive for a currency if they raise expectations of future economic growth in both absolute and relative terms.

From an historical vantage point, 2001 does not appear to be that unusual. Indeed, 2001 is not the first time that nominal U.S. short-term interest rates and the dollar's value have moved in opposite directions. Consider the Fed tightening episodes of 1972–1974, 1977–1980, 1986–1988, and 1994–1995. In all of those cases, the dollar actually fell, and in most cases, it did so quite sharply.

REAL LONG-TERM YIELD SPREADS AND THE DOLLAR'S VALUE

The seemingly anomalous relationship between nominal short-term interest rates and the dollar's value that occurred in 1972–1974, 1977–1980, 1986–1988, and 1994–1995 can be explained by the trend that real long-term interest-rate differentials took in all four episodes. In all of those cycles, real long-term yield spreads moved in favor of Germany, which supported the case for a weaker, not a stronger, dollar.

In 2001, the same thing happened, except in reverse. Even though nominal short-term yield spreads moved in Europe's favor, real long-term yield spreads actually moved modestly in favor of the dollar.

The conclusion one should draw from this historical analysis is that the level and trend in nominal short-term yield spreads may not be the best guide for explaining medium-term exchange-rate movements. Rather, it is the level and trend in real long-term yield spreads that do the best job in terms of explaining medium-term exchange-rate movements.

FORWARD-RATE BIAS

Numerous academic papers have investigated empirically whether the forward exchange rate has served as a reliable unbiased predictor of the future spot exchange rate. The forward-rate predictor hypothesis is usually tested by regressing the change in the exchange rate, $\dot{e}_{t+k}$, on the forward discount, $FD_{t,k}$:

$$\dot{e}_{t+k} = \alpha + \beta(FD_{t,k})$$

If the forward exchange rate were an unbiased predictor of the future spot rate, estimates of the regression coefficient, beta (β), would be equal to 1.0. If $\beta = 1.0$, then $\dot{e}_{t+k}$ would equal $FD_{t,k}$, on average, over time.

Interestingly, the academic evidence strongly rejects the hypothesis that the forward exchange rate is an unbiased predictor of the future spot exchange rate, with estimates of β that are often significantly less than 1. Indeed, β has often been found to be less than 0. In a survey of 75 published papers on the forward-rate predictor hypothesis, the average estimate of β was found to be -0.88.

This startling finding has the following implication for currency investment strategies. Currencies that trade at a forward discount, on average, tend to weaken less than the amount implied by the forward discount. If anything, there has been a tendency for such currencies to appreciate, not depreciate, over time. This means that the forward discount has been a biased predictor of future changes in the spot exchange rate. Hence, the term *forward discount bias*. The opposite applies for currencies that trade at a forward premium. From a strategy standpoint, if these findings on past performance were to remain valid in the future, investors would stand to benefit by overweighting currencies that trade at a forward discount and underweighting currencies that trade at a forward premium.

Various interpretations have been offered to explain these anomalous findings. One view holds that currencies that trade at a forward discount are more risky than those that trade at a forward premium. Hence, investors demand a higher risk premium to buy and hold such currencies, and the excess return earned by investing in such currencies merely represents the reward for accepting higher risk. Another view holds that the market simply makes repeated expectational errors, and that investors could exploit this by trading against the implicit views expressed in the forward exchange market.

Although excess returns could have been earned in the past by investors who sought to exploit the "bias" in the forward discount, the risk/return tradeoff is not always attractive for such strategies. Monthly returns can be and often are quite volatile for single-currency trades. In fact, single-currency trading strategies have not been attractive enough to justify risking large sums to trade the bias. (A single-currency strategy consists of buying, or going long, only the highest-yielding currency, that is, the currency with the largest forward discount, and funding it by borrowing (or going short) only the lowest-yielding currency, that is, the currency with the largest forward premium.)

Risk-adjusted excess returns from following diversified multicurrency approaches to exploit the bias, however, have been more impressive. Adopting a diversified strategy of going long the three highest-yielding currencies in the industrial world and funding that position by going short the three lowest-yielding currencies has yielded estimated Sharpe ratios averaging 0.7 to 0.8 for dollar, euro, and yen-based investors. That is nearly double the Sharpe ratios generated by buying and holding the shares of the S&P 500 Index.

TRADING THE BIAS

Our recommended approach to trading the forward-rate bias is to adopt a diversified strategy to exploit the fact that currencies trading at a forward discount tend to outperform those currencies trading at a forward premium. Consider a straightforward strategy involving the 11 major industrial currencies—the U.S. dollar, euro, Japanese yen, Swiss franc, British pound, Canadian dollar, Australian dollar, New Zealand dollar, Danish krone, Norwegian krone, and Swedish krona—in which an investor would go long the three highest-yielding currencies and simultaneously go short the three lowest-yielding currencies. Net long/short positions are put on at the beginning of each month and then closed at the end of each month. This process is repeated each month over time.

Figure 5–12 shows how the monthly recommendations for long and short currency positions for the 11 industrial country currencies can vary over time. At the beginning of 2001, a high-yield/low-yield currency investment strategy would have taken long positions in the Norwegian krone, New Zealand dollar, and U.S. dollar that were fully funded by short positions in the Swedish krona, Swiss franc, and Japanese yen (see Figure 5–13). By the end of 2001, with U.S. yields having fallen below those in most other markets, this strategy shifted in favor of being long the Norwegian krone, New Zealand dollar, and Australian dollar, and short the Swiss franc, U.S. dollar, and Japanese yen (see Figure 5–14).

FORWARD-RATE BIAS STRATEGY LONG-RUN TRACK RECORD FOR U.S. DOLLAR–BASED INVESTORS

An analysis of the risks and returns that would have been generated for a U.S. dollar–based investor following a diversified forward-rate bias strategy indicates that relatively attractive risk-adjusted returns could have been earned in the past 16 years. Over the 1986–2001 period, the average annual excess return from following the forward-rate bias strategy was around 5.6%, with an annualized standard deviation of 7.8% and a Sharpe ratio of 0.73. This Sharpe ratio compares favorably with the annualized Sharpe ratio on a buy-and-hold S&P 500 equity strategy of 0.3 to 0.4. At the end of January 2001, the cumulative excess return since 1986 of the diversified forward-rate bias strategy stood at 233% (see Figure 5–15).

FORWARD-RATE BIAS: THE ECONOMIC RATIONALE

Empirical evidence indicates that in the *very* long run, the cumulative returns on U.S. dollar–denominated and foreign-currency-denominated

FIGURE 5-12

Recommended Long and Short Positions versus the U.S. Dollar from Adhering to Long High-Yielders/Short Low-Yielders Currency-Investment Strategy

(January 2001-April 2002)

Month	AUD	CAD	DKK	EUR	JPY	NZD	NOK	SEK	CHF	GBP	USD
Jan-01	-	-	-	-	short	**long**	**long**	short	short	-	**long**
Feb-01	-	-	-	-	short	**long**	**long**	short	short	**long**	-
Mar-01	-	-	-	-	short	**long**	**long**	short	short	**long**	-
Apr-01	-	-	-	-	short	**long**	**long**	short	short	**long**	-
May-01	-	-	-	-	short	**long**	**long**	short	short	**long**	-
Jun-01	-	-	-	-	short	**long**	**long**	-	short	**long**	short
Jul-01	-	-	-	-	short	**long**	**long**	-	short	**long**	short
Aug-01	-	-	-	-	short	**long**	**long**	-	short	**long**	short
Sep-01	-	-	-	-	short	**long**	**long**	-	short	**long**	short
Oct-01	-	-	-	-	short	**long**	**long**	-	short	**long**	short
Nov-01	**long**	-	-	-	short	**long**	**long**	-	short	-	short
Dec-01	**long**	-	-	-	short	**long**	**long**	-	short	-	short
Jan-02	**long**	-	-	-	short	**long**	**long**	-	short	-	short
Feb-02	**long**	-	-	-	short	**long**	**long**	-	short	-	short
Mar-02	**long**	-	-	-	short	**long**	**long**	-	short	-	short
Apr-02	**long**	-	-	-	short	**long**	**long**	-	short	-	short
May-02	-	-	-	-	short	**long**	**long**	**long**	short	-	short

Note: Datastream is the source of the underlying data.

FIGURE 5-13

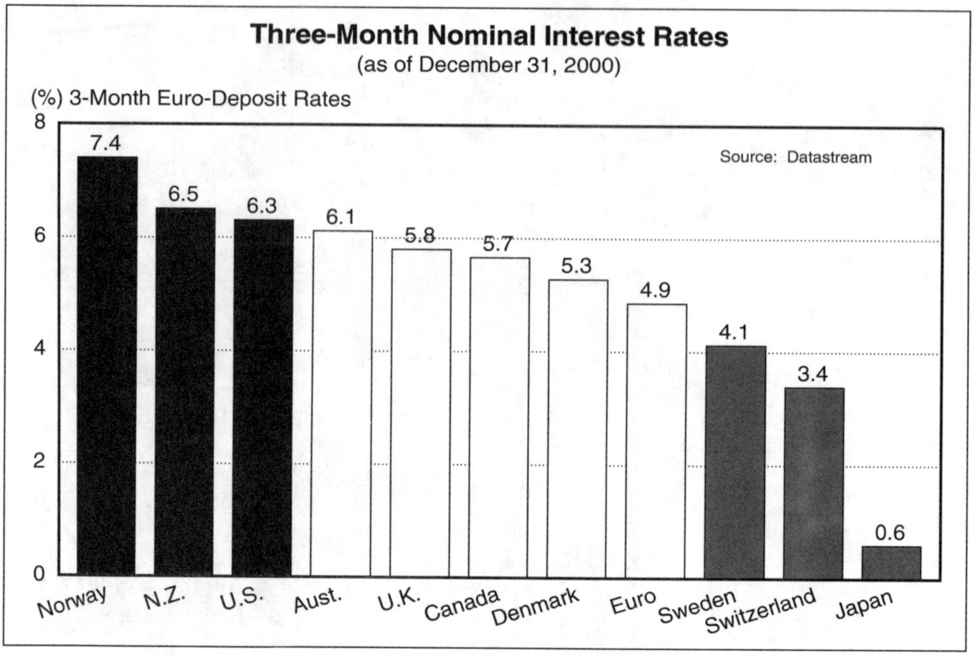

FIGURE 5-14

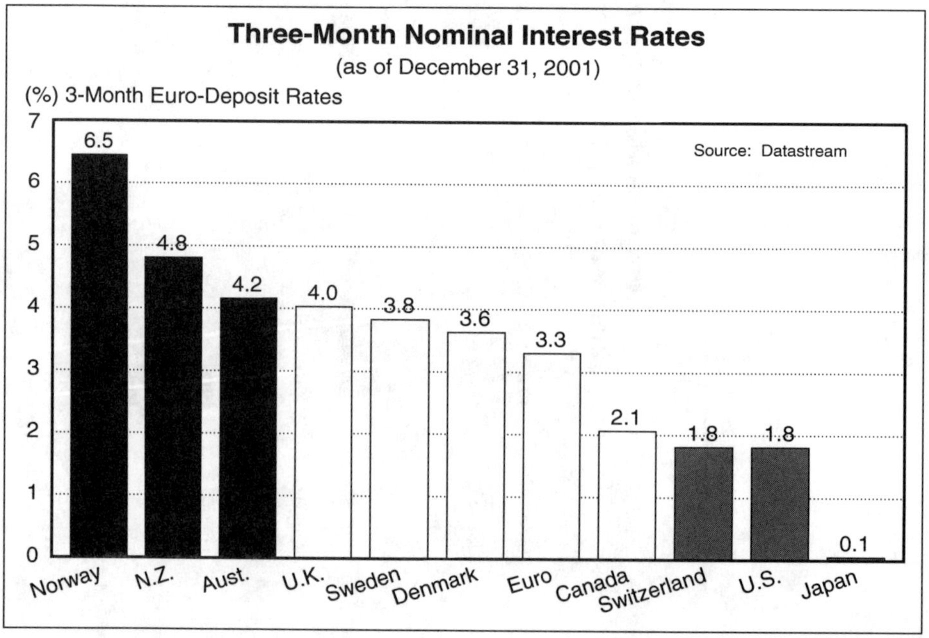

FIGURE 5-15

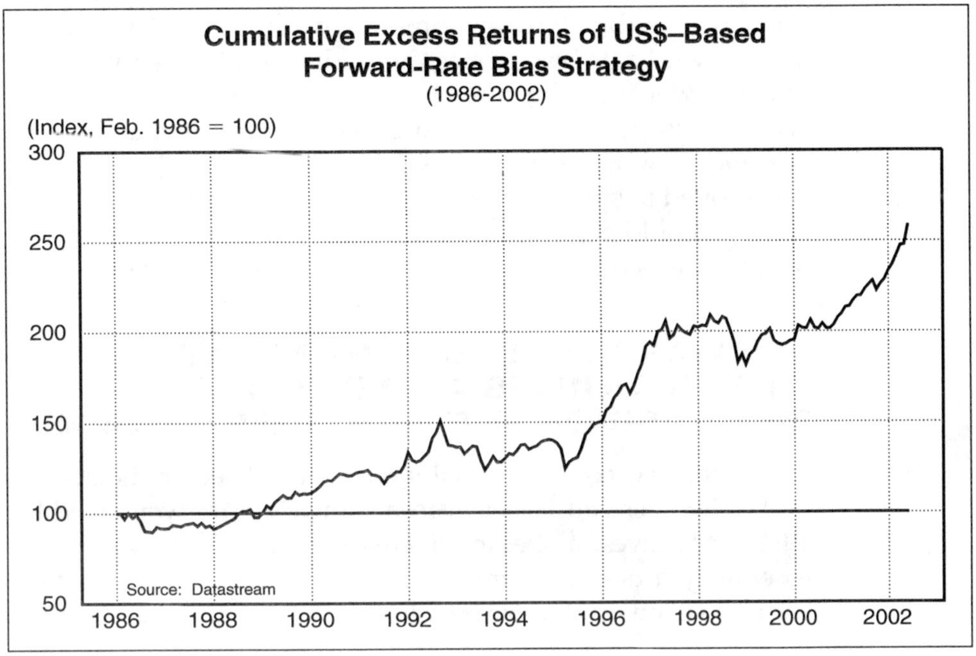

short-term fixed-income instruments are broadly the same. That is, high-yield markets have seen their currencies weaken over time, while low-yield markets have seen their currencies strengthen over time.

Indeed, consider the economic consequences if the cumulative returns on a persistently high-yielding market exceeded the cumulative returns on a persistently low-yielding market. One market could consistently outperform another market only if (1) its real yields were consistently higher, which would dampen that country's long-run growth prospects, or (2) its currency became progressively more overvalued on a PPP basis, which would dampen the country's long-run trade competitiveness. Eventually, a deterioration in growth and/or competitiveness would give rise to corrective moves on the interest-rate and/or exchange-rate fronts that would erase the cumulative excess returns. As shown in Figure 5–16, the cumulative returns of U.S. and foreign money-market instruments in U.S. dollar terms were virtually the same for the 1990–1999 period.

How, then, do forward-rate bias strategies generate such attractive risk-adjusted excess returns? The answer is that in the industrialized world, individual markets often trade places with other markets in terms of which market offers the highest or lowest yield (see Figure 5–17). Consider the following: When currency *A*'s yield rises above currency *B*'s yield, the widening of the *A–B* yield spread will likely contribute to a rise in currency *A*'s value. When currency *A*'s yield begins to fall relative to currency *B*'s yield, downward pressure on currency *A* is likely to materialize. The forward-rate bias strategy would generate positive excess returns if an investor went long currency *A* when its yield rose above currency *B*'s, and would also generate positive excess returns if that investor went short currency *A* when its yield fell below currency *B*'s, as long as the exchange rate moved in sympathy with the *A–B* yield spread. Thus, the forward-rate strategy could generate significant excess returns, even though the cumulative returns on currencies *A* and *B* might be the same in the long run.

FORWARD-RATE BIAS STRATEGY OPPORTUNITIES AND PITFALLS: THE CASE OF THE YEN CARRY TRADE

The monetary, fiscal, external, and financial-sector shocks that hit Japan in 1995–1998 were all largely yen-negative. As the yen steadily weakened in 1995–1998, investors became increasingly confident that the yen's path was essentially a one-way street, which encouraged fund managers to take on aggressive long-dollar/short-yen positions. As the yen weakened on a trend

FIGURE 5-16

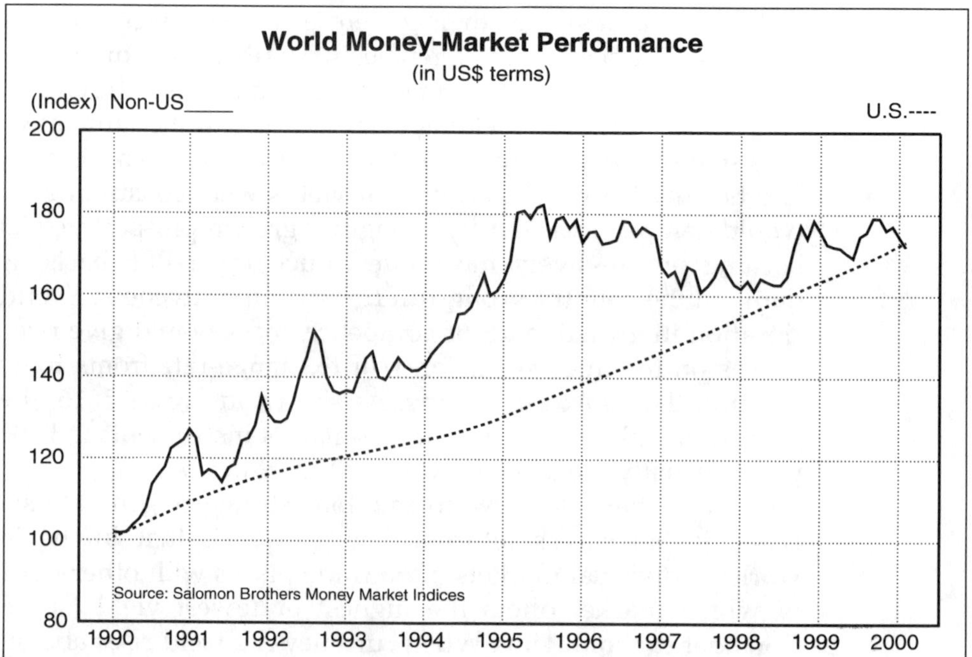

FIGURE 5-17

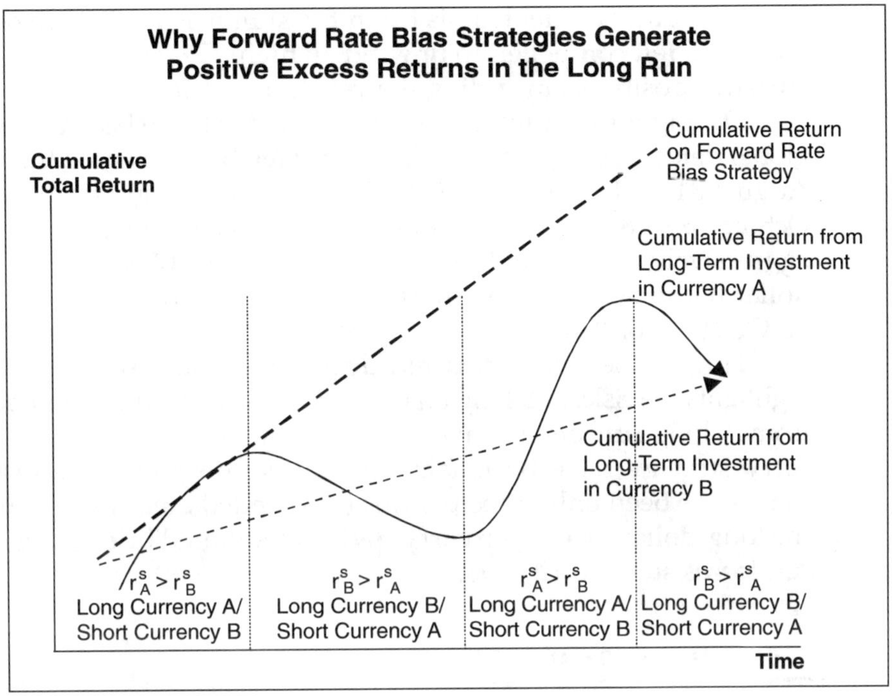

basis for 3½ straight years and with the U.S./Japan short-term yield spread averaging around 500 basis points, the "Yen Carry Trade" (borrowing in yen to invest in dollar-denominated securities) became enormously popular.

The yen carry trade generated large and persistent excess returns over the April 1995–August 1998 period. While it is difficult to quantify precisely how large the outstanding positions were at their peak, BIS data on foreign-exchange market turnover suggest that the yen carry trades were probably quite sizeable, given that the yen's share of total foreign-exchange turnover rose substantially between 1995 and 1998. As the BIS notes: "Between 1995 and 1998, the value of transactions involving the Japanese currency (at constant exchange rates) had grown at twice the rate of those involving the U.S. dollar or the Deutschemark, and 60% faster than global market turnover."

Excessive optimism or pessimism can often carry an exchange rate to extreme levels, and such was the case for the yen. The popularity of the yen carry trade had pushed the dollar into substantial overbought territory versus the yen by the summer of 1998.

Undervalued and oversold, the yen was, in retrospect, ripe for a corrective move upward. Although Japan's fundamental backdrop had not improved much, the existence of large, highly leveraged positions in the yen carry trade by the speculative community raised the risk that a sudden unwinding of those positions could drive the yen's value up sharply. When the Russian debt crisis hit in the summer of 1998, investors around the world felt compelled to unwind all highly leveraged fixed-income and currency positions, including the yen carry trade.

During the ensuing melee, the yen carry trade became a victim of the global deleveraging process. The dollar fell by 9% versus the yen between August 31 and September 7, 1998, and then fell an additional 12% from October 6 to 8 as highly leveraged long-dollar/short-yen positions were aggressively unwound. From a peak of ¥/US$ 147 on August 11, 1998, the dollar had fallen by 34 big figures in just 2 months to a low of ¥/US$ 113 on October 16, 1998.

Huge losses were incurred during the dollar sell-off of 1998, which highlights the risks of taking on leveraged positions in carry trades. However, from a long-run perspective, the cumulative excess returns on the yen-carry strategy have been fairly attractive, despite those losses. Indeed, there have been only three periods (the shaded areas in Figure 5–18) when the long-dollar/short-yen carry trade has suffered brief, albeit large, short-run losses since April 1995.

FIGURE 5-18

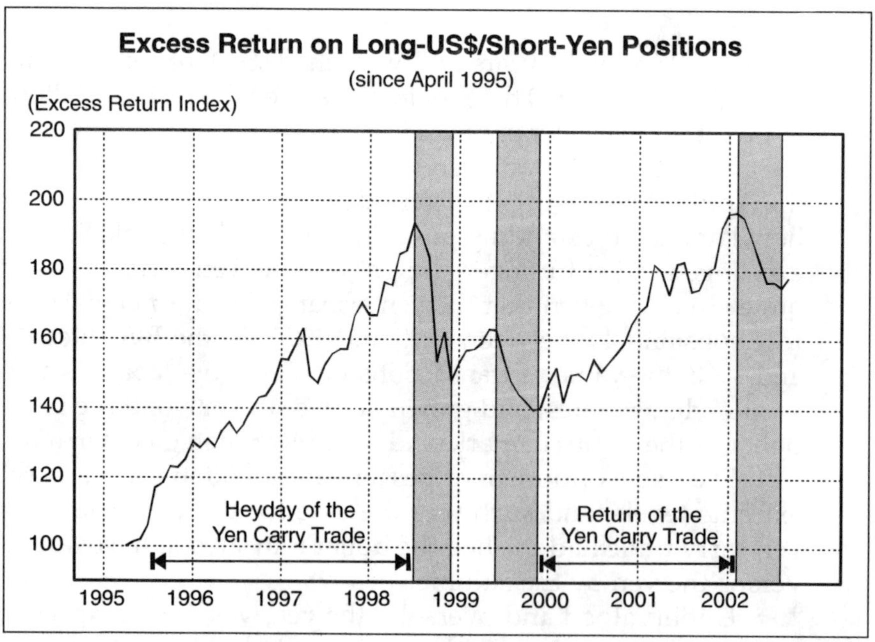

CHAPTER 6

Current-Account Imbalances and the Determination of Exchange Rates

Conventional wisdom holds that countries that run persistent current-account surpluses will see their currencies appreciate over time, while countries that run persistent current-account deficits will see their currencies depreciate over time.

Current-account imbalances can affect exchange rates through a variety of channels (see Figure 6–1). First, the existence of major external imbalances can influence the flow supply of and demand for individual currencies and thereby directly influence the paths that exchange rates take.

Second, major current-account imbalances can shift the residence of financial wealth among deficit and surplus nations, decreasing it in the former and raising it in the latter. Such shifts in the residence of financial wealth could then lead to shifts in global asset preferences, which, in turn, could influence the paths that exchange rates take.

Third, there is a general notion that there exists some limit on the ability of countries to run sizeable and persistent current-account deficits, because such deficits could lead to an unending rise in debt owed by deficit countries to foreign investors. If foreign investors view the rise in external debt as unsustainable, they would reason that at some point, a major depreciation of the deficit country's currency might be required to ensure that the current-account deficit narrowed and that the external debt stabilized at a level deemed sustainable.

In such a manner, the existence of a large current-account imbalance will tend to alter the market's notion of what level of the exchange rate constitutes a currency's real long-run equilibrium value, with ever-larger

FIGURE 6-1

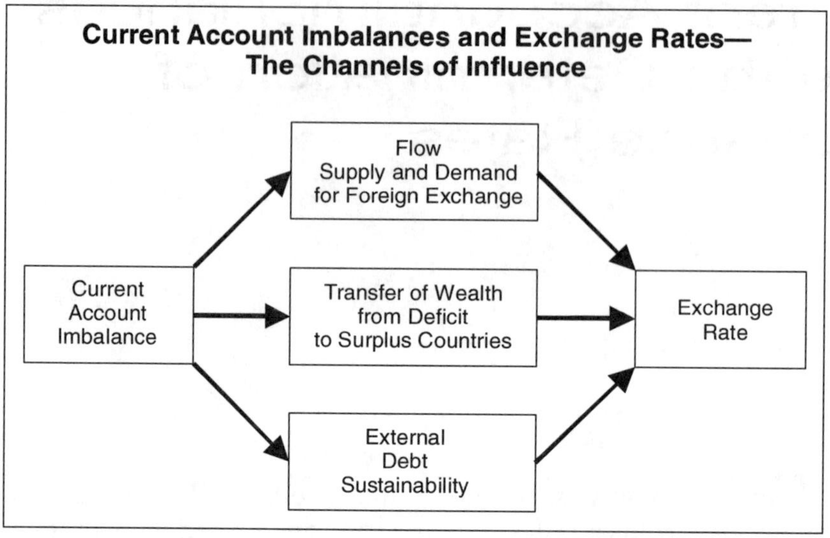

deficits and external debt levels giving rise to steady, downward revisions in market expectations of the real long-run equilibrium exchange rate.

BALANCE-OF-PAYMENTS FLOW MODEL OF EXCHANGE-RATE DETERMINATION

Most market participants view U.S. current-account trends as important for the dollar because such trends directly influence the flow supply of and demand for dollars in the foreign-exchange market. Using the traditional balance-of-payments flow model of exchange-rate determination, we can describe how current-account flows determine the supply of and demand for dollars.

Let's assume that the flow demand for dollars, $D_\$$, is generated by foreign demand for U.S. goods and services, while the flow supply of dollars, $S_\$$, is generated by U.S. demand for foreign goods and services. If current-account flows determine the supply of and demand for dollars, then it should be the case that when the U.S. current-account balance is in equilibrium, the supply of and demand for dollars will be in equilibrium as well. In terms of Figure 6–2, the dollar's equilibrium value, $\overline{q}_0$, would be determined by the intersection of the supply, $S_\$$, and demand, $D_\$$, curves for dollars at point *C*.

FIGURE 6-2

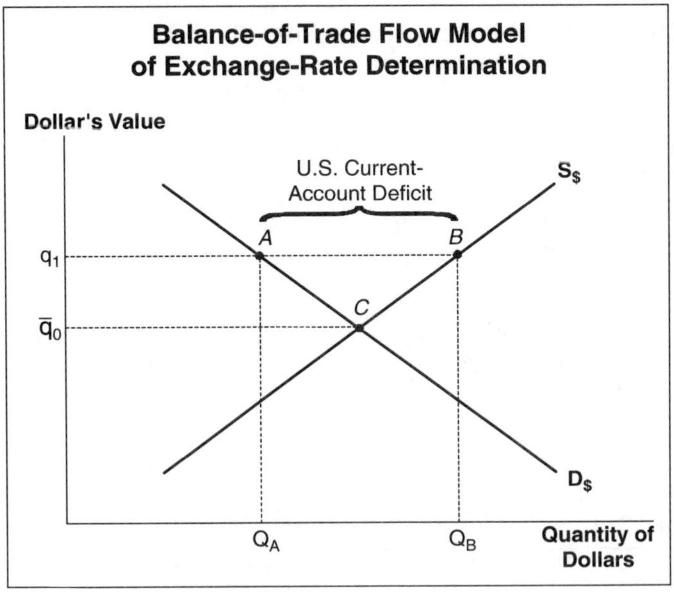

If, however, the United States were running a current-account deficit, perhaps because the value of the dollar was too high at q_1 relative to its equilibrium value, $\bar{q}_0$, then the supply of dollars, $S_\$$, on the foreign-exchange market would exceed the demand for dollars, $D_\$$. The excess supply of dollars, which is the foreign-exchange market counterpart of the U.S. current-account deficit, is represented as the gap between points *A* and *B*. The dollar's value at q_1 would clearly not be sustainable since the excess supply of dollars, *AB*, on the foreign-exchange market would exert continual downward pressure on the dollar's value. Once the dollar's value falls toward its long-run equilibrium value, $\bar{q}_0$, the supply of dollars would be brought back into line with the demand for dollars, and the U.S. current account would be brought back into balance at point *C*.

TRADE ELASTICITIES AND THE EXCHANGE-RATE/TRADE-BALANCE ADJUSTMENT PROCESS

The traditional balance-of-payments flow model posits that exchange rates will adjust until all current-account imbalances are corrected and

FIGURE 6-3

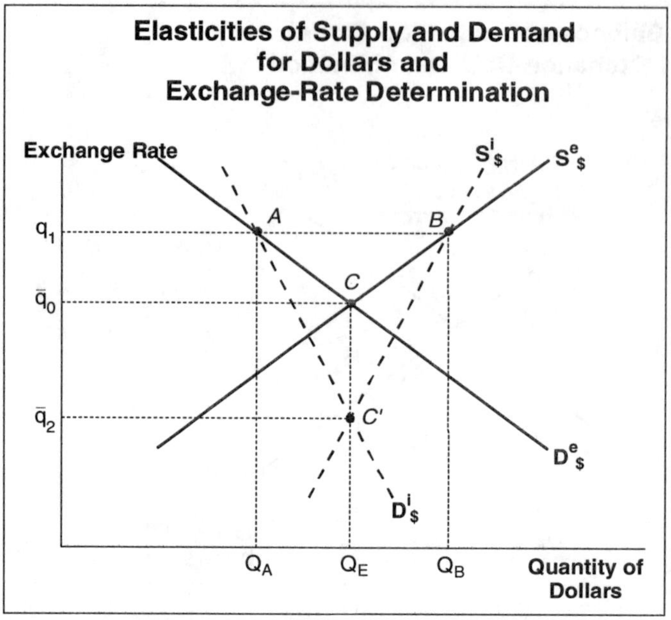

current-account equilibrium is restored. How much exchange rates must adjust to restore current-account equilibrium depends on the elasticities of the supply and demand curves for foreign exchange.

In Figure 6–3, we plot two sets of supply and demand curves for dollars—one set that is highly elastic ($S^e_\$$ and $D^e_\$$, respectively) and another set that is highly inelastic ($S^i_\$$ and $D^i_\$$, respectively). Initially, it is assumed that the U.S. is running a current-account deficit equal to *AB* at the prevailing exchange rate, q_1. The exchange-rate change necessary to correct the U.S. current-account imbalance will differ depending on whether the prevailing supply and demand curves for dollars are highly elastic or inelastic.

If the supply and demand curves for dollars were highly elastic, only a modest decline in the dollar's value to $\bar{q}_0$ would be required to restore equilibrium to the U.S. current account. If, instead, the supply and demand curves for dollars were highly inelastic, a large decline in the dollar to $\bar{q}_2$ would be required to restore equilibrium to the U.S. current account.

U.S. export and import price elasticities are estimated to be quite small, perhaps averaging only around −1.0 for exports and −0.3 for imports. Based on these rather low price elasticities, it would likely require a rather large depreciation of the dollar to restore a sizeable U.S. current-account deficit to a more sustainable level. Thus, the inelastic supply and demand curves shown in Figure 6–3 may be a more realistic picture of the potentially large dollar adjustment that might be required to restore equilibrium to the U.S. current-account balance.

ARE CURRENT-ACCOUNT DEFICITS NECESSARILY BEARISH FOR EXCHANGE RATES?

The dramatic appreciation of the dollar over the 1995–2001 period, despite a record deterioration of the U.S. current account, is clear evidence that a current-account deficit need not be bearish for a currency. Indeed, the same thing happened in the first half of the 1980s, when the dollar soared yet the current-account deficit steadily widened.

Current-account imbalances are typically driven by structural changes in international competitiveness, changes in the terms of trade, and long-term shifts in national savings-investment (S-I) balances. Consider the impact on exchange rates and the current account if a country underwent a major investment boom or undertook a long-term policy of fiscal expansion. In both cases, the S-I schedule would shift upward to the left (see Figure 6–4). The increase in investment relative to national savings would result in a wider current-account deficit and, at the same time, put upward pressure on the real exchange rate. That is pretty much what happened to the U.S. savings-investment balance, the current-account balance, and the dollar in both the 1980–1985 and 1995–2001 episodes. Hence, when the source of the deterioration in the current-account balance is a rise in investment relative to national savings, there is a high likelihood that the currency will strengthen over time, not weaken.

If the deterioration in a country's current-account balance were instead due to a long-run deterioration in that country's competitiveness, the CAB schedule would shift downward to the left relative to an unchanged S-I schedule (see Figure 6–5). In such a case, the deterioration of the current account would coincide with a long-term slide in the domestic currency's real long-run equilibrium value.

The message from all this is that certain economic disturbances may cause exchange rates and the current-account balance to move in the same direction while other disturbances may cause exchange rates and the current account to diverge. Consider the current-account/exchange-rate linkage that arises in response to fiscal and monetary policy changes. A country that pursues a highly expansionary monetary policy will likely see its current account deteriorate and its currency weaken at the same time. The question

FIGURE 6-4

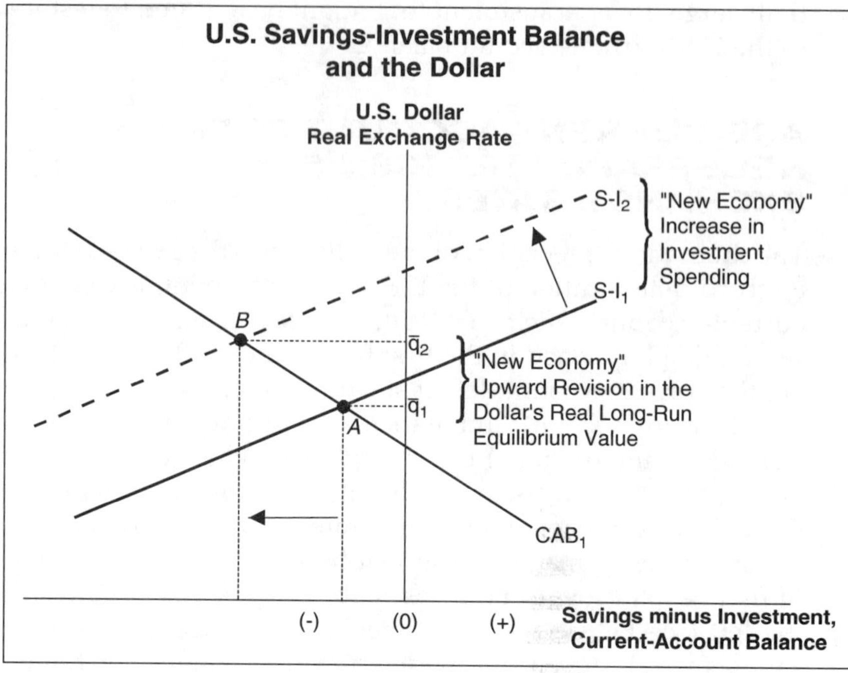

is whether the weakening of the currency is due to the easier monetary policy or the current-account deterioration or possibly both. In the case of a highly expansionary fiscal policy, the trend in the current account and the trend in the exchange rate may diverge as the current account deteriorates while the currency appreciates.

JAPAN'S CURRENT-ACCOUNT BALANCE AND THE YEN

Japan's tendency to run large and persistent current-account surpluses over time largely explains why the yen's trade-weighted value has risen on a secular basis. From a simple flow supply-and-demand perspective, one would expect larger and larger surpluses to give rise to successive increases in the demand for yen over time. Indeed, the rising trend in Japan's current-account surplus has moved in sympathy with the rising trend in the yen's value in the past 30 years (see Figure 6–6).

FIGURE 6-5

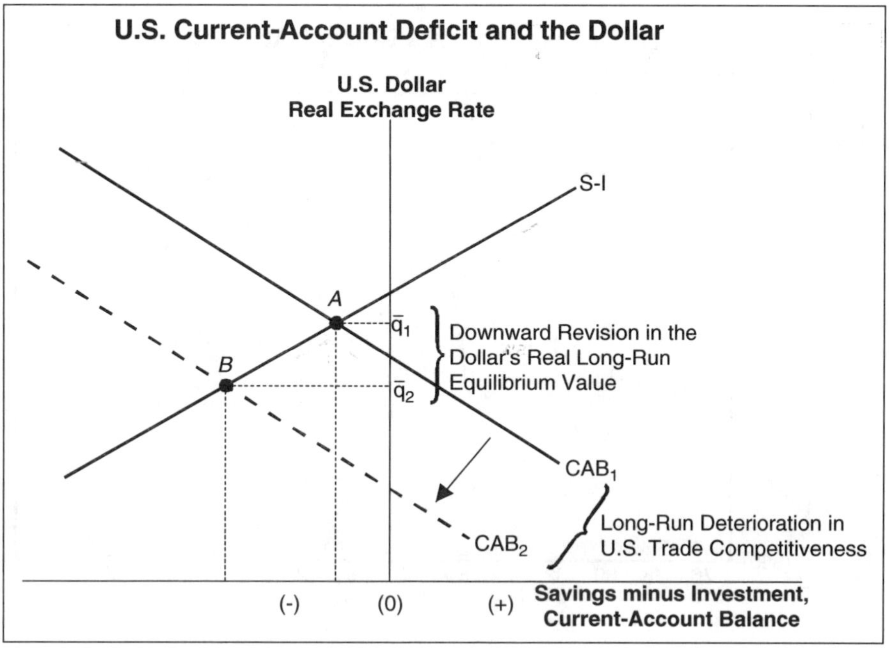

Related to this is the fact that Japan's cumulative current-account surpluses have allowed Japanese investors to acquire a rising claim on U.S. assets. To induce Japanese investors to acquire and hold onto those rising dollar claims, either U.S. interest rates needed to rise relative to those in Japan or the dollar needed to fall versus the yen to make dollar assets appear cheaper to Japanese investors, or some combination of the two was required. The evidence indicates the dollar bore the brunt of this adjustment, given that the yen's long-term trend moved sympathetically with the ratio of Japan's international investment position relative to the U.S. international investment position, as a percentage of their respective GDPs (see Figure 3–23).

In addition to the long-term financial pressure on the yen emanating from Japan's persistent current-account surpluses, Professor Ronald I. McKinnon of Stanford University makes the case that commercial tensions between the U.S. and Japan, including intermittent threats of an outright trade war, might have played an important role in driving the yen's real value higher over time. According to McKinnon, the United States—

FIGURE 6-6

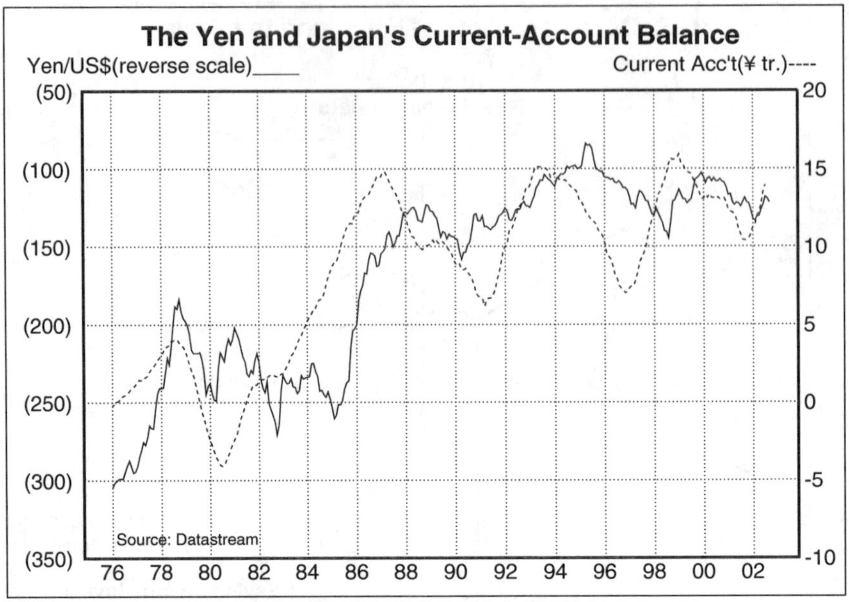

concerned about Japan's large and rising bilateral trade surplus versus the United States and frustrated by the inability of U.S. firms to penetrate Japan's relatively closed markets—pursued a policy of coupling protectionist threats with demands, implicit or explicit, for yen appreciation. With the yen the focus of both U.S. trade and exchange-rate policies, the Japanese authorities had to either tolerate an ever-rising yen or accept the wrath of American protectionists.

Repeated attempts to talk the dollar down versus the yen created, according to McKinnon, a syndrome of an ever-rising yen that had a pervasive influence on investor expectations in Japan. Concerned about possible large losses on their dollar-based investments, brought about by repeated attempts by U.S. officials to talk the dollar down, Japanese investors became increasingly reluctant to hold too large a proportion of their total portfolio in foreign assets. This meant that Japanese funds would effectively be bottled up inside Japan, with no safe passageway for Japan's current-account surpluses to exit through. This contributed to an ever-rising basic balance-of-payments surplus in Japan (the current account plus the long-term capital account) that generated a persistent excess demand for yen over time.

CORRECTING THE U.S. CURRENT-ACCOUNT DEFICIT: BELT TIGHTENING VERSUS DOLLAR DEPRECIATION

The United States can narrow its large current-account deficit in essentially three ways. First, the United States could pursue policies that encourage domestic savings and/or discourage domestic investment, perhaps via a tighter U.S. fiscal policy stance. Such a policy move would contribute to a leftward shift of the savings-investment (S-I) schedule in Figure 6–7. As illustrated, U.S. domestic demand would need to be pared back, perhaps significantly, to restore sustainable balance to the U.S. external account.

A second way to eliminate the unsustainable portion of the U.S. current-account deficit would be to engineer a major depreciation of the dollar to improve U.S. competitiveness, and thereby boost net exports. A major dollar depreciation would shift the export-import (Ex-Im) schedule to the right to Ex-Im_1 (see Figure 6–8) and that would narrow the deficit from point *A′* to a more sustainable level such as point *B′*. An even larger dollar

FIGURE 6-7

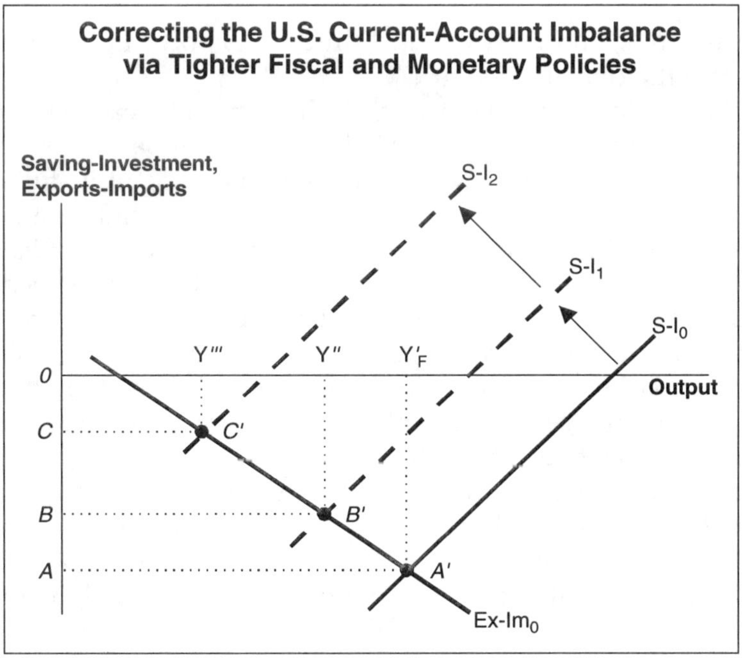

FIGURE 6-8

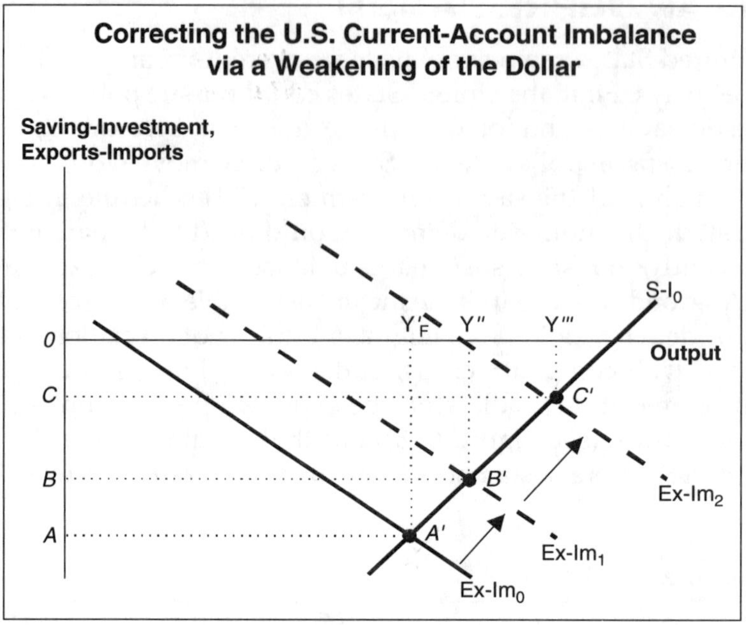

depreciation would be needed to shift the export-import curve to Ex-Im$_2$ to narrow the deficit to point C'.

The problem with this strategy is that it might create other problems for U.S. policymakers, and in all likelihood, might fail completely. That is because if the U.S. economy were already operating at its full employment level of output Y_F', then a dollar depreciation that shifts the export-import curve to the right would drive the level of U.S. output past its full employment potential. Since this would be highly inflationary, the Federal Reserve would need to tighten monetary policy, perhaps significantly. But if the Federal Reserve were forced to push U.S. interest rates up sharply, that would attract capital inflows to the U.S., which would then strengthen the dollar, thereby offsetting, perhaps completely, the initial depreciation of the dollar.

A third way to eliminate the unsustainable portion of the U.S. current-account deficit would be to combine belt-tightening and dollar-depreciation initiatives. A modest belt-tightening move on the fiscal policy front could shift the S-I curve to the left to S-I$_3$, while a modest dollar depreciation could work to shift the export-import curve to the right to Ex-Im$_3$ (see Figure 6–9). The combination of these two policy actions would leave the

FIGURE 6-9

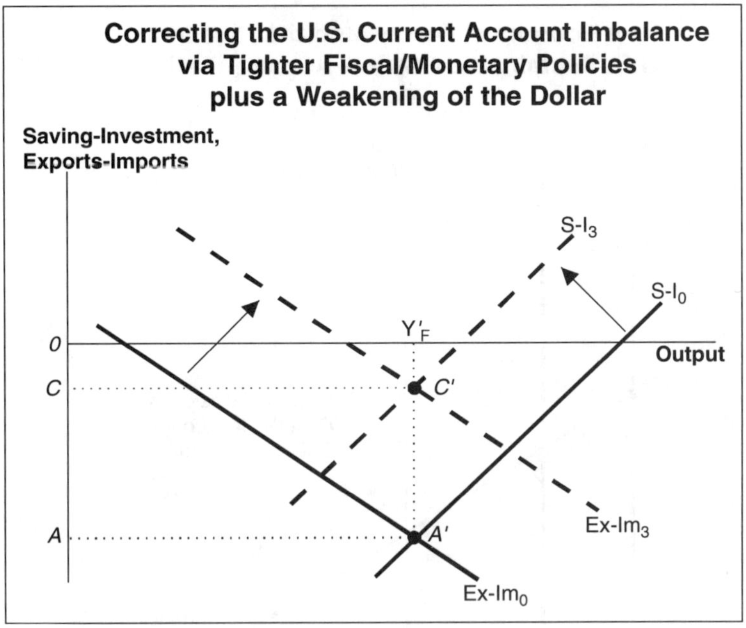

equilibrium level of output unchanged while narrowing the U.S. current-account deficit to a sustainable level.

U.S. CURRENT-ACCOUNT DEFICIT AND THE DOLLAR

Many pundits have argued that the record deterioration of the U.S. current-account deficit will inevitably lead to a hard landing for the dollar. But the dollar managed to defy such expectations over much of the 1995–2002 period.

One possible explanation for the dollar's resiliency was that a significant portion of the current-account deterioration might have been an *equilibrium* and not a *disequilibrium* phenomenon. If one views U.S. economic developments from a New Economy perspective, the revolutionary changes in information technology may have raised both the speed limit on sustainable U.S. GDP growth and the sustainable U.S. current-account deficit (see Figure 6-10).

With the return on capital on new technology investments highly attractive, foreign investors have been more than willing to finance a

FIGURE 6-10

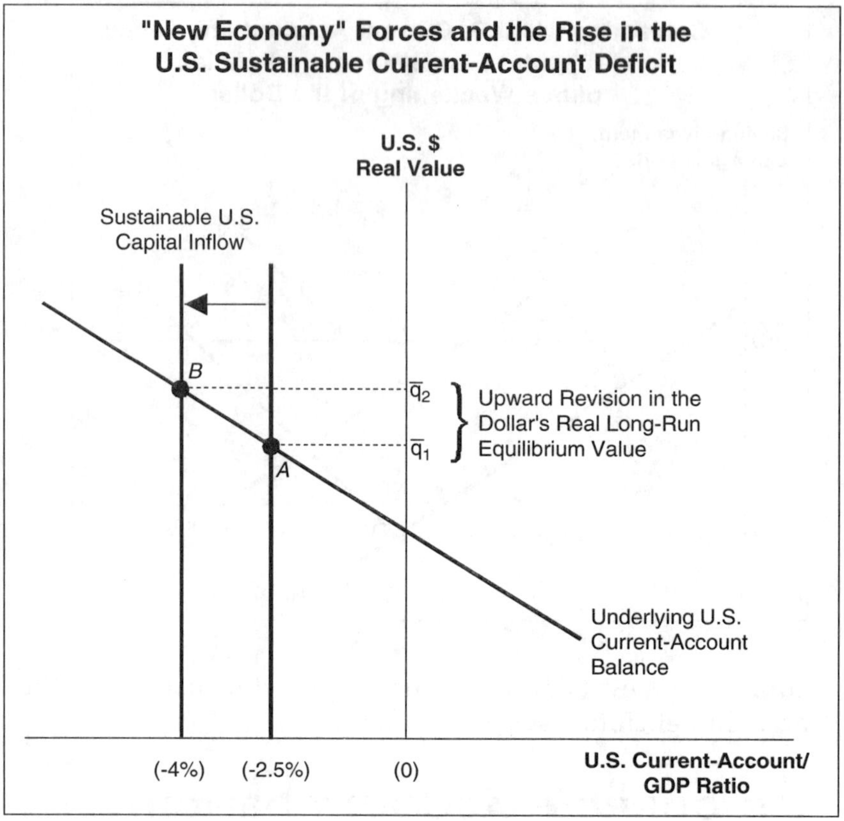

larger-than-normal gap between U.S. savings and investment. As a result, the inflow of foreign capital into the United States in recent years has exceeded the typical flow of capital that found its way to the United States in the past. Since, by definition, a country's current-account deficit equals its capital-account surplus, which also equals its savings-investment gap, it might be the case that the information technology revolution in the United States not only raised the speed limit on sustainable U.S. growth but also the size of the sustainable current-account deficit that the United States can safely run without triggering a dollar crisis.

While it might be true that the size of the sustainable current-account deficit has risen, there nevertheless must exist some threshold level for the U.S. current-account deficit that would trigger a decline in the dollar's value. The key question for investors then is, what might that new higher threshold level be?

ESTIMATING THE THRESHOLD LEVEL FOR THE U.S. CURRENT-ACCOUNT DEFICIT THAT WOULD TRIGGER A DECLINE IN THE DOLLAR'S VALUE

Based on an analysis of 17 episodes in industrial countries over the 1980–1995 period, Catherine L. Mann (1999) found that current-account deficits reaching 4.2% of GDP tended to set forces in motion—including corrective currency adjustments—for a reversal of the current-account shortfall. By the middle of 2002, the U.S. current-account deficit stood at 5% of GDP, well above the 4.2% average current-account-adjustment threshold.

Another study (Caroline L. Freund, 2000) examined a larger sample of industrial country current-account adjustment episodes and found that the median current-account deficit/GDP ratio that triggered corrective adjustments in the current account was around 4.9%. Those results are reported in Figure 6–11.

As shown by the median current-account adjustment process, an industrial-country deficit of 4.9% of GDP has, in the past, led to a 19% real depreciation of the deficit country's currency over a 3-year period, with the decline beginning 1 year prior to the peak in the current-account deficit and ending about 3 years after the peak. In conjunction with a slowdown in domestic demand, currency depreciation of this magnitude has typically helped bring about an 83% decline in the current-account imbalance.

IS THE U.S. CURRENT-ACCOUNT BALANCE A RELIABLE MEASURE OF U.S. TRADE COMPETITIVENESS?

After the experiences of the early 1980s and the late 1990s, when the dollar soared despite the significant widening of the U.S. current-account deficit, one could make the case that the U.S. current-account deficit might be overrated as a key determinant of the dollar. In fact, one could question whether the measurement problems associated with current-account data make them a reliable measure of U.S. trade competitiveness.

The reported current-account data omit the contribution that U.S. foreign affiliates make to the aggregate sales by U.S. firms in international markets. When allowance is made for the role played by U.S. foreign affiliates,

FIGURE 6-11

Current-Account Adjustment and Real Exchange-Rate Depreciation
(in 25 Episodes of Large Current-Account Adjustments, 1980-1995)

Date	Current Account/GDP Ratio at Peak (t_0)	3 Years after Peak (t_3)	Three-Year Percent Change	Real Exchange-Rate Depreciation	Relative to Peak Deficit Year (t_0), the Year in which Exchange-Rate Depreciation Began	Ended	Duration
Australia (1989)	-6.2%	-3.7%	40%	21%	1	5	4
Austria (1980)	-4.9%	0.4%	108%	19%	-1	2	3
Belgium (1981)	-4.2%	-0.1%	98%	51%	-3	4	7
Canada (1981)	-4.2%	-0.4%	91%	-	-	-	-
Canada (1993)	-3.9%	0.6%	114%	19%	-1	3	4
Denmark (1986)	-5.3%	-1.0%	81%	-	-	-	-
Finland (1991)	-5.5%	1.3%	124%	30%	-1	2	3
France (1982)	-2.2%	0.0%	100%	15%	-1	3	4
Greece (1985)	-8.1%	-1.5%	82%	21%	-2	2	4
Hong Kong (1980)	-5.0%	0.6%	111%	-	-	-	-
Ireland (1981)	-13.6%	-5.6%	59%	41%	-2	1	3
Israel (1982)	-8.7%	4.8%	155%	14%	2	6	4
Italy (1981)	-2.6%	-0.8%	70%	12%	-1	1	2
Italy (1992)	-2.5%	2.3%	194%	28%	0	4	4
Korea (1980)	-8.5%	-1.8%	78%	-	-	-	-
New Zealand (1984)	-13.6%	-8.0%	41%	11%	-1	1	2
Norway (1986)	-6.0%	0.2%	104%	5%	-3	1	4
Portugal (1981)	-16.8%	-2.8%	83%	8%	1	3	2
Singapore (1980)	-13.3%	-3.5%	74%	-	-	-	-
Spain (1981)	-2.9%	1.1%	139%	36%	-1	3	4
Spain (1981)	-3.8%	-1.4%	62%	17%	1	4	3
Sweden (1980)	-3.5%	-0.8%	77%	20%	1	4	3
Sweden (1992)	-3.6%	2.1%	160%	21%	1	4	3
United Kingdom (1989)	-4.4%	-1.8%	60%	15%	3	5	2
United States (1987)	-3.7%	-1.7%	56%	34%	-1	2	3
Median	**-4.9%**	**-0.8%**	**83%**	**19%**	**-1**	**3**	**3**

Source: Caroline L. Freund, "Current Account Adjustment in Industrial Countries," Federal Reserve Board, International Finance Discussion Paper, No. 692, December 2000.

one finds that U.S. firms' penetration of foreign markets actually exceeds the penetration of foreign firms in the U.S. market.

The U.S. Commerce Department reports that worldwide sales by U.S. companies to foreign residents (which include U.S. exports plus total sales by U.S. companies' foreign affiliates to nonresidents) amounted to $3.17 trillion in 1998 (latest data available), while total sales by foreign companies to U.S. residents (which include U.S. imports plus total sales by foreign firms' U.S. affiliates to U.S. residents) amounted to $2.81 trillion in the same period (see Figure 6–12). That means that worldwide sales by U.S. companies to foreign residents exceeded the sales of foreign firms to U.S. residents by $363 billion. Breaking the data down, the Commerce Department notes that of the $3.17 trillion in U.S. firms' worldwide sales, $930 billion represented U.S. exports of goods and services, while $2.24 trillion represented the sales by U.S. firms' foreign affiliates. Of the $2.81 trillion in foreign companies' sales to U.S. residents, $1.1 trillion represented U.S. imports of foreign goods and services, while $1.7 trillion represented the sales by foreign firms' U.S. affiliates.

What is clear from the data is that in 1998 although U.S. imports ($1.1 trillion) exceeded U.S. exports ($930 billion), leaving a wide U.S. trade deficit of $167 billion, the sales of U.S. firms' foreign affiliates ($2.24 trillion) far exceeded the sales of foreign firms' U.S. affiliates ($1.71 trillion), leaving a U.S. surplus on foreign affiliate operations of $530 billion.

Overall, despite the fact that the United States runs a large trade deficit, U.S. firms have had greater success in terms of penetrating foreign

FIGURE 6-12

Worldwide Sales by U.S. Companies versus Foreign Companies' Sales to the U.S.
(Latest Data, 1998)
(US$ Billions)

	Worldwide Sales by U.S. Firms	Sales by Foreign Firms to the U.S.	Difference
Total	$3,173	$2,810	+$363
Sales by Foreign Affiliates	$2,240 (71%)	$1,710 (61%)	+$530
Exports	$933 (29%)	$1,100 (39%)	-$167

Source: U.S. Commerce Department

markets than foreign firms have had in penetrating the U.S. market. The data show that, at the margin, U.S. firms tend to accommodate increases in foreign demand through their overseas affiliates (71% of worldwide sales) rather than through outright exports from the U.S. (only 29% of worldwide sales). In contrast, foreign firms, at the margin, tend to rely more on exports to the U.S. (39% of their U.S. sales) and a bit less on their U.S.-based affiliates (61% of their U.S. sales) to accommodate demand in the U.S. market.

What does this all imply for the U.S. current-account deficit's impact on the dollar? Does the dollar need to decline in order to balance U.S. exports and imports? Does the dollar have to be penalized because U.S. firms tend to accommodate foreign demand more through their overseas affiliates than via direct exports, particularly given the fact that U.S. firms do a better job in the aggregate than their foreign counterparts in terms of penetrating the other's market? Or should the dollar be rewarded to reflect the worldwide reach and strength that U.S. firms exhibit in today's global market?

CHAPTER 7

Capital Flows and Exchange Rates

Greater financial integration of the world's capital markets and the increased freedom of capital to flow across national borders have increased the importance of financial flows in the determination of exchange rates. The rise in the dollar's value in recent years was largely driven by strong increases in the demand for U.S. assets by overseas investors (see Figure 7–1). For example, Euroland investors had been structurally underweight equities for a long time, but beginning in the late 1990s they started to shift their portfolio allocations away from bonds and toward equities. Within their rising equity holdings, European investors also made the decision to increase the percentage allocated to U.S. equities and reduce the percentage allocated to Euroland equities. Overall, there was a marked rise in European investors' demand for U.S. equities in 1999–2001 that helped lift the dollar versus the euro.

Foreign demand for Japanese equities has also played an important role in influencing the medium-term direction of the yen (see Figure 7–2). The yen's weakness over the 1995–1998 period coincided with declining foreign demand for Japanese equities, and the yen's subsequent rebound in late 1998 and in 1999 coincided with a rise in foreign demand for Japanese equities. The drop-off in foreign demand for Japanese equities in 2000–2001 coincided with a sharp decline in the yen's value.

Foreign direct investment (FDI) and portfolio capital flows were highly positive for the dollar and negative for the euro in the latter half of the 1990s. As shown in Figure 7–3, Euroland's overall balance of payments

FIGURE 7-1

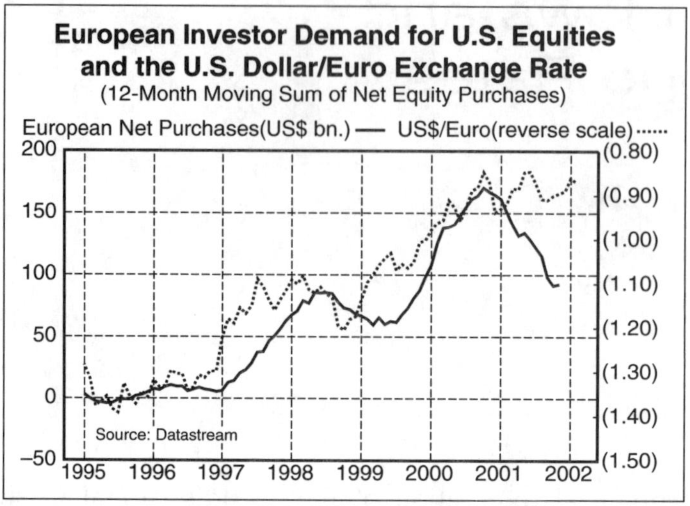

FIGURE 7-2

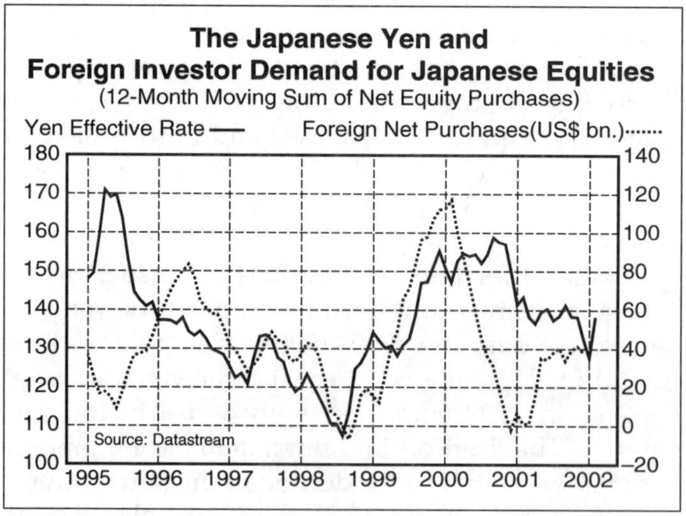

FIGURE 7-3

U.S., Euroland, and Japanese Balance of Payments
(1998-2000)
(US$ Billions)

	Current Account			FDI and Portfolio Flows			Overall Balance of Payments		
	1998	1999	2000	1998	1999	2000	1998	1999	2000
U.S.	–217	–331	–435	174	338	487	–43	7	**52**
Euroland	35	–7	–32	–218	–166	–144	–183	–173	**–176**
Japan	120	109	118	–63	–36	–60	57	73	**58**

was in huge deficit—because of sizeable FDI and portfolio outflows from Euroland—which is in stark contrast to the U.S. and Japanese overall balance-of-payments surpluses.

Although the United States has seen its current-account deficit double between 1998 ($217 billion) and 2000 ($435 billion), the United States over the same period was the recipient of massive FDI and portfolio inflows, which exceeded the size of the U.S. current-account deficit. As a result, the U.S. overall balance of payments swung from a deficit of $43 billion in 1998 to a surplus of $52 billion in 2000.

In contrast, Euroland saw its current account swing from a surplus to a deficit position, while FDI and portfolio flows recorded large outflows as well. As a result, Euroland ran overall balance-of-payments deficits averaging $173 to $183 billion per annum in 1998–2000, which weighed heavily on the euro during this period.

Despite all of the attention that capital flows receive in the FX market, there has not been much rigorous empirical testing to determine whether these flows have a statistically significant and quantitatively important impact on exchange rates, at least until lately. The International Monetary Fund recently published a report examining the impact that capital flows have had on the euro and the yen in the past decade. The IMF examined the trend in capital flows and other relevant indicators to determine whether they had statistically significant and quantitatively important effects on exchange rates (see Figure 7–4). The IMF's findings (based on an analysis of exchange rates over the 1988–2000 period) can be summarized as follows:

FIGURE 7-4

IMF Analysis of Factors That Explain Movements in the Euro and the Yen versus the U.S. Dollar
(1988-2000)

	Euro Coefficient	Yen Coefficient
Current Account & Capital Flows		
Current Account	Insignificant	Insignificant
Capital Account		
Net Bond Flows	Insignificant	Incorrect Sign
Net Equities Flows	**Significant**	Insignificant
Foreign Direct Investment	Insignificant	Insignificant
Traditional Underlying Factors		
Long-Term Interest Differential	**Significant**	**Significant** (Marginally)
Short-Term Interest Differential	Insignificant	Insignificant
Relative Current Growth	Insignificant	Insignificant
Alternative Underlying Factors		
Relative Stock Returns	Insignificant	Insignificant
Relative Expected Growth	**Significant**	Insignificant

Note: Coefficients of regression of change in the logarithm of the U.S. dollar exchange rate on a constant and the contemporaneous value of the explanatory variable using quarterly data since 1988. **Significant** denotes that the variable was both statistically significant and had the correct sign. All other variables were not statistically significant.

Source: Robin J. Brooks, Hali Edison, Manmohan S. Kumar, Torsten M. Slok, "Exchange Rates and Capital Flows," International Monetary Fund, *Research Department Series, Working Paper,* No. 01/190, May 2000, available on the IMF's Web site (www.imf.org).

1. "There is evidence that equity flows matter for the euro-dollar rate, but not for the yen-dollar rate."
2. Relative current and expected future growth rates derived from Consensus Economic Forecasts are correctly signed and statistically significant in explaining the euro, but not the yen.
3. Relative equity returns are not statistically significant in explaining either the euro or the yen.

4. Bilateral current-account trends vis-à-vis the United States are not statistically significant in explaining either the euro's or the yen's trend. However, the IMF notes that when multilateral, and not bilateral, current-account positions were investigated, there was some evidence of a positive effect of current-account trends on exchange rates.
5. "There is little evidence that merger and acquisition flows are important for exchange-rate determination. The coefficients on net foreign direct-investment (FDI) flows are correctly signed, but statistically insignificant for both the euro and yen." These results are consistent with the view that "the majority of cross-border merger and acquisition flows are financed through share-swaps that have no immediate impact on the demand for currencies."
6. "Net bond flows appear to have no significant effect on the euro- or yen-dollar rate."
7. "The movements of the euro-dollar and yen-dollar exchange rates are significantly correlated with the long-term interest-rate differential, but not their short-term equivalent." The IMF did note, however, that in the case of the euro, the explanatory power of the long-term spread is weaker than that for equity flows.

The IMF concluded that its findings were "supportive of the new conventional wisdom that net equity flows are important for the euro-dollar exchange rate, although long-term interest-rate differentials also appear to matter. For the yen, however, there is little evidence that net equity flows have been an important determinant of the bilateral exchange rate with the U.S. dollar." The IMF noted that the importance of equity flows for the euro might stem from the fact that European investors might have been diversifying their portfolios away from intra-European investments to U.S. equity investments.

EQUITY-MARKET TRENDS AND THE DOLLAR

Given the surge in the U.S. equity market in the second half of the 1990s, many observers have naturally associated the rise in the dollar's value over this period with the increase in U.S. equity values. Appearances, however, can be deceiving. As the Bank of International Settlements reports in its August 2000 *BIS Quarterly Review*, "There is little evidence of

FIGURE 7-5

Correlation Between Equity Market Trends and Exchange Rates
(Daily, Weekly, Monthly, and Quarterly Data)
(January 1983-May 2000)

Equity Market/ Exchange Rate	Correlation Coefficient			
	Daily	Weekly	Monthly	Quarterly
Dow Jones/ US$ Index	0.03	0.04	0.04	0.11
Dow Jones-Nikkei/ Yen/US$	0.04*	0.07*	0.08	0.11
Dow Jones-DAX/ DM/US$	0.17**	–0.15**	–0.25**	–0.22**

* Statistically significant at 5% level
** Statistically significant at 1% level
Source: *BIS Quarterly Review*, August 2000

a robust significant correlation between stock market indices and the major exchange rates." The BIS finds that the "correlation coefficient for the Dow Jones index and the nominal effective dollar rate is positive but very small and not statistically significant" (see Figure 7–5).

The BIS also reports that "a similar result holds for the co-movement of the return on the Dow Jones relative to the Nikkei and the percentage change of the bilateral yen/dollar rate." What was particularly surprising regarding the BIS findings was that "the correlation between the return on the Dow Jones relative to Germany's DAX equity index and movements in the Deutschemark/U.S. dollar exchange rate was negative and statistically significant." In other words, when the U.S. equity market has risen relative to the German equity market, the dollar has tended to fall, not rise in value versus the Deutschemark, as conventional reasoning would have suggested.

Not only did the BIS find a weak relationship between equity indices and exchange-rate movements, it also found a weak relationship between

FIGURE 7-6

Correlation Between International Portfolio Equity Flows and Exchange Rates
(Monthly Data)
(January 1983-May 2000)

Equity Market Flows/ Exchange Rate	**Correlation Coefficient**
U.S.-Japan Equity Flows/ Yen/US$	0.04
U.S.-European Flows/ DM/US$	0.05
Japan-European Flows/ Yen/DM	–0.26

Source: *BIS Quarterly Review*, August 2000

international portfolio equity flows and the trend in exchange rates. The correlation between U.S./Japan equity flows and the Japanese yen/U.S. dollar exchange rate was close to zero, as was the correlation between U.S./European equity flows and the Deutschemark/U.S. dollar exchange rate (see Figure 7–6). Contrary to conventional wisdom, the BIS found that the yen tended to strengthen versus the Deutschemark when equity flows moved in favor of Europe, although the reported correlation coefficient was not statistically significant.

Given the historically weak relationship between equity-market trends and exchange rates, why has the foreign-exchange market become so fixated on equity-market developments? One reason may be that in the late 1990s the correlation between the Dow Jones Industrial Average and the dollar was in fact highly positively correlated (even though the long-run correlation between the Dow Jones index and the dollar has averaged close to zero). The high correlation in the late 1990s may have led market observers to believe that this trend would continue into the future. This proved not to be the case over the 2000–2001 period, however, as the correlation between the Dow Jones index and the dollar plummeted.

FIGURE 7-7

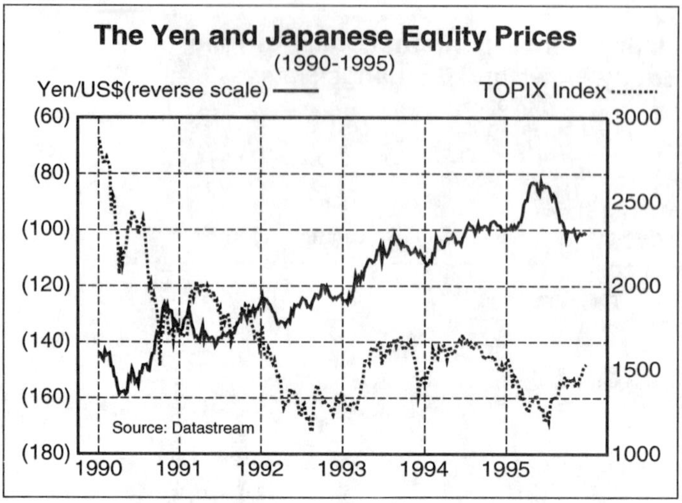

EQUITY-MARKET TRENDS AND EXCHANGE RATES: AN UNSTABLE RELATIONSHIP

Although exchange rates and equity markets will move in sync from time to time, the relationship between equity-market trends and exchange rates is not stable (see Figures 7–7 and 7–8). For instance, between 1990 and 1995, the U.S. dollar fell despite a strongly performing U.S. equity market, while the Japanese yen soared despite a weakly performing equity market. In both cases the correlation between local equity-market performances and the local currency's value was negative. In contrast, between 1995 and 2001, the correlation between local equity-market performances and the local currency's value turned highly positive. The U.S. dollar soared in tandem with a rising U.S. equity market, at least up until late 1999, while the yen weakened in tandem with a trend decline in the Japanese equity market. Such instability makes it difficult to form judgments on possible future currency moves based solely on expected equity-market performances.

FOREIGN DIRECT-INVESTMENT FLOWS AND EXCHANGE RATES

The market's fixation with foreign direct-investment flows as an explanatory variable in projecting future exchange-rate movements is a phenomenon that derives largely from large acquisitions of U.S. firms by European

FIGURE 7-8

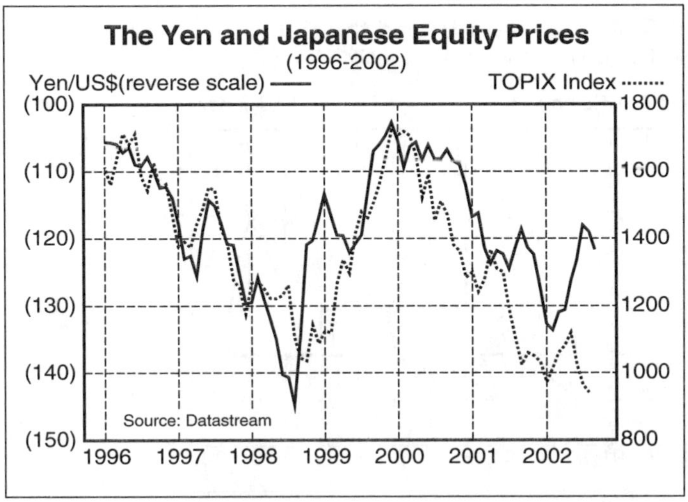

corporations in the late 1990s and the surge in the dollar that appeared to accompany those acquisitions. But the relationship between FDI flows and the dollar is not robust over time (see Figure 7–9).

A careful reading of the trend in the U.S. dollar trade-weighted index plotted against the smoothed trend (four-quarter moving sum) in U.S. net FDI flows reveals that U.S. net FDI flows were actually negative from 1991 to mid-1998, yet the dollar was strong during a considerable portion of that time. In the fourth quarter of 1998, net FDI flows into the United States were quite large yet the dollar fell during that period. Since then, FDI flows have been quite volatile—large in one quarter and then modest in the next—and the trend in the dollar has clearly not moved in sympathy with the quarterly pattern in net FDI flows. Overall, the correlation between quarterly net FDI flows and the dollar's value since 1981 is a low 0.05.

MERGER AND ACQUISITION FLOWS AND THE DOLLAR: 1999–2001

A recent BIS study entitled "The Impact of Transatlantic M&A Activity on the Dollar/Euro Exchange Rate" finds that over the 1999–2000 period, merger and acquisition (M&A) announcements of European firms' acquisitions of U.S. firms had a statistically significant impact on the dollar's value versus the euro and that the size of this impact was independent of

FIGURE 7-9

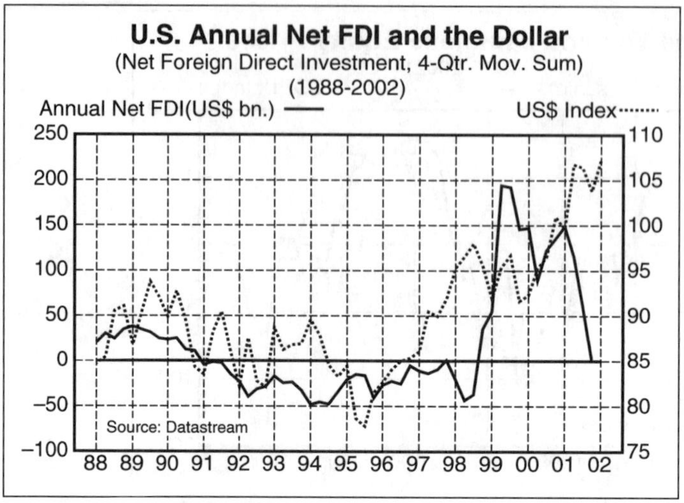

how the deal was financed (see Figure 7–10). Interestingly, M&A deals involving U.S. firms' acquisitions of Euroland firms were found not to have a statistically significant impact on the dollar's value versus the euro.

This asymmetric response suggests that the influence of M&A deals on the dollar's value over the 1999–2001 period may have less to do with the FX flows, if any, generated by such deals, and more to do with the way the market perceived the underlying rationale for those deals. That is, the market may have perceived the steady acquisition of U.S. firms by Euroland firms as a sign that Euroland firms had greater confidence in the long-run growth prospects of the United States relative to Euroland. The fact that the pace of transatlantic activity slowed sharply in 2001, yet the dollar remained remarkably resilient, suggests that the linkage between M&A activity and the dollar may be less robust when viewed over longer time horizons.

THE IMPACT OF EMERGING-MARKET CAPITAL FLIGHT ON THE DOLLAR: 1997–2001

It is widely believed that part of the dollar's strengthening trend in recent years can be explained by the dramatic surge in foreign direct investment and portfolio flows into the United States from overseas markets. Many assume that this surge in capital inflows reflected a newfound optimism in

FIGURE 7-10

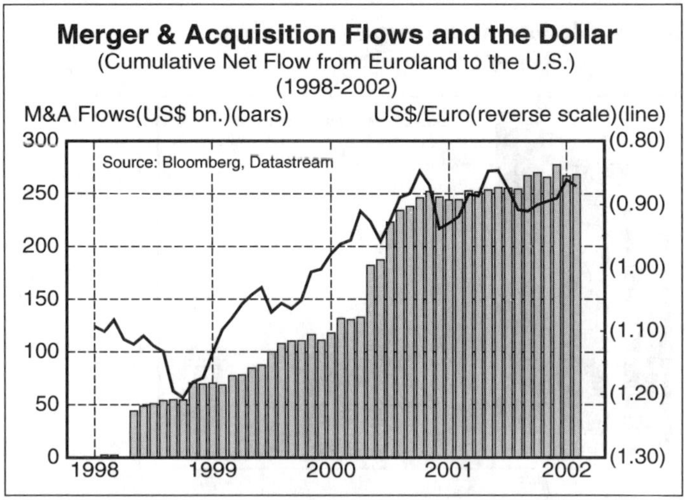

the health and vigor of the U.S. economy and financial markets. While this is undoubtedly true, it may also be the case that a significant portion of the capital flow that has found its way to the United States simply reflected capital flight from other parts of the world, notably emerging markets.

The evidence suggests that a series of crises in emerging markets—from Asia to Russia to Brazil to Turkey to Argentina—persuaded investors to exit from emerging-market investments and look for more stable returns in the industrialized markets (see Figure 7–11). Given the U.S. dollar's dominant position as a global medium of exchange and store of value, the United States naturally benefited from that capital flight. Net private capital flows into emerging markets peaked at $233 billion in 1996, just prior to the Asian financial crisis of 1997. Since then, private capital flows to emerging markets have plummeted, with the 2000 inflow amounting to only $9.0 billion. Where did all that capital go? Assuming most of it found its way to the United States, this could have played a major role in driving the dollar higher in 1997–2000.

THE LATIN AMERICAN DEBT CRISIS AND THE SURGE OF THE DOLLAR: 1982–1985

The 1997–2000 episode did not mark the first time that capital flight from emerging markets has played an important role in contributing to a major rise in the dollar's value. A similar development occurred in the first half

FIGURE 7-11

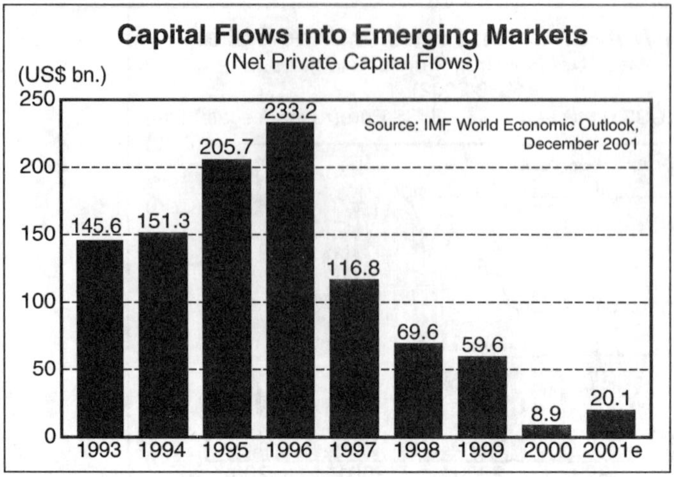

of the 1980s, when the dollar underwent a dramatic upside overshoot that could not be adequately explained by U.S., European, or Japanese economic fundamentals.

One reason the dollar might have overshot its equilibrium level in 1982–1985 was that the United States had become a major recipient of massive capital flight from Latin America following the onset of the Latin American debt crisis in 1982. Evidence on Latin American capital flight and dollarization ratios indicates that a large and sustained increase in the demand for dollars by Latin American residents occurred at that time (see Figures 7–12 and 7–13).

FINANCING THE U.S. CURRENT-ACCOUNT DEFICIT

The United States was the beneficiary of a structural shift in capital inflows in the 1995–2001 period, both from the emerging markets and from Europe (see Figure 7–14). The rise in capital flows from emerging markets to the United States began with the flight of capital from Asia following the Asian financial crisis in 1997. Capital flows to emerging markets dried up as well in 1998 following the Russian/LTCM crisis and have yet to recover. It is assumed that most of those flows found their way to the United States.

FIGURE 7-12

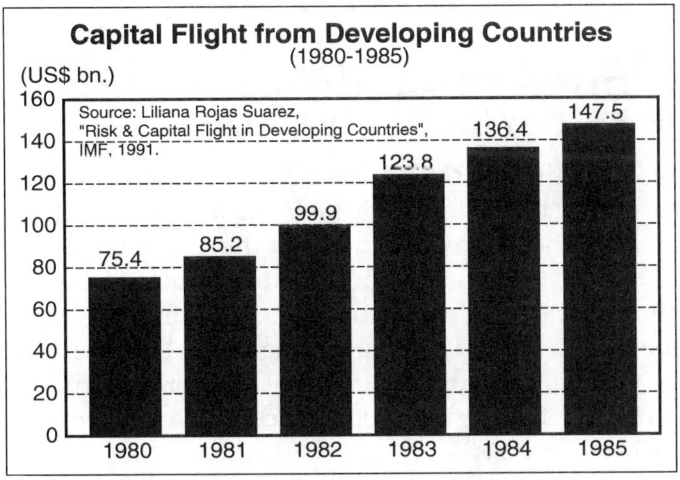

FIGURE 7-13

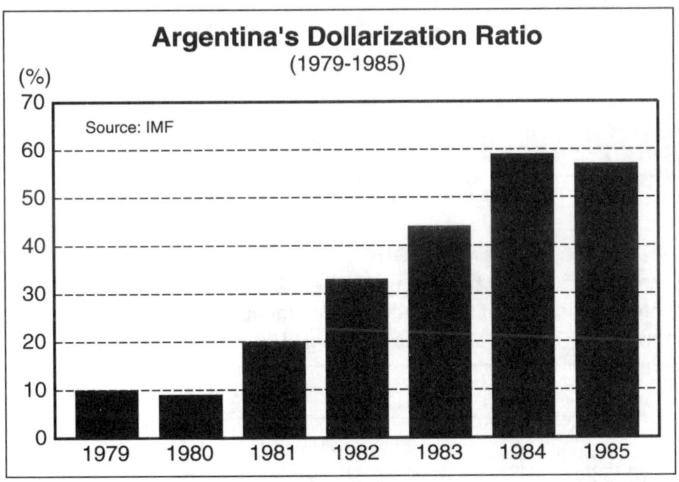

The inflows from Europe came in the form of surges in foreign direct investment into the United States, stepped-up foreign purchases of U.S. equities by Euroland investors, and huge increases in European purchases of U.S. corporate bonds. Foreign direct investment and equity flows slowed dramatically in 2001, but this was more than offset by a major surge in foreign purchases of U.S. corporate bonds. These inflows helped drive the dollar steadily higher over the 1995–2001 period despite a record deterioration of the U.S. current-account deficit.

THE U.S. CURRENT-ACCOUNT DEFICIT AND U.S./FOREIGN YIELD SPREADS

Under normal conditions, U.S. interest rates would have been required to rise relative to foreign interest rates in order to attract greater capital inflows to finance the steady widening of the U.S. current-account deficit. As shown in Figure 7-15(*a*), the equilibrium value for the dollar is shown to be determined at the point where the U.S. savings-investment schedule (S-I) and the underlying U.S. current-account balance schedule (CAB) intersect. As shown in Figure 7-15(*b*), the U.S./foreign interest-rate spread required to finance the current-account deficit and attract the necessary capital flows is $(r_{US} - r_F)_1$.

An increase in U.S. investment, such as the one experienced by the U.S. during the 1990s, would have shifted the S-I schedule to the left, which under normal circumstances would have required a relative rise in U.S. interest rates in order to induce foreign investors to finance the wider U.S. current-account deficit. Higher U.S. interest rates would, in turn, have led to wider U.S./foreign yield spreads, from $(r_{US} - r_F)_1$ to $(r_{US} - r_F)_2$.

FIGURE 7-14

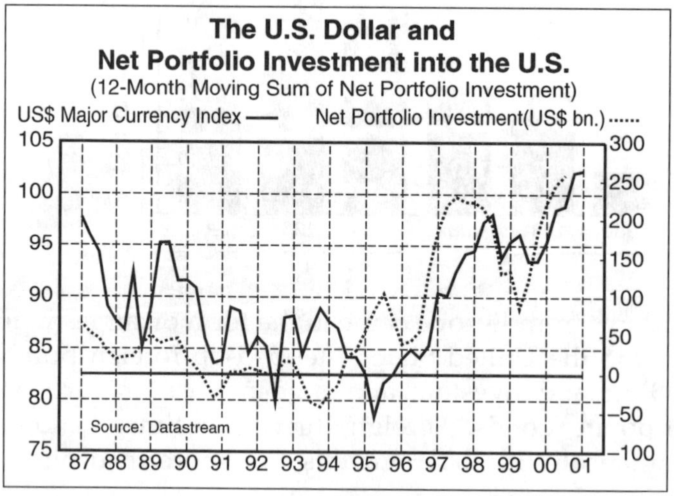

FIGURE 7-15

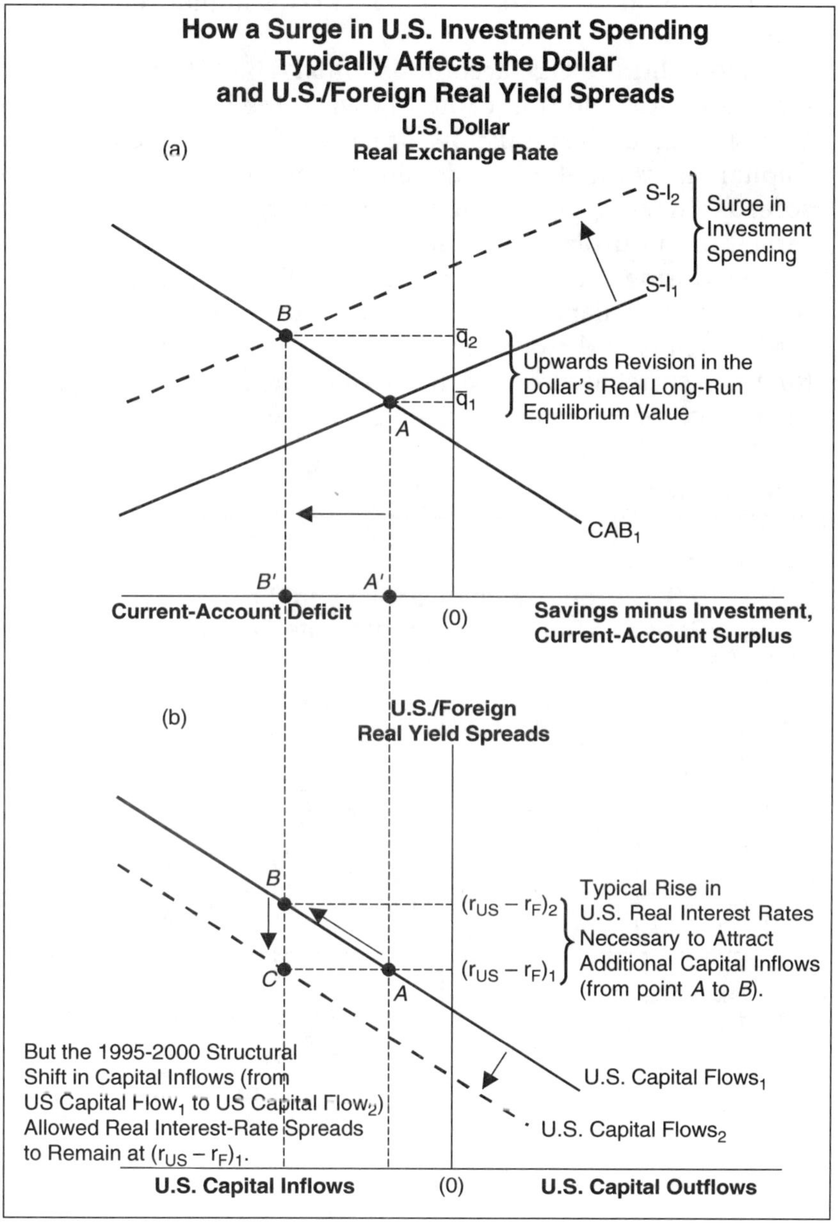
How a Surge in U.S. Investment Spending Typically Affects the Dollar and U.S./Foreign Real Yield Spreads
(a)
U.S. Dollar Real Exchange Rate
S-I2
S-I1
Surge in Investment Spending
B
A
q̄2
q̄1
Upwards Revision in the Dollar's Real Long-Run Equilibrium Value
CAB1
B'
A'
Current-Account Deficit
(0)
Savings minus Investment, Current-Account Surplus
(b)
U.S./Foreign Real Yield Spreads
B
C
A
(rUS – rF)2
(rUS – rF)1
Typical Rise in U.S. Real Interest Rates Necessary to Attract Additional Capital Inflows (from point A to B).
But the 1995-2000 Structural Shift in Capital Inflows (from US Capital Flow1 to US Capital Flow2) Allowed Real Interest-Rate Spreads to Remain at (rUS – rF)1.
U.S. Capital Flows1
U.S. Capital Flows2
U.S. Capital Inflows
(0)
U.S. Capital Outflows

It was truly remarkable during the 1999–2002 period that the United States was able to finance a record deterioration in its current-account deficit without having to push U.S. interest rates higher relative to interest rates overseas.

How did the U.S. accomplish this? The U.S. was the beneficiary of a major structural shift in capital flows to the U.S. (shown in Figure 7–15(*b*) as a shift of the capital flow schedule from U.S. Capital Flows_1 to U.S. Capital Flows_2) that was independent of any change in U.S./foreign yield spreads. Indeed, capital flight from emerging markets and the inflow of capital from Euroland actually allowed nominal and real yield spreads to narrow during the dollar's run-up in 1999–2002 (see Figure 7–16). Hence, the normally reliable, positive correlation between trends in U.S./foreign yield spreads and trends in the dollar's value broke down. At the same time, the correlation between the trend in U.S./foreign yield spreads and the U.S. current-account deficit broke down as well.

FIGURE 7-16

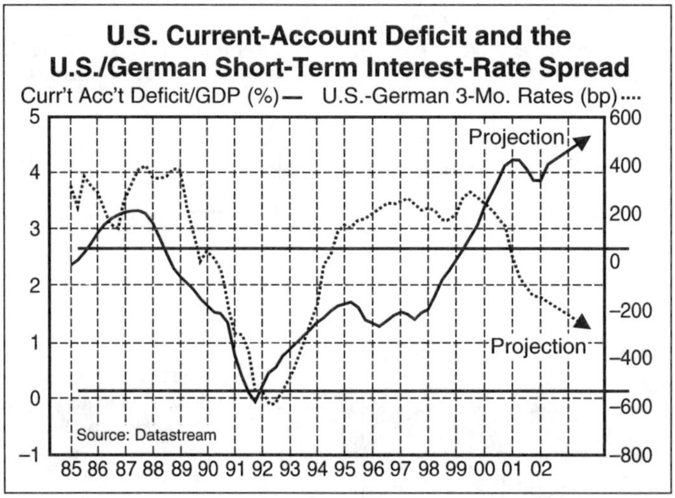

CHAPTER 8

The Mundell-Fleming Model of Exchange-Rate Determination

Our understanding of the impact that monetary and fiscal policy changes have on exchange rates owes much to the pioneering work of Robert A. Mundell and J. Marcus Fleming. The Mundell-Fleming (MF) model has become the textbook standard that most students today use to study the role of monetary and fiscal policy in an open economy (see Figures 8–1 and 8–2).

In the MF model, the degree of capital mobility plays a pivotal role in determining the exchange rate's response to a change in fiscal or monetary policy. For example, an expansionary monetary policy will lead to a depreciation of the domestic currency in large part because the induced decline in domestic interest rates will generate an outflow of capital that puts downward pressure on the domestic currency. The more sensitive capital flows are to changes in interest rates, the greater will be the outflow of capital in response to the interest-rate decline. Hence, the more mobile capital is, the more the currency will depreciate in response to a monetary expansion.

Fiscal policy's impact on the exchange rate is a bit ambiguous. If capital is highly mobile, an expansionary fiscal policy will likely give rise to an appreciation of the domestic currency. If capital is relatively immobile, then an expansionary fiscal policy could lead to a decline in the domestic currency's value. This is because an expansionary fiscal policy typically results in a rise in domestic interest rates and an increase in economic activity. The rise in domestic interest rates should attract an inflow of capital from abroad, which should be positive for the domestic currency, but

FIGURE 8-1

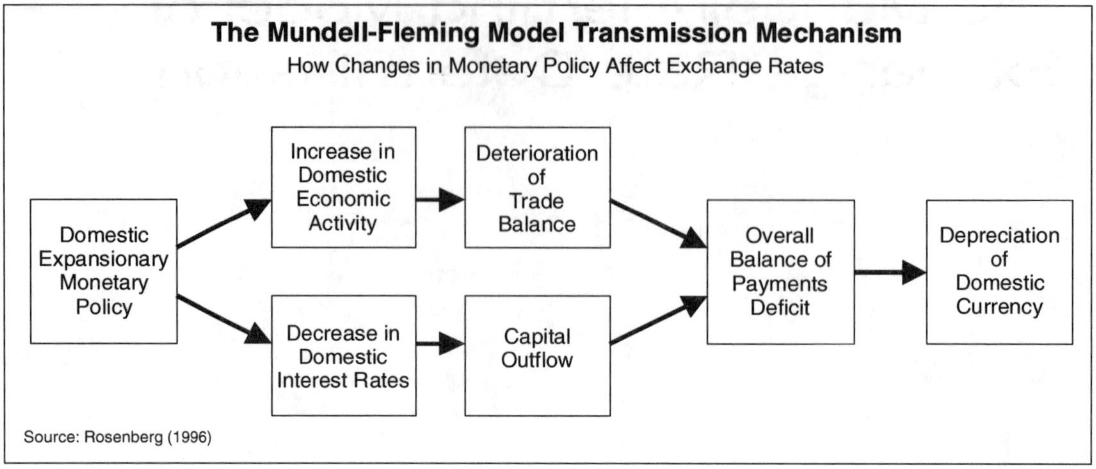

FIGURE 8-2

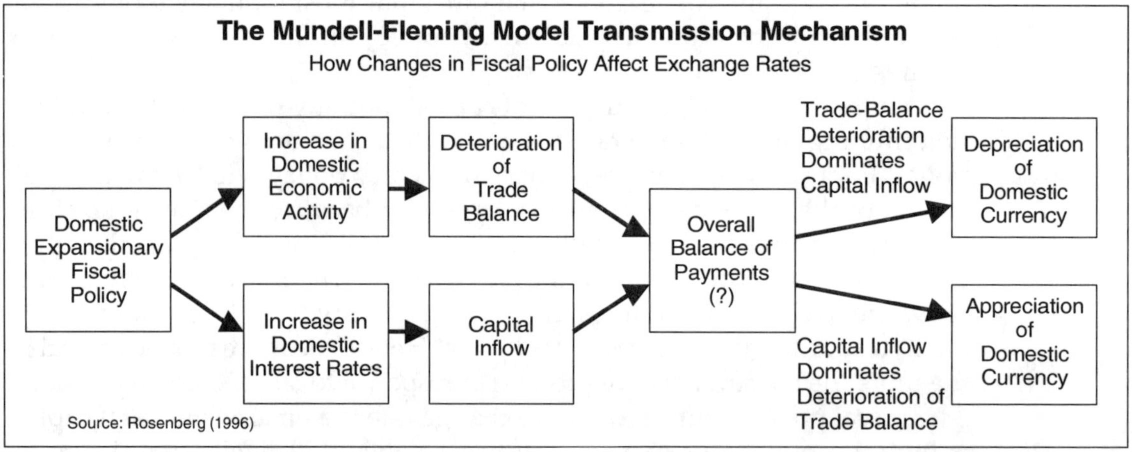

at the same time, the consequent rise in domestic economic activity will contribute to a deterioration of the trade account, which should be negative for the domestic currency.

Whether the exchange rate rises or falls in response to a fiscal expansion will depend on how sensitive capital flows are to changes in interest rates. If capital flows are highly mobile, the induced inflow of capital from abroad should dominate the deterioration in trade, and thus the domestic currency should appreciate in value. If capital flows are relatively immobile, the opposite will be the case.

MONETARY POLICY'S IMPACT ON EXCHANGE RATES IN THE MF MODEL

In the MF model, an expansionary domestic monetary policy will exert downward pressure on a domestic currency's value while a restrictive domestic monetary policy will exert upward pressure on a domestic currency's value (see Figure 8–3). The more mobile is capital, the greater will be the exchange-rate response.

In an IS-LM context, an expansionary domestic monetary policy will shift the LM (liquidity) curve downward and to the right to LM_1, resulting

FIGURE 8-3

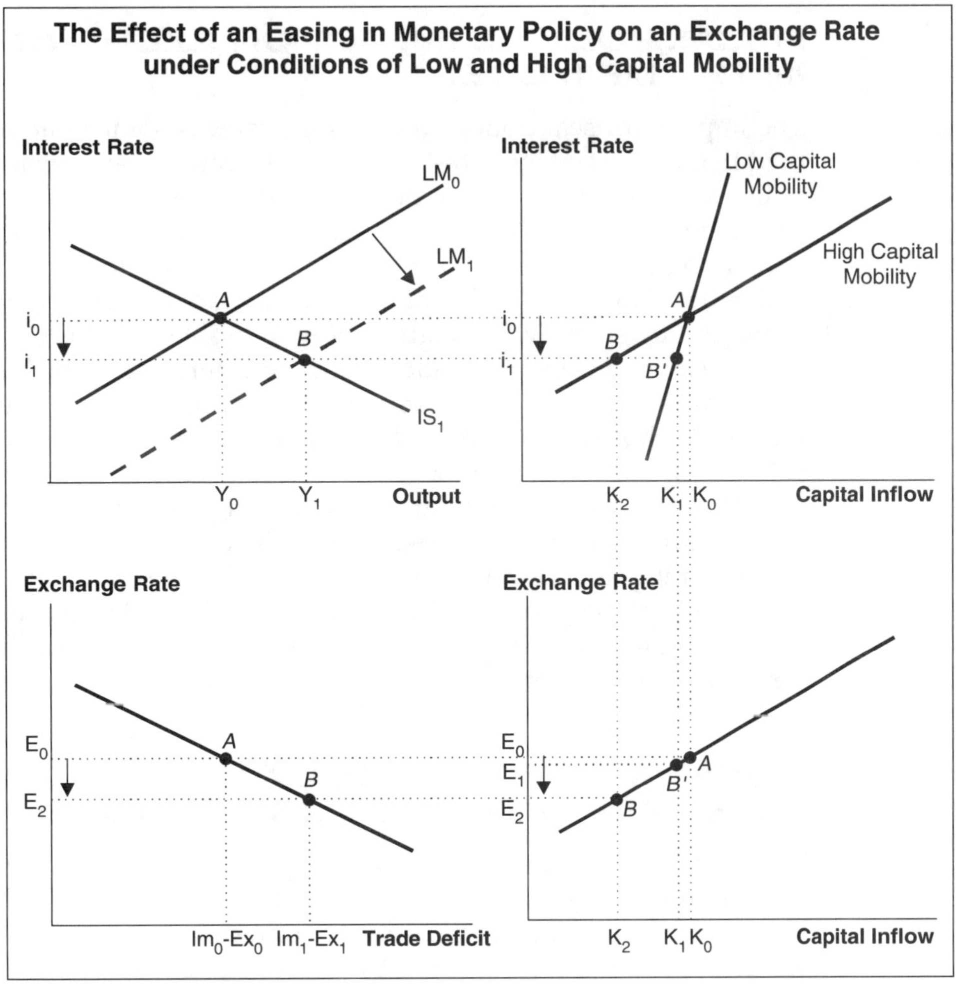

in a decline in domestic interest rates and a rise in domestic demand. The decline in domestic interest rates will cause capital to flow abroad, while the rise in domestic demand will cause the trade balance to deteriorate. The combined deterioration of the trade and capital accounts will lead to a deterioration of the overall balance of payments and, in the process, exert downward pressure on the domestic currency.

Under conditions of low capital mobility, the interest-rate-induced outflow of capital should be modest (from K_0 to K_1). A modest capital outflow in turn should result in a modest decline in the domestic currency's value (from E_0 to E_1). Under conditions of high capital mobility, the interest-rate-induced outflow of capital should be large (from K_0 to K_2), and the resultant decline in the domestic currency's value (from E_0 to E_2) should be large as well.

FISCAL POLICY'S IMPACT ON EXCHANGE RATES IN THE MF MODEL

The impact of fiscal policy on exchange rates is somewhat ambiguous in the MF model (see Figure 8–4). In an IS-LM context, an expansionary fiscal policy will give rise to a rightward shift of the IS (investment-savings) curve to IS_1, resulting in a rise in domestic interest rates from i_0 to i_1 and a rise in domestic demand from Y_0 to Y_1. The rise in domestic interest rates will attract an inflow of capital from abroad, which should drive the domestic currency's value higher (from E_0 to E_2) while the rise in domestic demand should cause the trade balance to deteriorate, which should cause the domestic currency to weaken (from E_0 to E_1). The equilibrium exchange rate could thus be either E_1 or E_2 following a fiscal expansion, that is, the resulting change is ambiguous.

Under conditions of high capital mobility, the induced inflow of capital should dominate the deterioration in trade, and thus the currency should strengthen significantly. If capital mobility is not that high, then the exchange-rate response will be more muted. Under certain conditions when capital mobility is extremely low, the deterioration in trade may dominate and the domestic currency could weaken.

FISCAL/MONETARY POLICY MIX AND THE DETERMINATION OF EXCHANGE RATES

The specific mix of monetary and fiscal policies that a country pursues can have a profound impact on exchange rates (see Figure 8–5). In a world of high capital mobility, an expansionary domestic fiscal policy will give rise to an appreciation of the domestic currency's value. Similarly, a tight

FIGURE 8-4

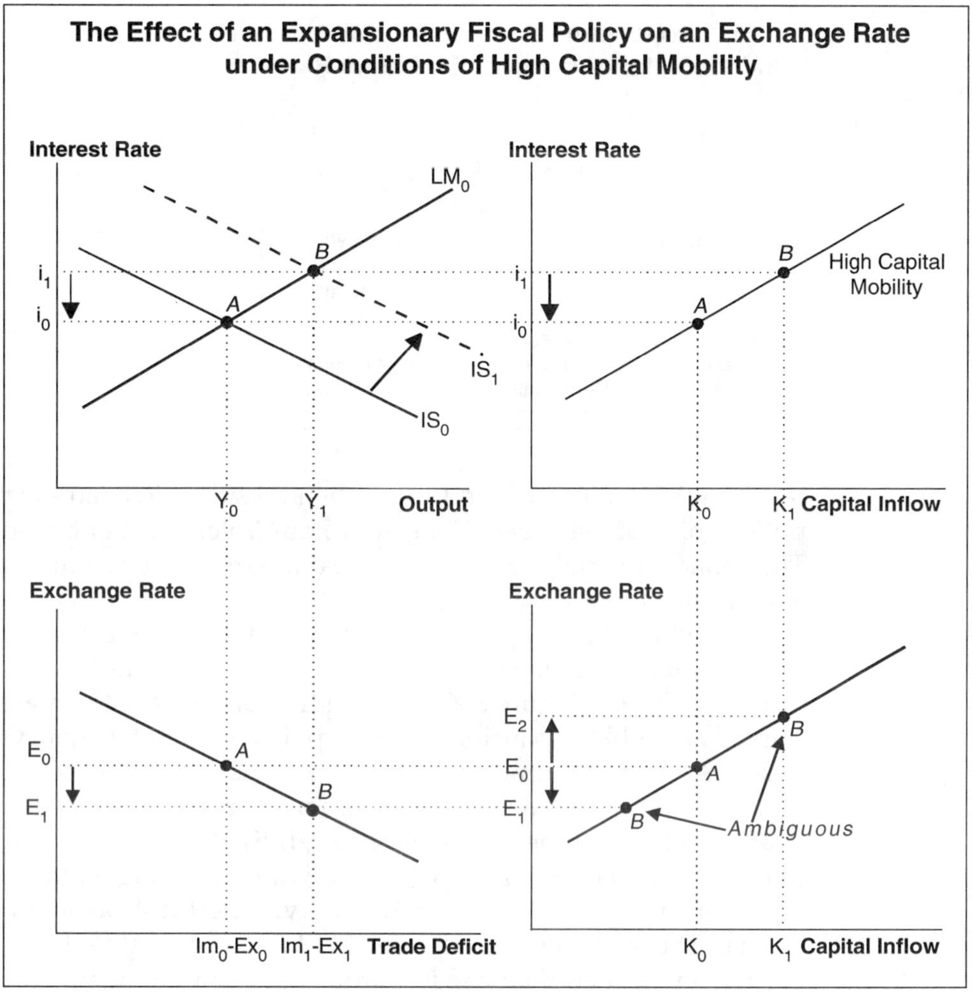

domestic monetary policy will give rise to an appreciation of the domestic currency's value when capital flows are highly mobile. Thus, the combination of an expansionary fiscal policy and a restrictive monetary policy should be extremely bullish for a currency when capital mobility is high. Conversely, the combination of a restrictive fiscal policy and an expansionary monetary policy should be extremely bearish for a currency. When both monetary and fiscal policies are expansive or restrictive at the same time, the impact on exchange rates is ambiguous.

The classic example of how an expansive fiscal/tight monetary policy mix contributed to a sharp rise in a currency's value is the case of the United

FIGURE 8-5

The Monetary/Fiscal Policy Mix and the Determination of Exchange Rates

	Expansionary Monetary Policy	Restrictive Monetary Policy
Expansionary Fiscal Policy	Ambiguous	Domestic Currency Appreciates
Restrictive Fiscal Policy	Domestic Currency Depreciates	Ambiguous

States in the first half of the 1980s, when President Reagan's expansive fiscal policy collided with Fed Chairman Paul Volcker's tight monetary policy. That policy mix helped drive U.S. real interest rates and the dollar's value to extraordinarily lofty levels.

Another classic episode in which a dramatic shift in the policy mix caused equally dramatic changes in exchange rates was the case of Germany in 1990–1992 (see Figure 8–6). During that period, the German government pursued a highly expansionary fiscal policy to help facilitate German unification. At the same time, the Bundesbank pursued an extraordinarily tight monetary policy to combat the inflationary pressures associated with unification. The combined expansive fiscal/tight monetary policy mix drove interest rates sharply higher in Germany, and those higher interest rates were then transmitted to the rest of Europe via the ERM pegged exchange-rate regime. Those higher interest rates led to a marked slowdown in European growth and to a marked rise in European unemployment. European central banks found it difficult to keep interest rates high enough to defend the ERM pegs and at the same time encourage a rebound in economic activity. Recognizing that this deterioration in the European economic climate was unsustainable, currency speculators waged an attack on the ERM regime and eventually toppled it.

EUROLAND'S FISCAL/MONETARY POLICY MIX IN THE 1990S AND THE LONG-TERM DECLINE IN THE EURO'S VALUE

The (synthetic) euro's decline over the 1992–2000 period provides an example of how an adverse fiscal/monetary policy mix can have a negative

FIGURE 8-6

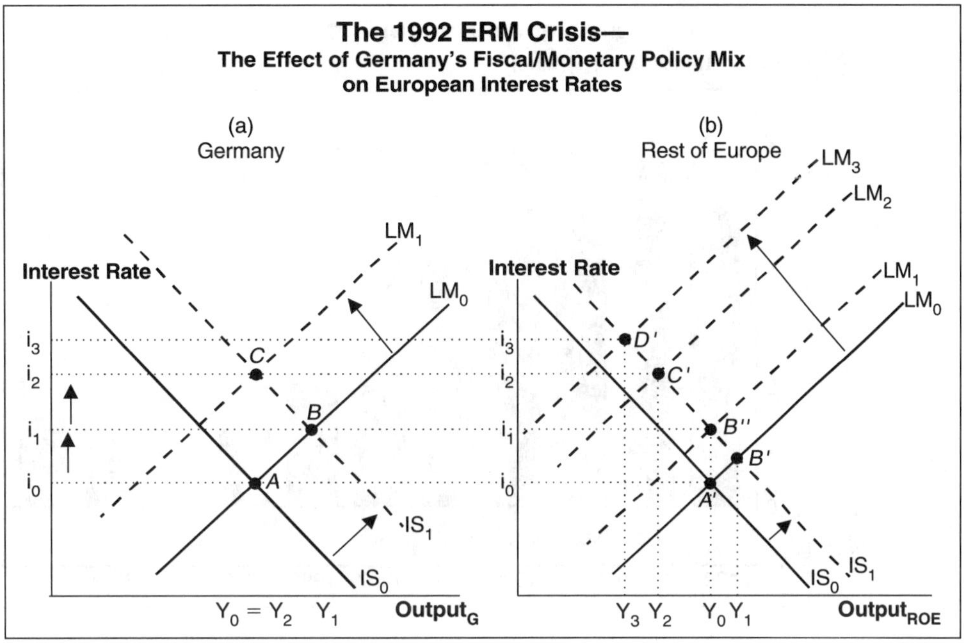

impact on a currency's value (see Figures 8–7 and 8–8). In the run-up to European Monetary Union (EMU), Europe's overall fiscal stance leaned toward significant restraint as most governments in Europe steadily trimmed their structural budget deficits to satisfy the EMU admission criteria on budget deficits and debt levels set out in the Maastricht Treaty. All else being equal, fiscal restraint would have been negative for the euro.

To counteract the negative economic consequences of Europe's relatively restrictive fiscal policy stances, most European central banks felt compelled to pursue relatively easy monetary-policy stances. Real short-term interest rates in Europe were pushed steadily lower in the 1990s. All else being equal, the pursuit of a relatively easy monetary policy should have exerted downward pressure on the euro's value.

A tight fiscal or an easy monetary policy alone would have been enough to depress the euro's value in the 1990s. But the combination of the two proved to be deadly. As illustrated in the IS-LM diagram in Figure 8–9, the pursuit of an easy monetary policy in Europe resulted in a rightward shift in Europe's LM schedule from LM_0 to LM_1, while the pursuit of a tight fiscal policy in Europe resulted in a leftward shift in Europe's IS schedule from IS_0 to IS_1. The intersection of the newly shifted IS_1 and LM_1 curves at point *C* indicates that Europe's policy mix drove European real interest

FIGURE 8-7

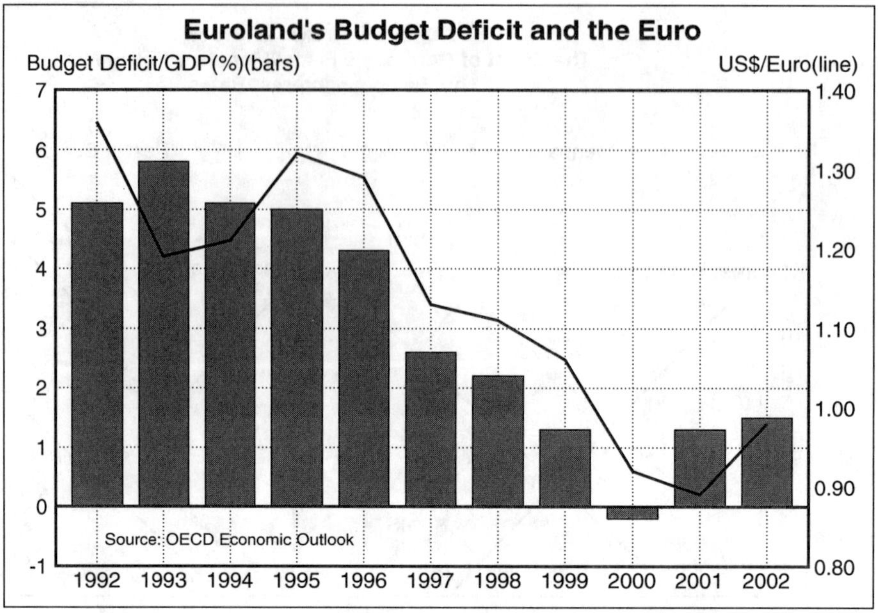

FIGURE 8-8

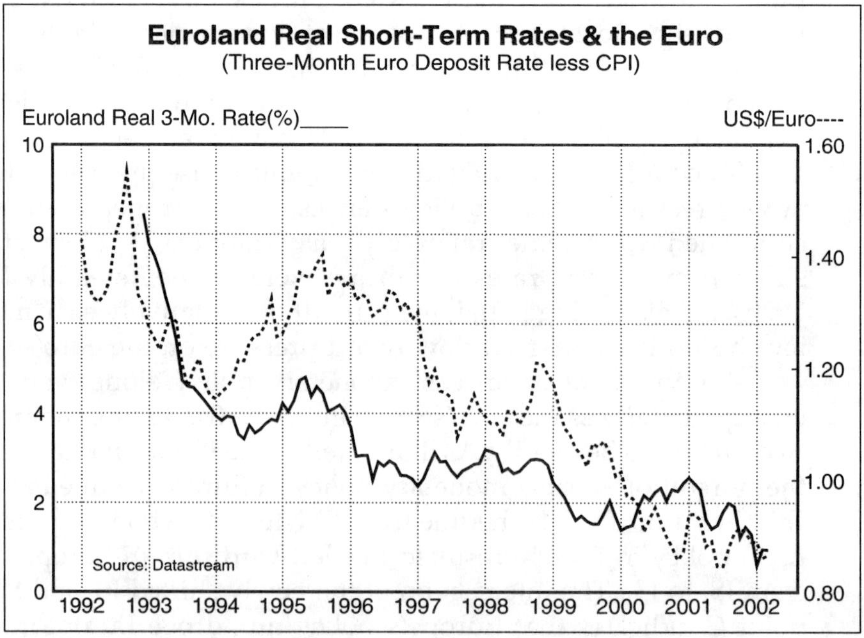

rates lower, and those lower real rates then contributed to a decline in the euro's value from point A' to point C'.

JAPAN'S MONETARY/FISCAL POLICY MIX DEBATE AND THE YEN'S VALUE IN 1999-2000

The Japanese yen's response to changing monetary/fiscal policy conditions during 1999–2001 provides another example of the influence of policy mixes on exchange rates. In 1998–1999, a number of prominent economists offered policy prescriptions to help Japan out of its decade-long economic slump. Adam Posen, of the Institute for International Economics in Washington, D.C., wrote a book entitled *Restoring Japan's Economic Growth* (1998), in which he recommended that the Japanese government should undertake a major fiscal stimulus initiative to reverse the decline in Japanese economic activity. Posen argued that Japan's fiscal stance had been too austere in the 1990s, particularly after the 1997 hike in Japan's consumption tax. Therefore, massive fiscal stimulus was needed to offset the contractionary forces underway in Japan. In an IS-LM context, Posen's solution amounted to shifting the IS curve as far to the right as possible (see Figure 8–10).

Paul Krugman of Princeton University offered a different policy prescription. Krugman (1998) argued that Japan had fallen into a liquidity trap and stressed that the Japanese economy needed a negative real interest rate

FIGURE 8-9

The Effect of Europe's Fiscal/Monetary Policy Mix on the Euro

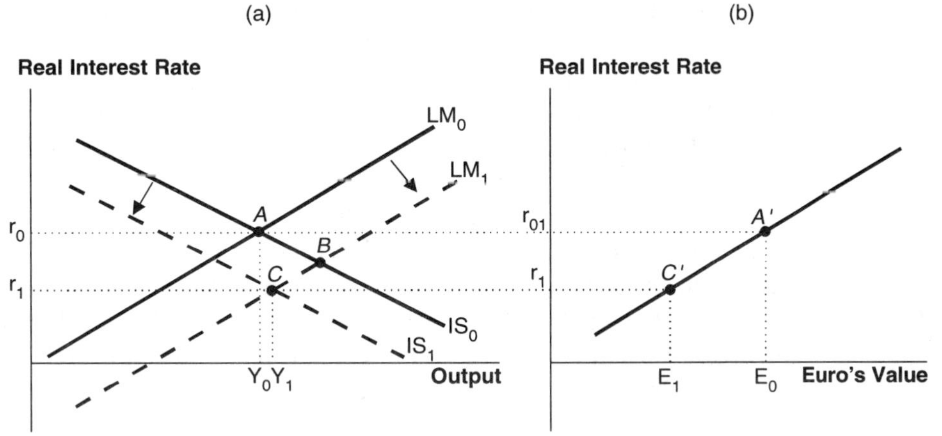

FIGURE 8-10

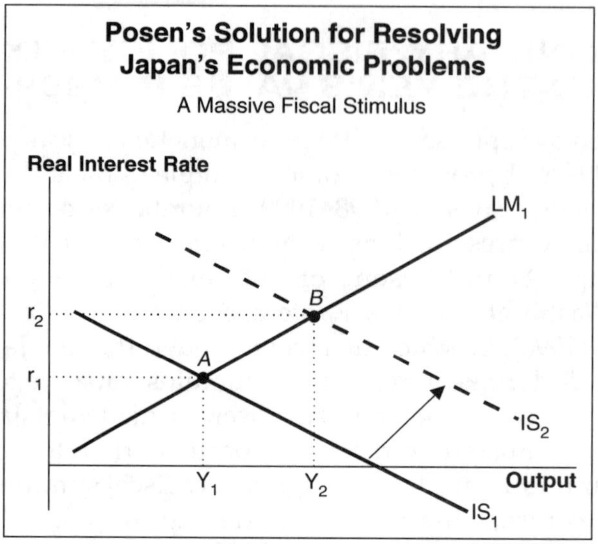

to restore economic growth. Since nominal interest rates were already near zero and could not move into negative territory, Krugman asserted that Japan needed to generate expectations of higher inflation to drive real interest rates into negative territory. That could be accomplished only if the Bank of Japan made a credible commitment to expand the rate of growth of the money supply now and in the future. In an IS-LM context, Krugman's solution amounted to shifting the LM curve downward and to the right, so that it intersected the IS curve in negative real interest-rate territory (see Figure 8–11).

A combination of fiscal and monetary stimulus probably would have been the most desirable policy, allowing Japan's real growth to expand by more than would have been possible with either fiscal or monetary stimulus alone. In addition, the impact of such a policy mix would have been broadly neutral for the yen. An expansive fiscal policy stance would have been yen supportive, while an expansive monetary policy stance would have been yen negative, leaving the yen's value largely unchanged.

In the end, the Japanese authorities chose to follow the policy recommendations suggested by Posen and engineered a powerful fiscal stimulus over the 1998–1999 period. The Bank of Japan did not adopt an aggressive policy of monetary easing, as recommended by Krugman but rather leaned toward monetary restraint over much of the 1999–2000 period. So instead of Japan's LM curve shifting to the right, it appears that the LM curve shifted to the left in 1999 and remained there in 2000 (see Figure 8–12).

FIGURE 8-11

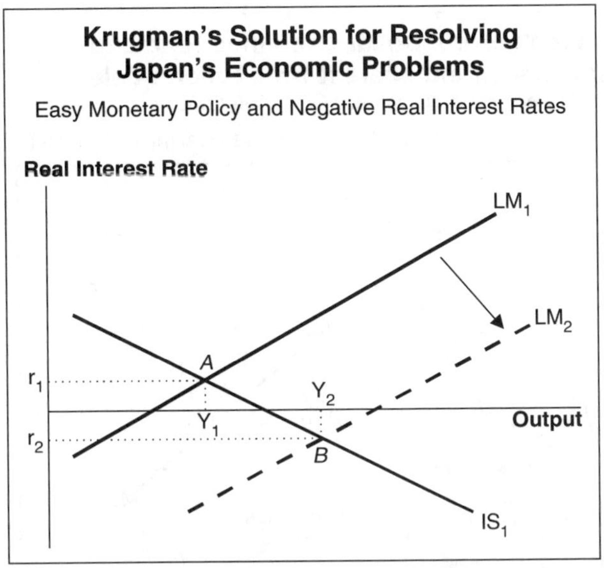

FIGURE 8-12

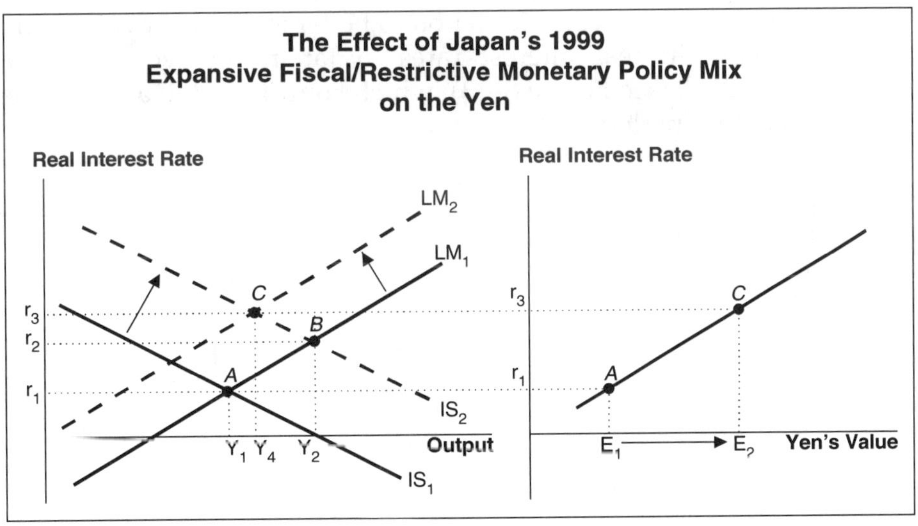

The result of this expansive fiscal/tight monetary policy mix was that Japan's LM curve shifted leftward while its IS curve shifted rightward, which had the effect of driving real interest rates higher instead of lower. As shown in Figure 8–12, the increase in output associated with this policy mix is normally quite modest (shown as a rise from Y_1 to Y_4), while the

FIGURE 8-13

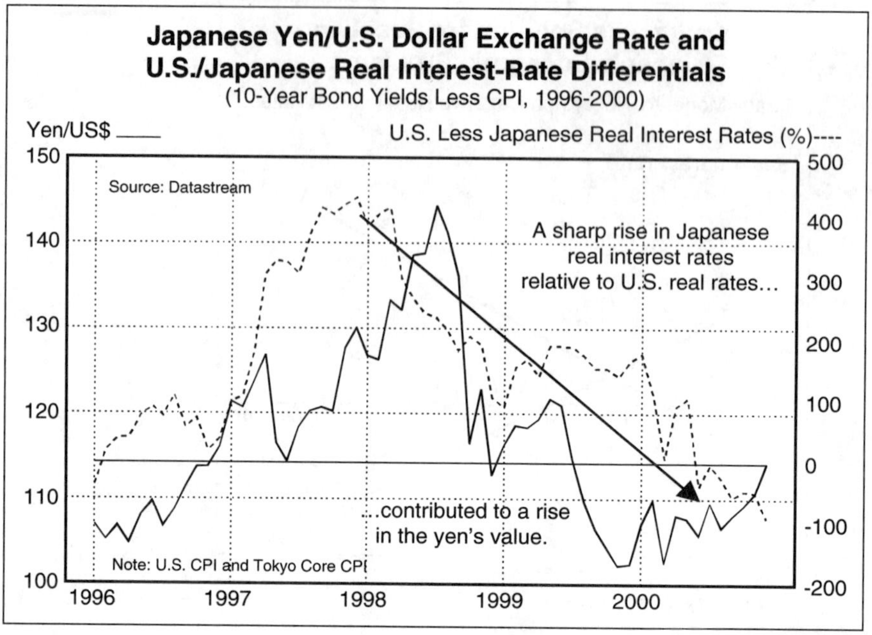

rise in real interest rates tends to be large. There was indeed a very sharp increase in real interest rates in Japan relative to U.S. real rates in 1999–2000 (see Figure 8–13), which contributed to a rise in the yen's value over that period.

CHAPTER 9

The Monetary Approach to Exchange-Rate Determination

Historically, changes in monetary policy have had a profound impact on exchange rates. In the case of the dollar, relatively easy monetary policies pursued by the United States during the Carter administration contributed to a sharp decline of the dollar in 1977–1978. The dramatic tightening in U.S. monetary policy by the Volcker-led Federal Reserve in the early 1980s helped drive the dollar dramatically higher between 1981 and 1985. In the case of the yen, a relatively tight monetary policy by the Bank of Japan in the early 1990s contributed to a major strengthening of the yen during that period. Then beginning in 1995 and continuing until 1998, the Bank of Japan pursued an extraordinary easy monetary policy that contributed to a weaker yen. In 2001, the Bank of Japan also engaged in a very dramatic easing in monetary policy, and the yen fell commensurately. Finally, in the case of many emerging-market currencies, overly easy monetary policies have often been the catalyst for currency-crisis episodes.

The monetary approach asserts that changes in the supply of and demand for money are the primary determinants of exchange-rate movements. Although the monetary approach is widely regarded as an incomplete theory of exchange-rate determination because it ignores other important explanatory variables, it nevertheless correctly warns that the pursuit of overly expansionary monetary policies will exert downward pressure on a currency's value, and vice versa.

The monetary model of exchange-rate determination can be derived from a basic model of the demand for money. If it is assumed that purchasing power parity (PPP) holds at all times, the equilibrium exchange rate can be shown to be completely determined by trends in relative money-supply growth (see Figure 9–1), relative GDP growth (see Figure 9–2), and relative interest-rate differentials. According to the monetary model, a relative increase in domestic monetary growth, a relative decrease in domestic GDP growth, and a relative rise in domestic interest rates will exert downward pressure on a domestic currency's value.

THE MONETARY MODEL'S TRACK RECORD: JAPANESE MONETARY POLICY AND THE YEN

While the monetary model has not been highly successful, broadly speaking, in explaining exchange-rate trends, it nevertheless has done a fairly good

FIGURE 9-1

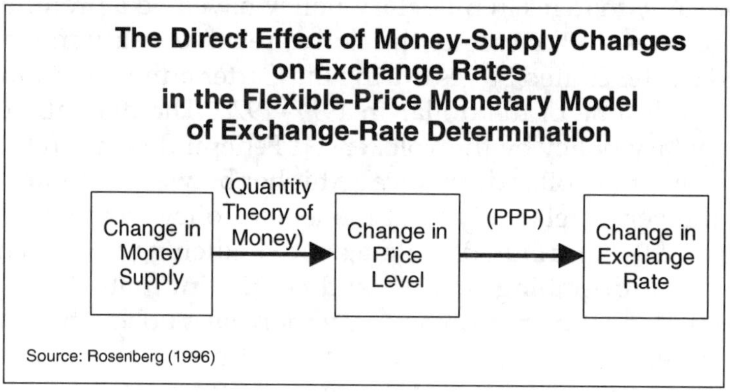

FIGURE 9-2

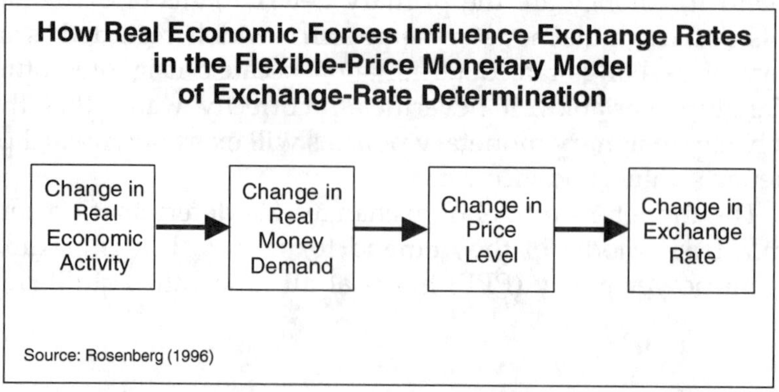

job of explaining the yen's medium-term cycles over the past 12 years. Since 1989, the yen has tended to strengthen on a trend basis when Japanese monetary-base growth has decreased relative to the U.S. monetary-base growth, and vice versa.

For example, monetary conditions in Japan were quite lax in 1988–1989 and this helped foster a weakening of the yen during that period. Over the 1990–1995 period, Bank of Japan (BoJ) policy was especially tight compared to a rather loose Federal Reserve. That relatively tight BoJ stance helped contribute to a stronger yen in 1990–1995. The BoJ then turned easy again over the 1995–1998 period and the yen weakened in tandem. BoJ policy then turned restrictive in 1998–2000 and the yen strengthened in response. Beginning in 2001 and carrying over into 2002, BoJ policy turned easy again, and the yen weakened accordingly. All in all, the yen's medium-term cycles of the past dozen years were largely determined by the path that the Japan/U.S. monetary-base ratio took (see Figure 9–3).

Some observers might find it difficult to accept that BoJ policy was too tight in 1998-2000 when Japanese short-term interest rates were hovering around zero. We would argue, however, that nominal interest rates were a misleading guide as to how tight the Bank of Japan truly was. In fact, our

FIGURE 9-3

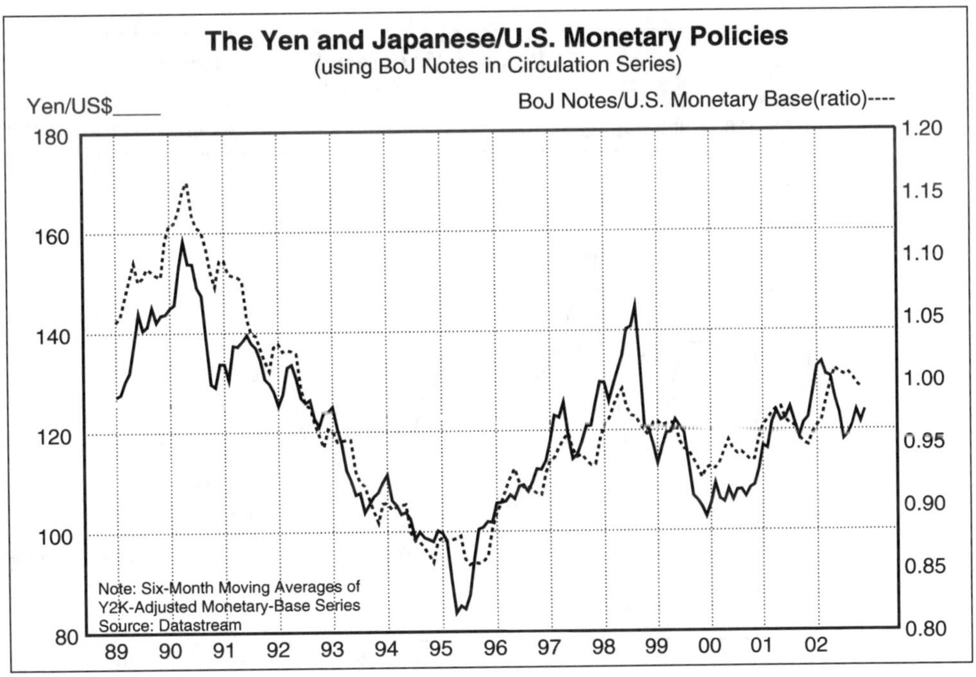

FIGURE 9-4

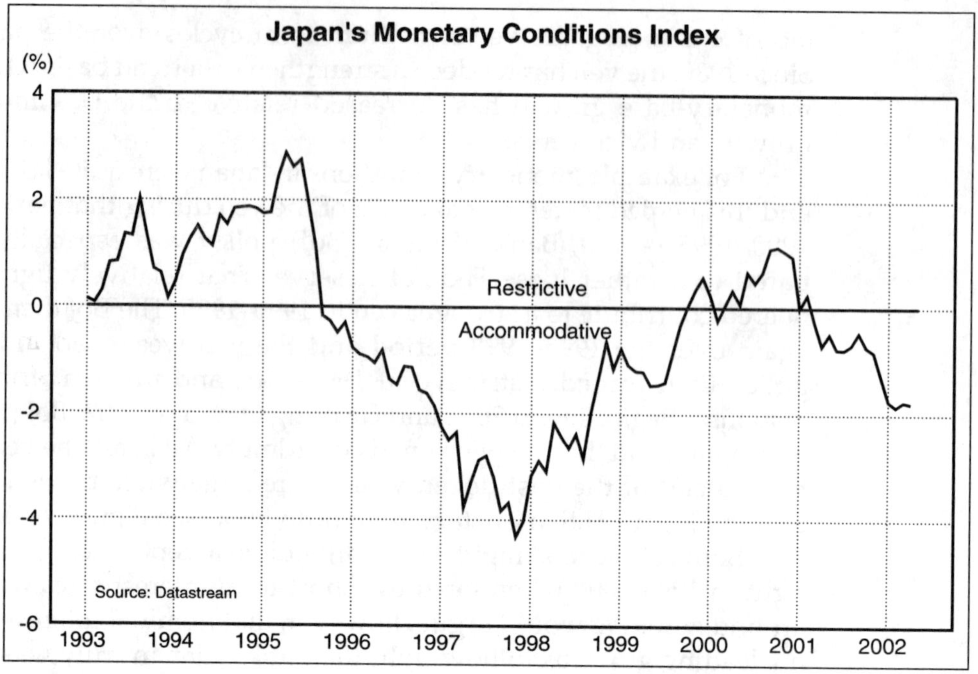

FIGURE 9-5

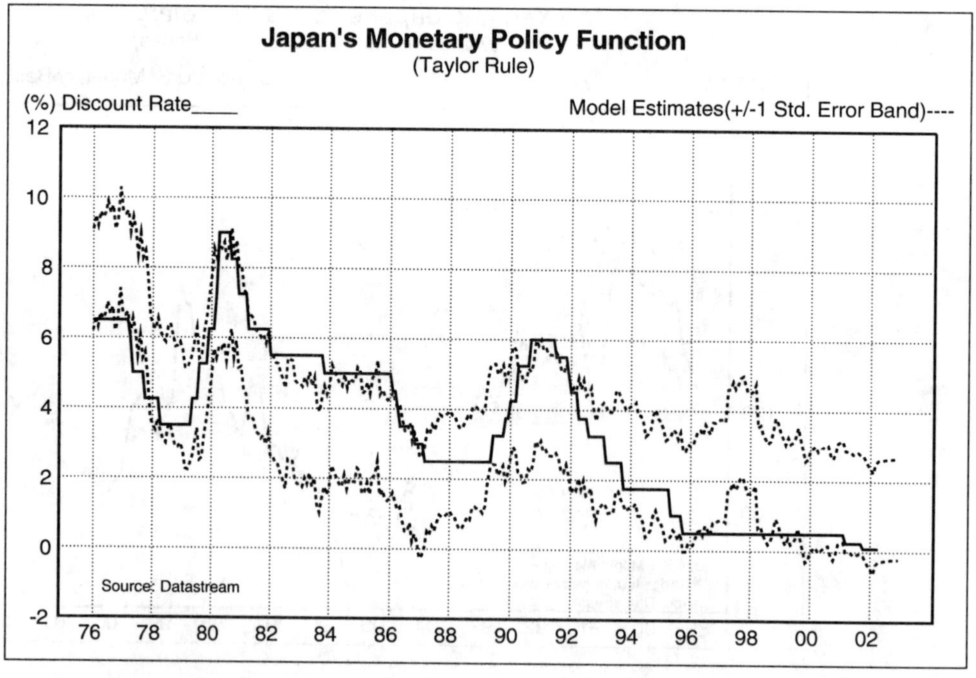

monetary conditions index for Japan (see Figure 9–4) shows that the BoJ shifted from an accommodative policy stance toward a restrictive policy stance in 1998–2000, and a standard Taylor Rule model (see Figure 9–5) suggests that negative nominal rates would have been more appropriate than the BoJ's zero interest-rate policy.

If one accepts the monetarist proposition that "inflation is always and everywhere a monetary phenomenon," then it must also be true that deflation is always and everywhere a monetary phenomenon. If so, the existence of outright deflation in Japan would be evidence that BoJ policy had been too tight. Indeed, Japan's GDP deflator had been declining for nearly 4 years and had recently fallen to −2%, a near record pace of outright deflation (see Figure 9–6).

Another indicator suggesting that BoJ policy was too tight in 1998–2000 was the rising trend in real short-term interest rates (see Figure 9–7). With Japan's GDP deflator falling and nominal short-term interest rates stable at around 0 percent, this had the effect of driving Japan's real short-term interest rates higher on a trend basis. Other evidence of tight monetary and credit conditions include the decline in Japanese bank lending and the steady erosion in equity prices and land values (see Figures 9–8 to 9–10).

FIGURE 9-6

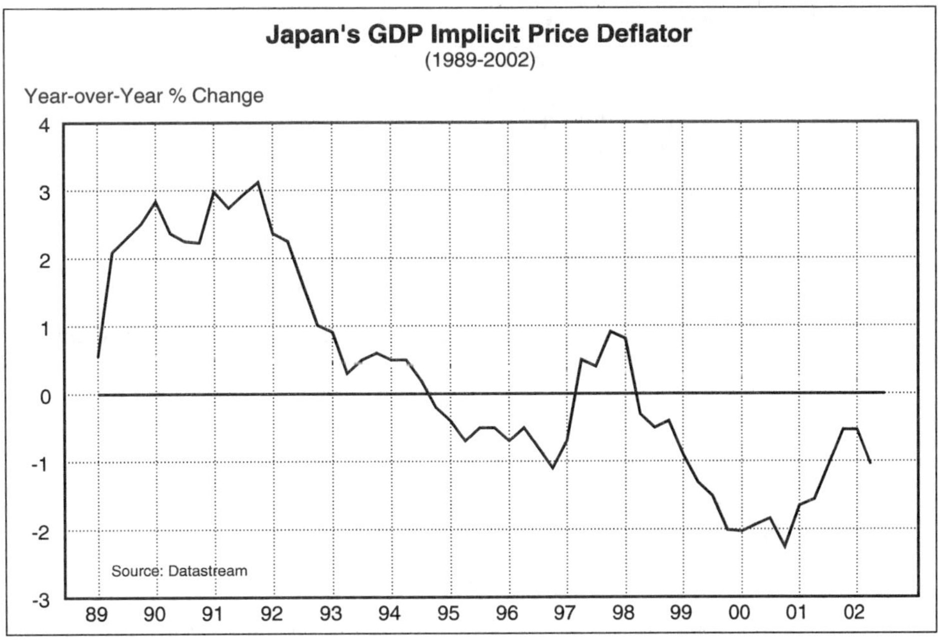

FIGURE 9-7

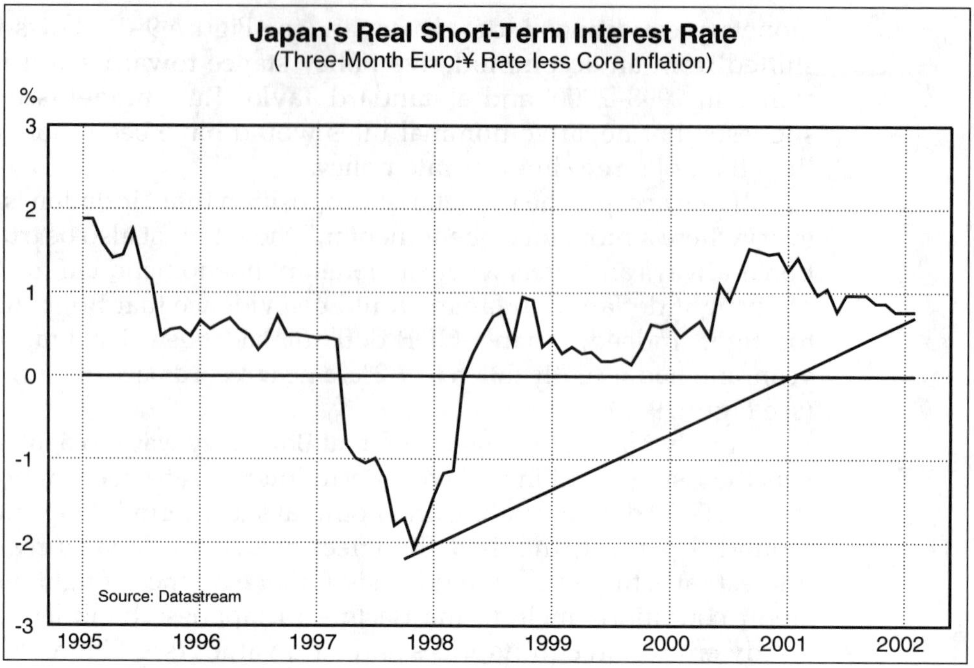

FIGURE 9-8

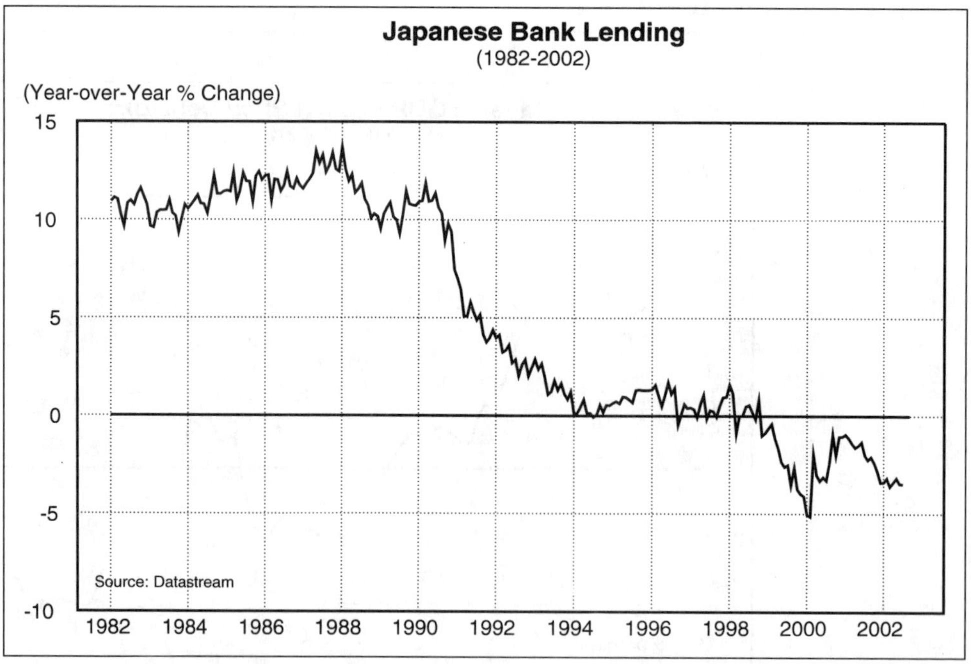

FIGURE 9-9

FIGURE 9-10

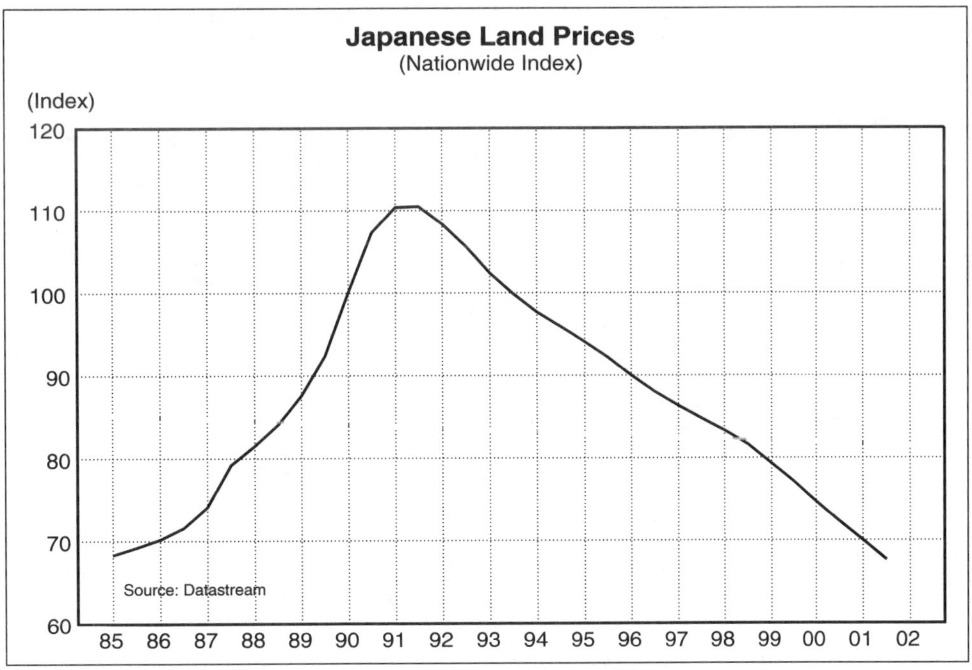

WHY MONETARY AND CREDIT CONDITIONS IN JAPAN BECAME TOO TIGHT IN THE PAST DECADE

Monetary policy typically affects economic activity through a variety of channels: (1) an interest-rate channel, (2) a bank-lending or credit channel, (3) an exchange-rate channel, (4) an inflation-expectations channel, and (5) a wealth-effect channel (see Figure 9–11). Under normal circumstances, an easier monetary policy will lead to lower short-term interest rates, and as lower short-term rates are transmitted to lower rates across the entire yield curve, investment spending will tend to rise. If, however, nominal short-term interest rates are already at zero, as has been the case in Japan, an easier policy stance will not be able to drive short-term interest rates any lower, thereby rendering the interest-rate channel ineffective.

FIGURE 9-11

The Channels of Monetary Policy

How Monetary Policy Changes Are Transmitted to Economic Activity

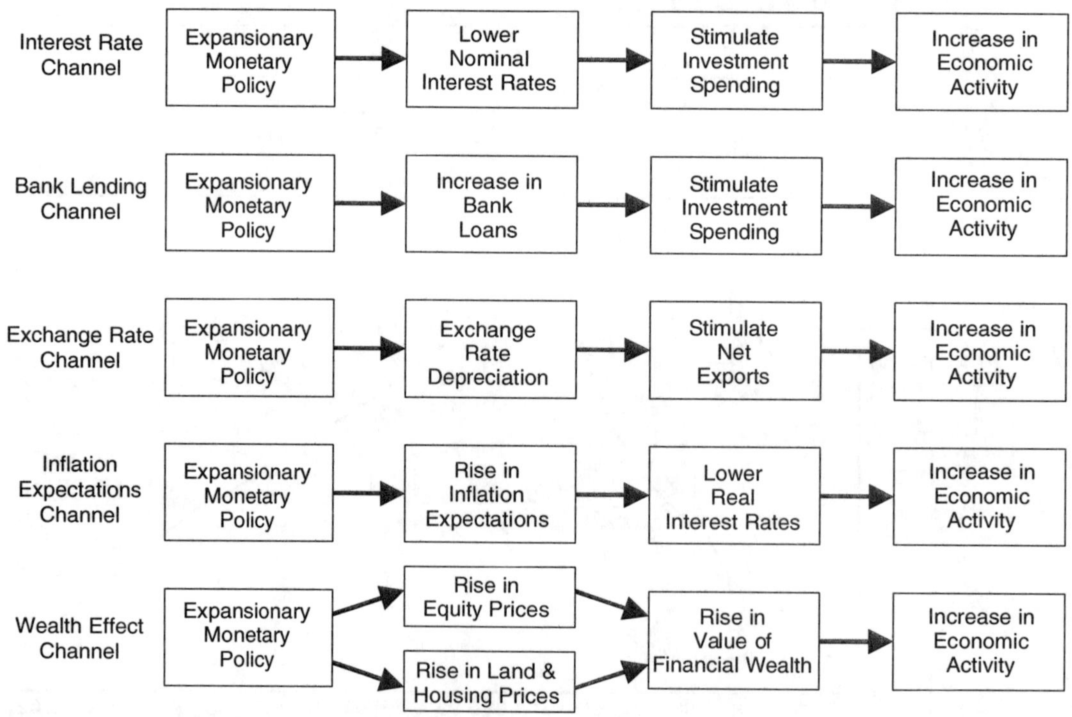

Adapted from Frederick Mishkin, "The Channels of Monetary Transmission: Lessons for Monetary Policy," NBER Working Paper, No. 5464, February 1996.

The bank-lending channel in Japan has also been rendered ineffective as the Bank of Japan's attempt to ease policy has been blunted by the financial problems besetting the banking industry. Indeed, since Japanese bank lending has outright contracted in the past 4 years, this channel has been effectively closed. And if bank-share prices are any indication of what is in store, the banking system's problems are not likely to go away anytime soon.

The exchange-rate channel has also failed to operate properly in Japan. Normally an easy monetary policy gives rise to a depreciation of the exchange rate and that, in turn, contributes to a rise in net exports and therefore economic activity. Up until recently, the yen was fairly strong, suggesting that monetary policy in Japan had been tight in the first place. Given the yen's firmness in 1999–2000, it is obvious that this channel did not function properly during that period.

When nominal short-term interest rates are zero, monetary policy can still be effective if the money supply is expanded at a sufficiently rapid rate so as to raise the expected inflation rate. A higher expected inflation rate will then lower the *real* short-term interest rate, even if *nominal* rates are zero. In theory, those lower real interest rates should stimulate investment spending as outlined in the conventional interest-rate channel. Many outside observers have recommended that the Bank of Japan engineer a quantitative easing in policy and adopt a positive inflation target. But Japan's deflationary pressures remain intact, thereby rendering the inflation-expectations channel inoperative over the last decade.

Finally, the wealth-effect channel in Japan has not been operative for some time now. Normally, an easier monetary policy can be transmitted to the domestic economy through rising equity prices and real estate values, which then increases net wealth and, in turn, helps boost consumption. But with the Tokyo stock market and real estate values down significantly on a trend basis, there has been a trend decline in net financial wealth over time. Indeed, the inability of equity and real estate prices in Japan to rally raises questions whether monetary policy has been truly easy even when interest rates have hovered near zero.

With the traditional channels of monetary policy not functioning properly, the Bank of Japan's policy actions have not been as accommodative as would have been the case under normal conditions. The end result of all this is that the Bank of Japan has been too tight, perhaps inadvertently, and this has given rise to a stronger-than-desired Japanese yen.

CHAPTER 10

Portfolio-Balance Model of Exchange-Rate Determination

The portfolio-balance model posits that exchange rates are determined by the supply of and demand for all financial assets. The monetary model is actually a subset of the broader portfolio-balance model in that the monetary model narrowly focuses on the supply of and demand for money as the key determinant of exchange-rate movements. The portfolio-balance model broadens the menu of assets that can determine the path that exchange rates take. In addition to relative changes in money supply and demand, the portfolio-balance model focuses on relative changes in bond supply and demand (domestic as well as foreign) as key determinants of exchange-rate movements.

In the portfolio-balance model, global investors are assumed to hold a diversified portfolio of domestic and foreign bonds. Their desired allocation to domestic and foreign bonds is assumed to vary in response to changes in expected return and risk considerations. In the portfolio-balance framework, a steady increase in the supply of domestic bonds outstanding, generated by a continued widening of the government budget deficit, will be willingly held only if asset holders are compensated in the form of a higher expected return or risk premium. The higher risk premium could come in the form of higher domestic interest rates or an immediate decline in the domestic currency's value, or some combination of the two (see Figure 10–1). The major insight one draws from this is that in the long run, governments that run large budget deficits on a sustained basis will eventually see their currencies decline in value.

FIGURE 10-1

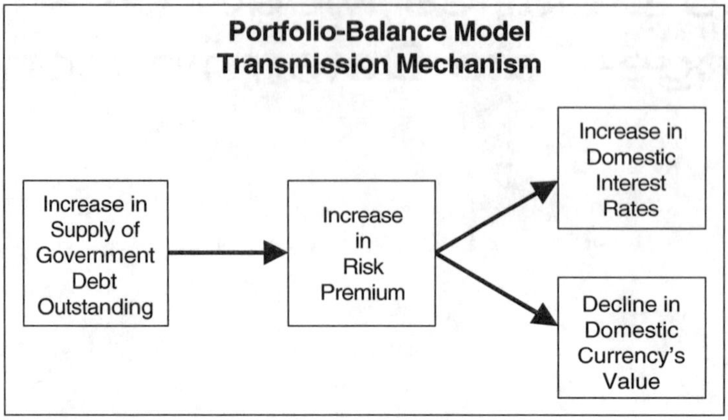

EXTERNAL DEBT, PORTFOLIO BALANCE, AND EXCHANGE-RATE DETERMINATION: THEORY

According to the portfolio-balance model, a rising net external debt burden will, in the long run, have negative consequences for domestic interest rates and/or the domestic currency's value (see Figure 10–2). That is because, in the long run, foreign investors will demand a higher risk premium to buy and hold increasing claims on the debtor country's assets. That higher risk premium could come in the form of wider domestic/foreign interest-rate spreads and/or a weaker domestic currency. If the external debt becomes particularly burdensome, the domestic currency may have to weaken sharply, thereby allowing foreign investors to buy the debtor country's assets at fire-sale prices.

Figure 10–3 illustrates what normally happens when a country undergoes a rapid deterioration in its net external debt position. The risk premium on a debtor country's assets, $Ø_1$, is determined at point *A*, where the outstanding stock of external debt, D^S_1, is willingly held by foreign investors. If the outstanding stock of debt rises to D^S_2, foreign investors will demand a higher risk premium, $Ø_2$, to buy and hold that debt (at point *B*). The result would be a widening in domestic/foreign yield spreads and/or a weakening of the domestic currency.

DEBT TRAP DYNAMICS AND THE EQUILIBRIUM EXCHANGE RATE

Just how long can a country run large and persistent current-account deficits (or surpluses) before there is a required adjustment in the exchange

FIGURE 10-2

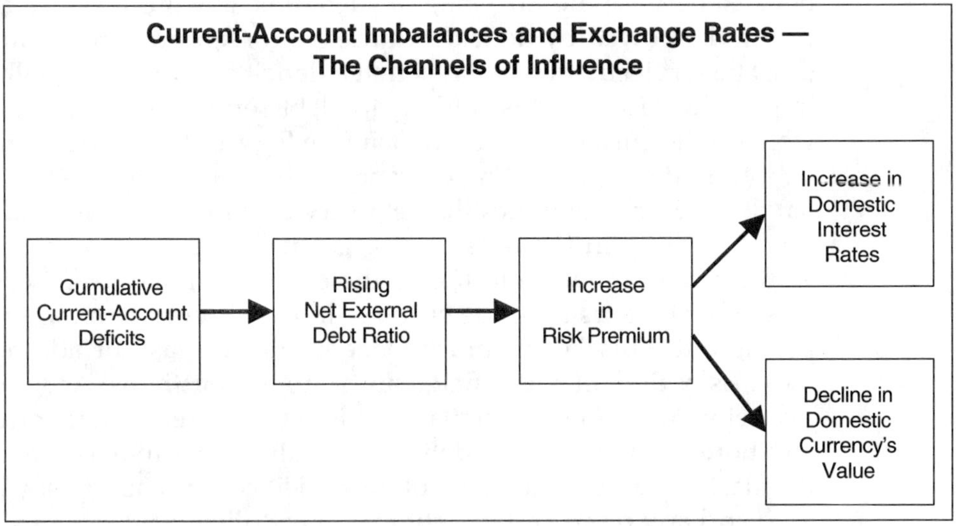

FIGURE 10-3

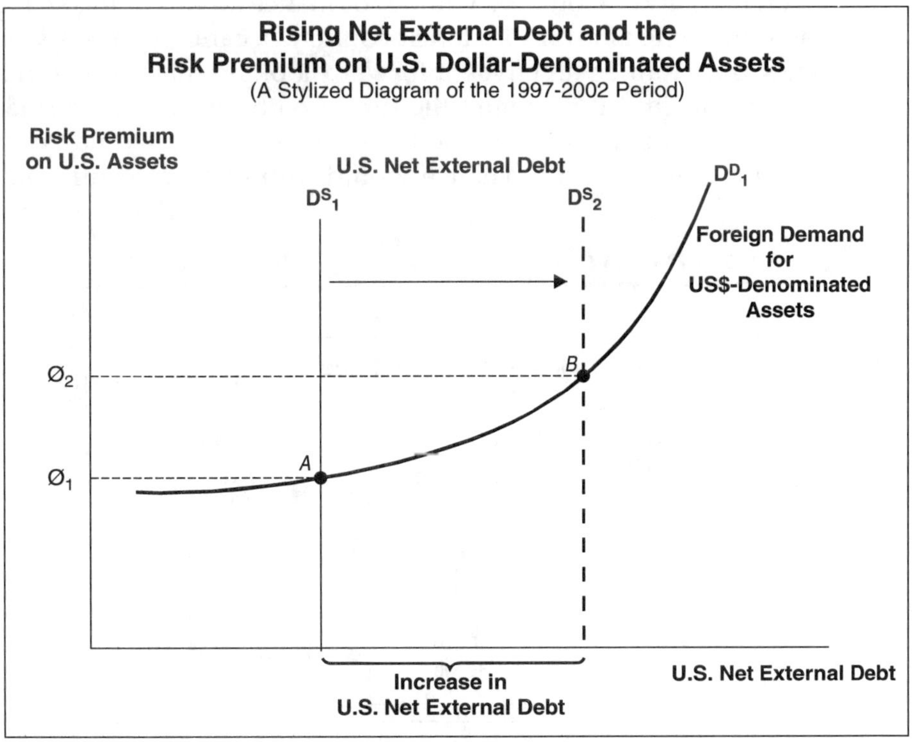

rate to correct the growing external imbalance? There must be some limit on the ability of a country to run sizeable and persistent current-account deficits, because the financing of such deficits would lead to an unending rise in debt owed by deficit countries to foreign investors. Since that debt must be serviced, there is a risk that a deficit country could fall into a "debt trap" with rising debts adding to debt-service obligations, which then worsens the current-account deficit (see Figure 10–4). Once entrenched in a debt trap, the deteriorating current-account trend adds to the rising external debt, which magnifies the debt-service burden further, and so on.

The trend in the outstanding external debt as a percentage of GDP would rise without limit, unless the country's rising debt-service burden was offset by a rising trade surplus. In the absence of an improving trade position, the market would be faced with the task of adding more and more risky debt of the deficit country to its portfolios. At some point, the market would probably demand a higher risk premium to induce it to buy and hold onto that rising debt. Eventually, there may come a time when the market perceives the debt of the deficit country as so risky that it refuses to add any more of that debt to its portfolios.

Thus, although it may be difficult to quantify precisely, there will clearly be a limit on just how long a country can run large and persistent current-account deficits (or surpluses). It is unlikely that an efficient forward-looking market would be willing to finance an unending string of current-account deficits until the deficit country became hopelessly engulfed in a debt trap. Rather, an efficient forward-looking market would look far into the future, and if it judged the future path of the net external debt/GDP ratio to be unsustainable, then the exchange rate would adjust sooner to ensure that the trade balance would improve by a sufficient amount to

FIGURE 10-4

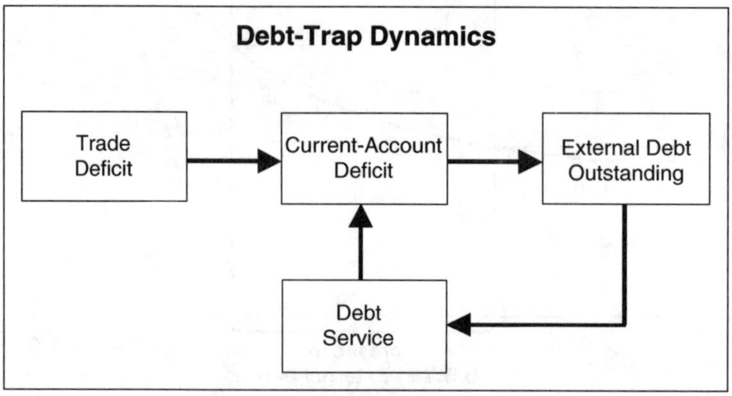

offset the rising debt-service burden and thus stabilize the net foreign debt/GDP ratio at a level that was deemed sustainable.

Using the sustainability criterion to determine a currency's real long-run equilibrium level, the equilibrium real exchange rate could be defined as that rate that will ensure a stable net external debt/GDP ratio in the long run. One would then expect to find a positive (negative) relationship between a currency's real value and the trend in the net external asset (liability) position of that country, and long-run equilibrium would be attained only when the net investment position stabilized.

THE U.S. EXTERNAL DEBT PROBLEM AND THE DOLLAR: THEORY VERSUS PRACTICE

The U.S. net external debt did not change much over the 1997–1999 period despite a record deterioration in the U.S. current-account deficit. The reason for this was that favorable valuation factors on U.S.-owned assets abroad offset increases in foreign holdings of U.S. assets. In recent years, however, negative valuation adjustments, coupled with record increases in foreign holdings of U.S. assets, have contributed to a mammoth deterioration in the U.S. net external debt position (see Figure 10–5).

The portfolio-balance model would have predicted that the dollar should have fallen and U.S./foreign yield spreads should have widened in response to the deterioration in the U.S. net external debt position. This did not happen. Instead, U.S./foreign yield spreads actually narrowed, not

FIGURE 10-5

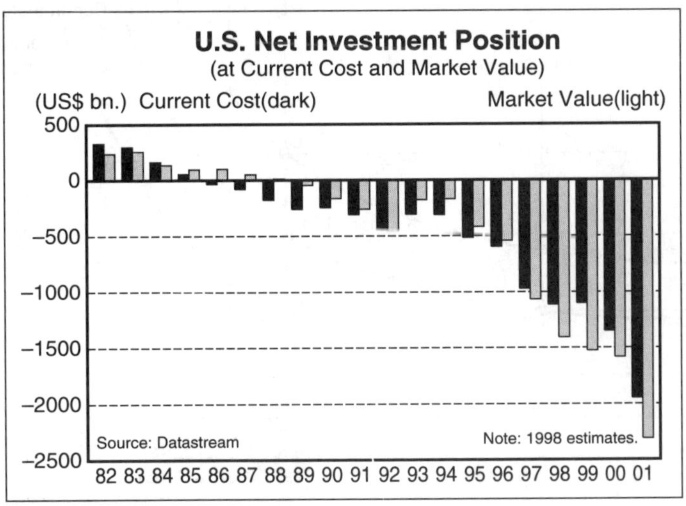

widened, while the dollar's value soared, not weakened, as the portfolio-balance model would have predicted. This would suggest, if anything, that the risk premium on dollar-denominated investments must have fallen, not risen in recent years.

RECENT TRENDS IN THE RISK PREMIUM ON U.S. DOLLAR–DENOMINATED ASSETS

Perhaps Figure 10–6 better characterizes the recent trend in the U.S. risk premium. In this diagram, let's assume that the U.S. net external debt position during 1997–1999 stood at U.S. Net External Debt$_{1997\text{-}99}$. Since the U.S. net external debt position did not change much in 1997–1999, we assume that the outstanding stock of foreign-held U.S. debt remained fixed at that level. Given the prevailing Foreign Demand for U.S. Assets$_1$ that existed in 1997, the U.S. risk premium is assumed to have initially stood at $Ø_1$ in 1997.

Between 1997 and 1999, foreign demand for U.S. assets began to rise. This rise was attributable to increased European investor demand for U.S.

FIGURE 10-6

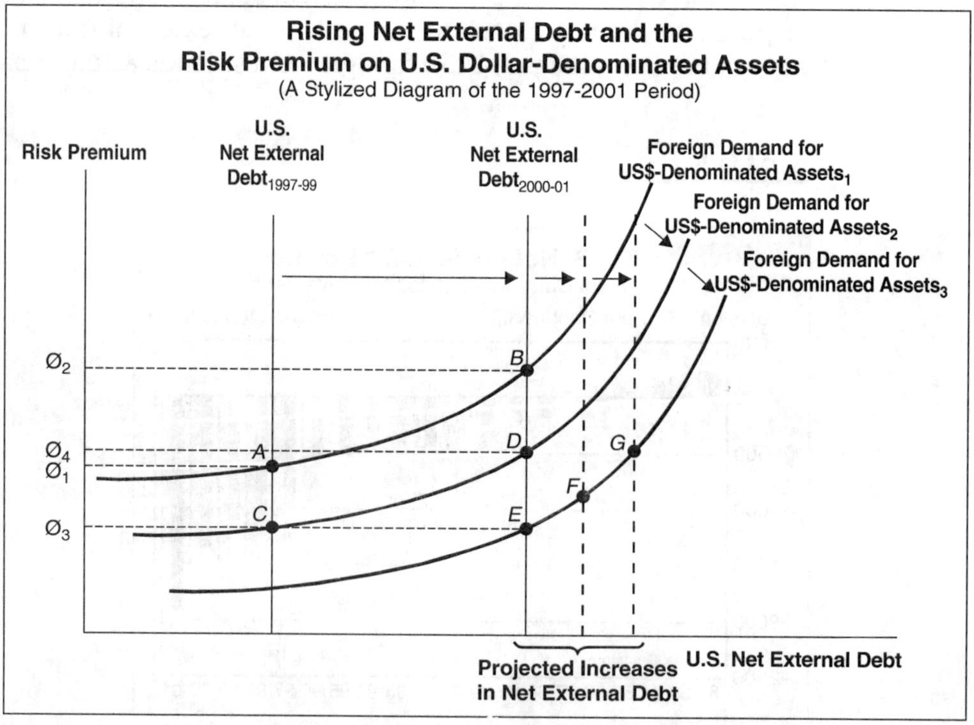

equities and bonds, record FDI flows into the United States, and capital flight from emerging markets to the United States as investors looked for a refuge from the Asian and Russian financial crises. This increased demand for U.S. assets is shown as a rightward shift in the Foreign Demand for U.S. Assets schedule to Foreign Demand for U.S. Assets_2. That shift in overseas demand helped drive the risk premium on dollar-denominated assets down from $Ø_1$ to $Ø_3$ (or from point *A* to point *C*).

As the U.S. net external debt soared from U.S. Net External $\text{Debt}_{1997\text{-}99}$ to U.S. Net External Debt_{2000} in 2000–2001, one might have expected the risk premium on dollar-denominated assets to have risen to perhaps $Ø_4$ (or point *D*), but that was not the case. With U.S./foreign yield spreads continuing to narrow and the dollar remaining firm, the risk premium on dollar-denominated assets must have fallen further in 2000–2001. This implies that although the U.S. net external debt position rose in 2000–2001, the demand for U.S. assets by foreign investors must have risen commensurately, say to Foreign Demand for U.S. Assets_3.

SHIFTS IN EQUITY MARKET CAPITALIZATION RATIOS AND THE TREND IN EXCHANGE RATES

Analysts attribute the rise in the dollar's value versus the euro in the second half of the 1990s to a wide range of factors including strong productivity gains in the United States, structural shifts in portfolio flows from Euroland to the United States, increased M&A flows from Euroland to the United States, structural rigidities in Euroland, New Economy forces in the United States, relative economic growth rates, policy mixes, and euro-changeover risk. The portfolio-balance model offers an additional explanation—the increase in wealth generated by the U.S. equity-market rally in the second half of the 1990s and its impact on U.S. domestic demand.

While it is true that both the U.S. and Euroland equity markets rallied strongly in the second half of the 1990s, U.S. equity-market capitalization as a percentage of GDP rose by a larger amount than the comparable capitalization ratio in Euroland (see Figure 10–7). According to the IMF, U.S. market capitalization rose from about 60% of GDP in 1994 to 160% in 1999, while the comparable capitalization ratio in Euroland rose from 30% of GDP to 90% of GDP. Thus, the capitalization ratio in the United States rose a full 100%, while Euroland's capitalization rose just 60%. Since U.S. households have a higher propensity to consume out of equity wealth than do their Euroland counterparts, the greater increase in U.S. wealth relative to Euroland wealth had a larger impact on the rise in U.S. demand relative to Euroland demand in the second half of the 1990s (see Figure 10–8).

FIGURE 10-7

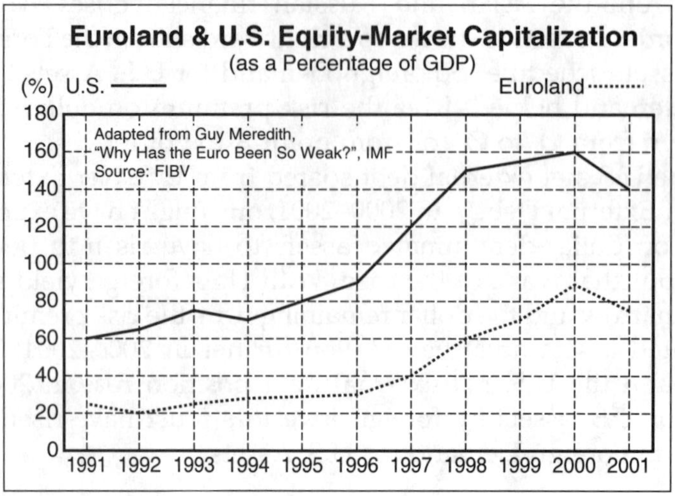

FIGURE 10-8

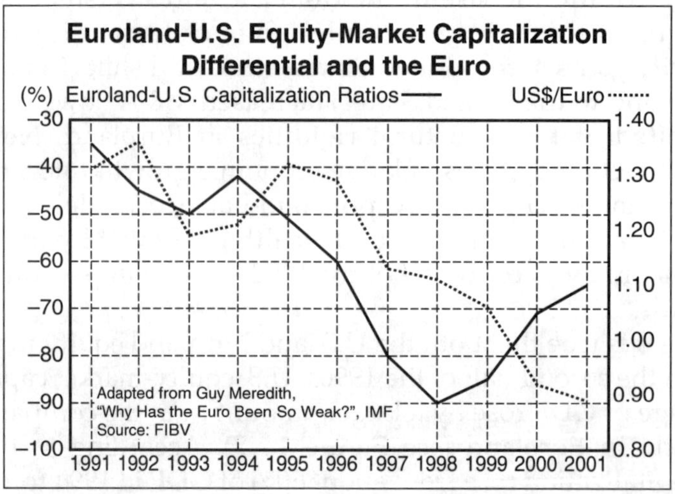

EURO-DENOMINATED DEBT ISSUANCE AND THE VALUE OF THE EURO

At the outset of the euro's launch, EMU optimists predicted that global investors and central banks would attempt to build their holdings of euro assets at the expense of their dollar holdings. It was widely felt that such portfolio shifts would be extremely bullish for the euro.

What was not considered by EMU optimists at the time was the possibility that issuers might also find the euro as an attractive vehicle in which to fund their operations. If the issuance of euro-denominated debt exceeded the demand for that debt, then the euro would weaken, not strengthen.

That is pretty much what happened to the euro over the 1999–2001 period. Issuance of euro-denominated debt by nonresidents soared between 1999 and 2001, both in absolute terms and as a share of all foreign-currency denominated debt. As shown in Figure 10–9, the share of international debt denominated in euros rose from 17% prior to the euro's launch to around 27% in 2000. Most of that increase in debt was purchased by Euroland residents, as little was purchased by international investors.

Overall, the increased issuance of euro-denominated debt, the increased demand for foreign equities by euro-area residents, and the stepped-up acquisition of U.S. firms by European firms resulted in a large flow of capital out of Euroland, which acted to depress the euro's value over the 1999–2001 period.

FIGURE 10-9

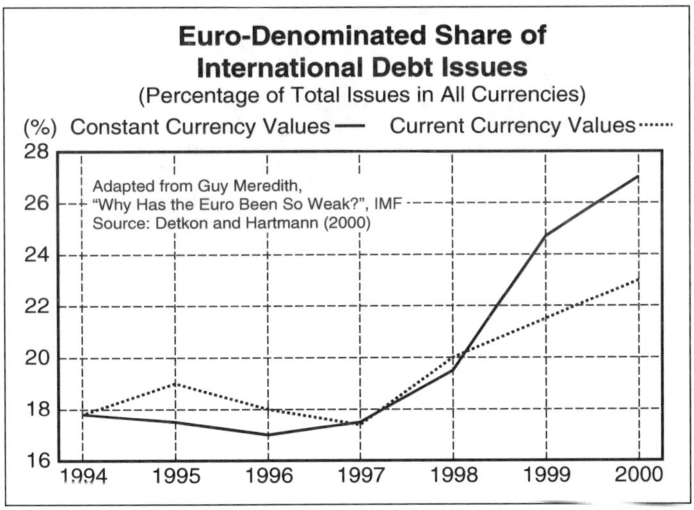

CHAPTER 11

Fiscal Policy and Exchange Rates

There is no universal agreement among economists on the role that fiscal policy plays in the determination of exchange rates. The reason for disagreement is that fiscal impulses are transmitted to exchange rates through a variety of channels, some of which generate positive influences on a currency's value, while others generate negative influences.

For example, in the Mundell-Fleming model, an expansionary fiscal policy typically gives rise to higher domestic interest rates and an increase in domestic economic activity. The rise in domestic interest rates will induce a capital inflow that should contribute to a rise in the domestic currency's value, but the consequent rise in domestic economic activity will also contribute to a deterioration of the trade account, which should put downward pressure on the domestic currency's value. How sensitive capital movements are to the rise in domestic interest rates will determine whether the induced capital inflow will dominate the deterioration of the trade balance or vice versa.

In the portfolio-balance model, a steady string of rising budget deficits will result in a rising stock of government debt outstanding. If risk-averse investors balk at buying and holding an ever-rising stock of government debt, then investors would need to be induced to buy and hold that debt through higher domestic interest rates, an immediate decline in the domestic currency's value, or some combination of the two.

Perhaps one could combine the Mundell-Fleming and portfolio-balance models into a single integrated framework by asserting that a stimulative fiscal policy is likely to be positive for a currency in the short run, but negative in the long run (see Figure 11–1). After the currency's initial appreciation during the period when the stimulative fiscal policy is put into place, budget deficits will rise and total debt outstanding will grow. As the government's debt obligation rises, the market will begin to wonder how that debt will be financed, and if the mountain of debt is sizeable, the market may believe that pressure will eventually be brought to bear on the central bank to monetize the debt. That clearly would lead to a rapid reversal of the initial currency appreciation.

Alternatively, the market may believe that the government's fiscal stance will eventually have to shift toward significant restraint to restore longer-run balance to its fiscal position. A reversal of the fiscal stance that initially drove the currency higher would, by definition, set forces in motion for a reversal of the initial currency appreciation.

U.S. FISCAL POLICY AND THE DOLLAR

One of the best examples of how a stimulative fiscal policy can have a favorable impact on a currency is U.S. President Reagan's Economic Recovery and Tax Act of 1981. The dollar rose sharply following the passage of the act, as it contributed to both a rise in the dollar's real long-run equilibrium level and a significant rise in U.S./foreign real interest-rate differentials.

The U.S. 1981 tax bill included cuts in marginal tax rates for individuals and investment tax credits and accelerated depreciation allowances for

FIGURE 11-1

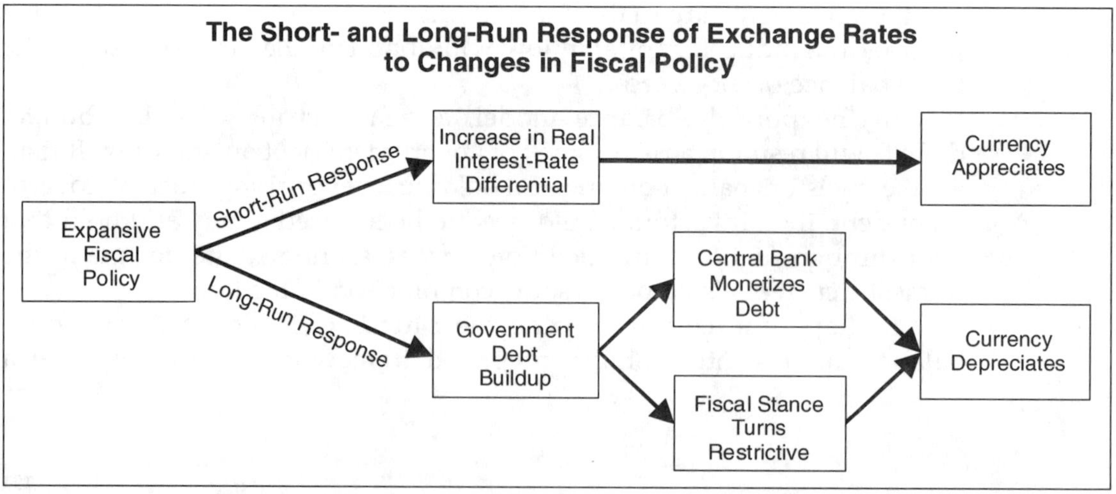

corporations to help spur business investment. From an exchange-rate determination standpoint, the business-oriented tax cuts helped boost the dollar's real long-run equilibrium value because they made U.S. industry more competitive. But the dollar got its real boost when U.S. government spending soared at the same time that taxes were cut. That pushed the U.S. budget deficit as a percentage of GDP from 1.6% up to a high of 6.1% in just four years in the early 1980s (see Figure 11–2). Along with an extremely tight monetary policy during the early 1980s, this helped drive U.S./European real yield spreads up sharply, thereby sending the dollar up sharply as well.

JAPAN'S FISCAL POLICY AND THE YEN

Japan's fiscal deficit—at both the central and local authority level—has been swelling in recent years, partly because of past stimulus efforts and partly because government revenue growth has been weak during Japan's decade-long slump (see Figure 11–3). Japan already has the industrial world's largest government debt outstanding as a percentage of GDP, and that debt burden seems certain to mount in future years, according to OECD projections. Even those debt projections probably understate Japan's true

FIGURE 11-2

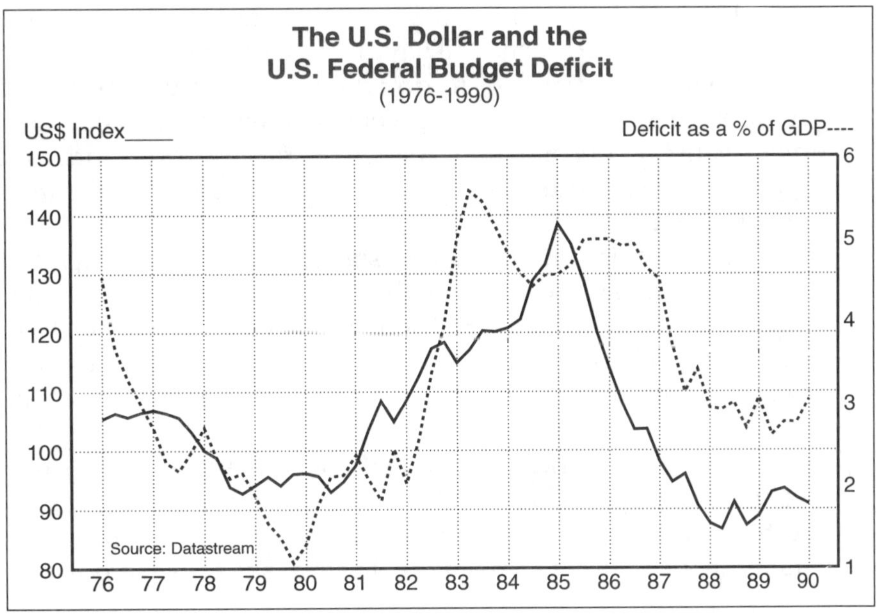

FIGURE 11-3

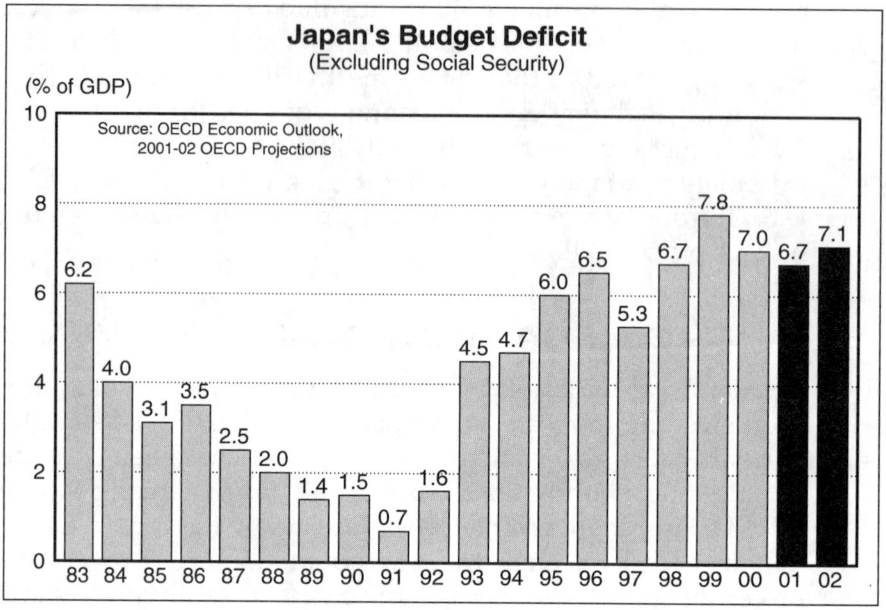

debt burden by a sizeable amount, given Japan's seriously underfunded social security and public pension systems, as well as other off-balance-sheet liabilities that the government will be obliged to underwrite.

The path for Japanese debt is clearly not sustainable. In the long run, the Japanese government will have to do what every other government in the industrial world has had to do when faced with a similar set of circumstances. That is, the Japanese government will have to engineer a multiyear plan of fiscal consolidation—either by raising taxes and/or by curtailing government spending—to bring the budget deficit/GDP ratio down to sustainable levels.

Changes in Japan's fiscal stance have historically had a marked impact on Japan's GDP growth rate, with stimulative policies boosting GDP growth higher and restrictive policies dragging GDP growth lower (see Figure 11–4). Therefore, as Japan's fiscal stance is tightened, pressure will come to bear on the Bank of Japan to turn more accommodative to sustain economic growth.

As a result of these anticipated policy changes, Japan's fiscal/monetary policy mix appears destined to shift toward a stance of significant fiscal restraint and considerable monetary ease. Hence, Japan's policy mix should therefore be highly yen negative. Indeed, since such a policy mix will need

FIGURE 11-4

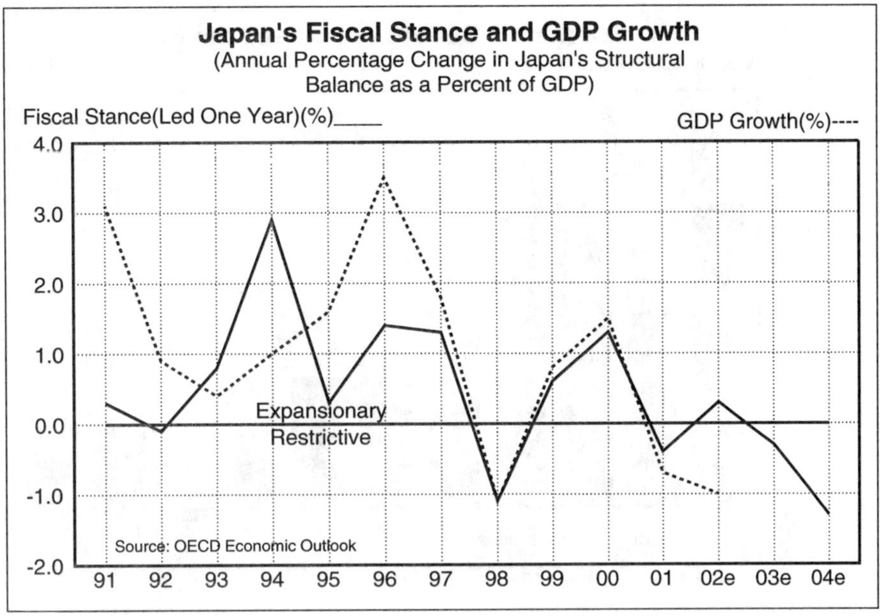

to be put in place for a number of years, the yen appears destined to weaken on a long-term basis.

THE EXPERIENCE OF OTHER COUNTRIES WITH RESTRICTIVE FISCAL POLICIES IN THE PAST 10 YEARS

A number of currencies—notably the Canadian dollar, euro, Australian dollar, and Swedish krona—weakened on a trend basis over the past 10 years as their respective governments engineered major fiscal consolidations to rein in excessively wide budget deficits (see Figures 11–5 and 11–6).

In all cases, pressure was brought to bear on the respective central banks to pursue highly accommodative monetary policies during those extended periods of fiscal consolidations. Therefore, the policy mix in each of those cases exerted significant downward pressure on the respective currencies.

FIGURE 11-5

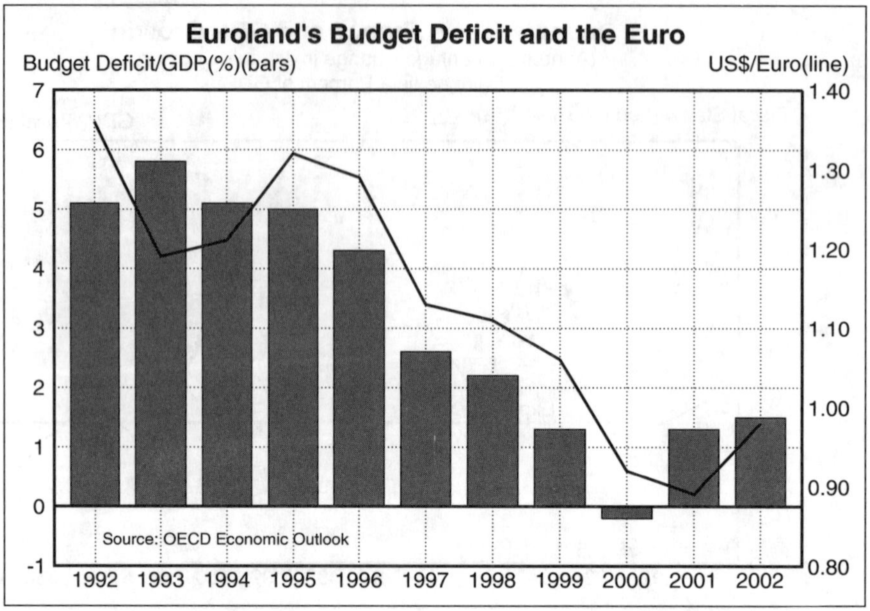

FIGURE 11-6

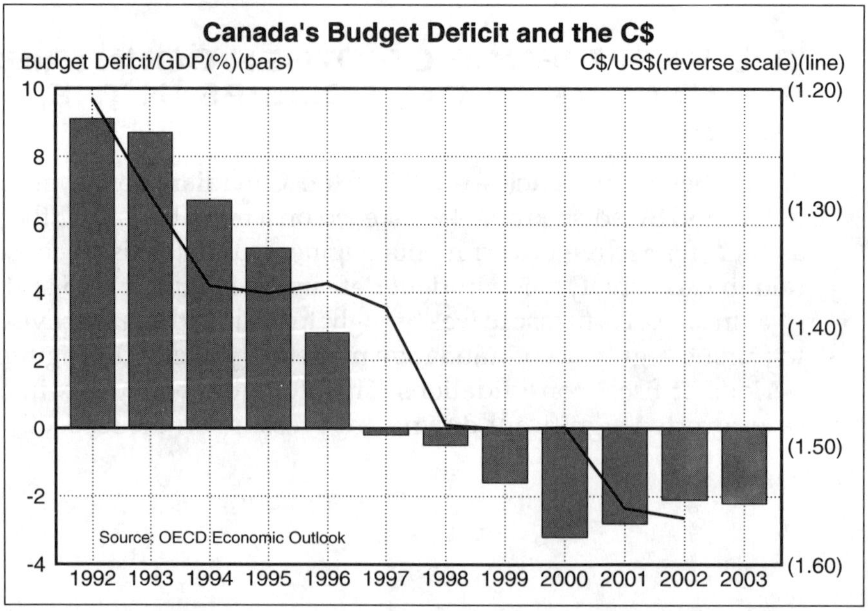

CHAPTER 12

Economic Growth and Exchange Rates

Is a strongly growing domestic economy bullish or bearish for a currency? According to the monetary model of exchange-rate determination, an increase in domestic economic activity will give rise to an increase in the demand for domestic money, and the increased demand for money (everything else being equal) should then lead to an appreciation of the domestic currency (see Figure 12–1). In contrast, in the Mundell-Fleming and balance-of-payments flow models, an increase in domestic economic activity will give rise to an increase in import demand, which should cause the trade balance to deteriorate (see Figure 12–2). The deterioration of the trade balance should then exert downward pressure on the domestic currency.

One could combine the conclusions drawn from these two models by arguing that in the short and medium run, a strongly growing domestic economy should be bullish for a domestic currency because increases in economic activity are often associated with attractive investment opportunities that should attract significant inflows of capital from abroad. But in the long run, the balance of payments may place a constraint on how rapidly a domestic economy can grow relative to growth overseas. If strong domestic demand gives rise to a significant deterioration of the trade balance that is deemed unsustainable, then either domestic demand will have to be restrained or the domestic currency's real value will have to fall to bring the trade/current-account imbalance back to sustainable levels.

FIGURE 12-1

How Changes in Economic Activity Influence Exchange Rates in the Monetary Model of Exchange-Rate Determination

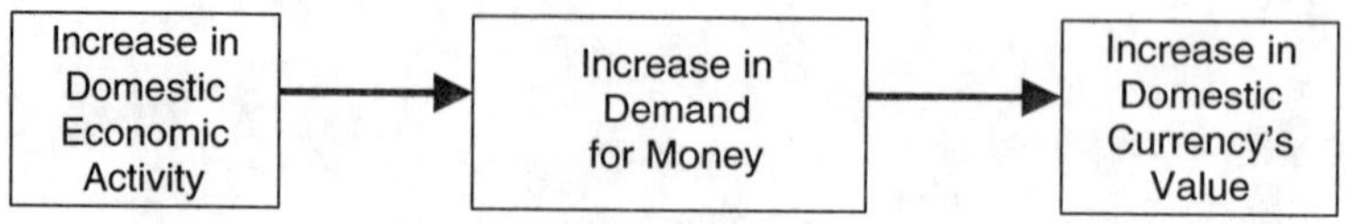

FIGURE 12-2

How Changes in Economic Activity Influence Exchange Rates in the Balance of Payments Flow (Mundell-Fleming) Model of Exchange-Rate Determination

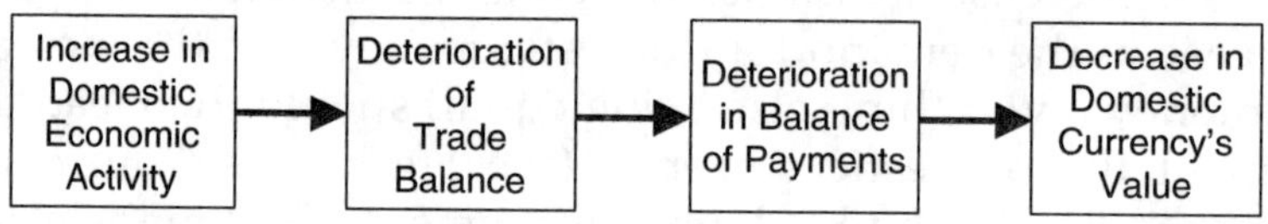

HOW CHANGES IN ECONOMIC ACTIVITY HAVE INFLUENCED RECENT TRENDS IN EXCHANGE RATES

Trends in economic activity have been a key determinant of exchange-rate trends in recent years. For example, the trend in the euro has been found to be highly correlated with the difference in U.S./Euroland *expected* GDP growth rates since the euro's inception in 1999 (see Figure 12–3).

Other currencies have also exhibited a tendency to move in tandem with relative economic performances. For instance, there has been a close relationship in recent years between the yen and the OECD's leading indicator of Japanese economic activity, with weaker Japanese growth prospects negative for the yen and vice versa (see Figure 12–4). In the case of the British pound, the ratio of German/U.K. unemployment rates has served as a good guide to sterling's prospects (see Figure 12–5). All things being equal, a decline (rise) in the U.K. unemployment rate relative to the German unemployment rate has been bullish (bearish) for sterling.

FIGURE 12-3

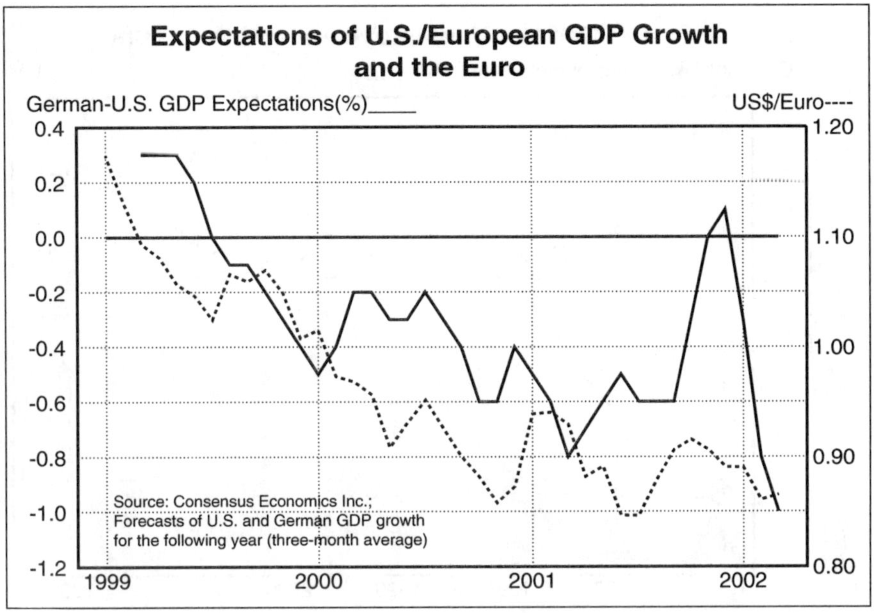

FIGURE 12-4

FIGURE 12-5

FIGURE 12-6

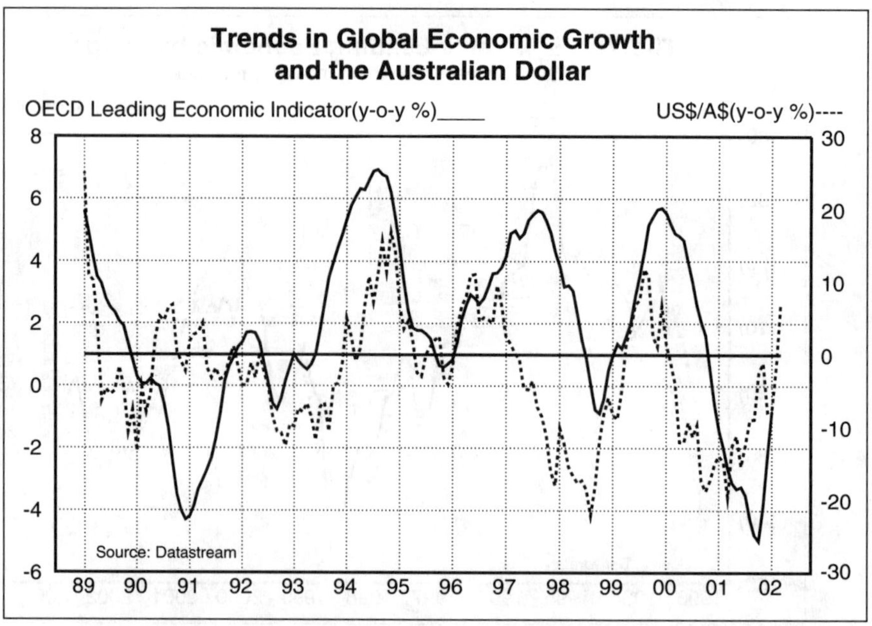

Finally, in the case of Australia, the Australian dollar's fortunes have often been tied to global economic prospects, with strong global growth positive for the Australian dollar, and vice versa (see Figure 12–6). Evidently, strong global growth boosts the world's demand for commodities, which is positive for Australia's trade balance, and thus the Australian dollar.

STRUCTURAL RIGIDITIES, LONG-TERM GROWTH, AND LONG-TERM TRENDS IN EXCHANGE RATES

It is not too difficult to unearth the reasons for the dollar's rising trend over the 1995–2001 period. The U.S. economy grew two to three times faster than either the German or Japanese economies (see Figure 12–7), with New Economy forces in the United States widely credited for the relative strength of the U.S. economy, and thus the dollar.

According to the New Economy view, the surge in U.S. investment spending and the consequent rise in U.S. productivity helped push U.S. growth significantly above the pace of overseas growth, which, in turn, raised the dollar's real long-run equilibrium value versus the euro. This view appears to be shared by many economists. However, what is open to dispute is (1) by how much did the dollar's real long-run equilibrium value actually rise, and (2) did the dollar's rise in 2000–2001 push it above its new long-run equilibrium level?

(Note that the German economy did not fare much better than the Japanese economy over the 1993–2002 period. Given that the 1990s have often been characterized as Japan's lost decade, they could just as easily have been characterized as Germany's lost decade as well.)

FIGURE 12-7

U.S., German, and Japanese Real GDP Growth
Annual Percentage Growth Rates
(1993-2002)

	1993	1994	1995	1996	1997	1998	1999	2000	2001p	2002p	1993-2002 Average
U.S.	2.7	4.0	2.7	3.6	4.4	4.3	4.1	4.1	1.2	2.3	**3.3**
Germany	-1.1	2.3	1.7	0.8	1.4	2.0	1.8	3.0	0.6	0.9	**1.2**
Japan	0.5	1.1	1.5	3.6	1.8	-1.0	0.7	2.2	-0.4	-1.0	**0.9**

Source: IMF

INDICATORS OF GLOBAL COMPETITIVENESS AND LONG-TERM VALUE IN FX MARKETS

The persistent underperformance of the German and Euroland economies has, according to the BIS, given rise to an asymmetry in the response of global investors to favorable and unfavorable data releases out of Euroland. When Euroland data releases are disappointing, the market tends to react negatively and the euro declines in value. However, when Euroland data releases are favorable, the investment community has been reluctant to reward the euro by driving it higher. Evidently, investors have become accustomed to longer-term disappointing data out of Euroland, and therefore treat favorable data releases as transitory events and unfavorable data releases as more permanent events. Given the market's asymmetric behavior, the euro has tended to trade with a sustained downward bias.

Market participants often place the blame for Euroland's and Japan's sluggish growth on structural rigidities that inhibit their long-term economic potential. As shown in Figure 12–8, the major European economies and particularly Japan fare poorly in various independent surveys of global competitiveness, entrepreneurship, attracting foreign direct investment, and opacity/transparency. The fact that Europe's and Japan's poor standing is consistent across a wide range of independent surveys suggests that structural rigidities could act as a major drag not only on Europe's and Japan's long-term growth prospects but on the euro's and yen's value as well. While there has been some improvement in recent years in Euroland's standing in the World Economic Forum rankings, Japan's standing in that survey has steadily fallen (see Figure 12–9). That may explain why the yen fell sharply versus the euro in 2001–2002.

FIGURE 12-8

How Germany and Japan Rank in Independent Surveys of Global Competitiveness

Rank	World Economic Forum	Institute Management Development	Japan Center for Economic Research	Babson College Global Entrepreneurship Monitor	A. T. Kearney Foreign Direct Investment Confidence Index	PriceWaterhouse Coopers Opacity Index
1	**U.S.**	**U.S.**	**U.S.**	Brazil	**U.S.**	Singapore
2	Singapore	Singapore	Singapore	Korea	China	**U.S.**
3	Luxembourg	Finland	Netherlands	**U.S.**	Brazil	Chile
4	Netherlands	Netherlands	Finland	Australia	U.K.	U.K.
5	Ireland	Switzerland	Hong Kong	Norway	Mexico	Hong Kong
6	Finland	Luxembourg	Norway	Canada	Germany	Mexico
7	Canada	Ireland	Sweden	Argentina	India	Italy
8	Hong Kong	Germany	Australia	India	Italy	Hungary
9	U.K.	Sweden	U.K.	Italy	Spain	Israel
10	Switzerland	Iceland	Switzerland	U.K.	France	Uruguay
11	Taiwan	Canada	Canada	Germany	Poland	Greece
12	Australia	Denmark	Germany	Denmark	Canada	Peru
13	Sweden	Australia	N.Z.	Spain	Singapore	Egypt
14	Denmark	Hong Kong	Belgium	Israel	Thailand	Lithuania
15	Germany	U.K.	Denmark	Finland	Australia	South Africa
16	Norway	Norway	**Japan**	Sweden	Czech Rep.	**Japan**
17	Belgium	**Japan**	Iceland	Belgium	S.Korea	Colombia
18	Austria	Austria	Ireland	France	Netherlands	Argentina
19	Israel	France	Taiwan	Singapore	Taiwan	Taiwan
20	N.Z.	Belgium	Austria	**Japan**	**Japan**	Brazil
21	**Japan**	N.Z.	France	Ireland	Hungary	Pakistan

FIGURE 12-9

U.S., Euroland, and Japan's Global Competitiveness Rankings

World Economic Forum Rankings

(1996-2001)

Country	2001	2000	1999	1998	1997	1996
Finland	1	6	11	15	19	16
U.S.	**2**	**1**	**2**	**3**	**3**	**4**
Canada	3	7	5	5	4	8
Netherlands	8	4	9	7	12	17
Ireland	11	5	10	11	16	26
U.K.	12	9	8	4	7	15
Germany	**17**	**15**	**25**	**24**	**25**	**22**
Austria	18	18	20	20	27	19
Belgium	19	17	24	27	31	25
France	20	22	23	22	23	23
Japan	**21**	**21**	**14**	**12**	**14**	**13**
Spain	22	27	26	25	26	32
Portugal	25	23	27	26	30	34
Italy	26	30	35	41	39	41
Luxembourg	NA	3	7	10	11	5

Source: World Economic Forum, www.weforum.org

CHAPTER 13

Central Bank Intervention

The argument most often made to justify official intervention in the FX markets is that the exchange rate is simply too important a price to be left to the market. Intervention advocates contend that financial markets cannot be trusted to get the exchange rate "right" (see Figure 13–1). They argue that intervention is necessary to keep exchange rates broadly in line with their long-run fundamental equilibrium value. Thus, the case for intervention relies largely on the belief that the authorities can do a better job than the market in terms of driving exchange rates toward their long-run equilibrium value. This assumes that government officials have better information and greater knowledge than the market, which, of course, is highly debatable.

No precise rules govern the conduct of FX intervention, but the IMF has established guidelines to prevent one country from unfairly manipulating its exchange rate to gain an unfair advantage over others (see Figure 13–2).

Numerous empirical studies have been conducted to assess whether intervention operations have a statistically significant and quantitatively important impact on exchange rates. In most studies, the results have been negative. In those cases where a statistically significant relationship between intervention and exchange rates has been found, it has generally been the case that the impact was not quantitatively important, that is, the effect of the intervention effort was neither sizeable nor lasting. The major reason for such findings is that intervention operations are typically small relative to the volume of foreign exchange that changes hands on a daily

FIGURE 13-1

Why FX Intervention Advocates Believe That the Market Cannot Be Trusted to Get the Exchange Rate "Right"

- FX market may fail to use "all" existing information.
- FX market may be dominated by noise (trend-following) traders.
- Excessive speculation.
- Excessive risk aversion (shortage of speculation).
- FX market may be using a defective model of exchange-rate determination.
- Market perceptions of the future may be flawed or inappropriately skewed.
- FX market may be pre-occupied with extraneous information.
- FX market may be subject to persistent mood swings, shifting from excessive optimism to excessive pessimism, and then back.

FIGURE 13-2

Acceptable Forms of FX Intervention That Help Foster Orderly Market Conditions

- Simple smoothing operations to limit erratic short-run fluctuation in exchange rates.
- Counter excessive speculation or market overreaction to news.
- Trend-breaking operation to put an end to an undesirable uptrend or downtrend in a currency's value.
- Counter excessive risk aversion.
- Intervention to target a currency's value to some specific level or range.
- Intervention to prevent large and persistent misalignments.

basis in the FX markets. Daily intervention efforts typically average in the hundreds of millions or perhaps only several billion. This contrasts with average daily FX turnover of $1.2 trillion. While episodes of successful intervention can be found, no systematic relationship exists between official intervention efforts and the trend in exchange rates.

U.S. INTERVENTION POLICY

U.S. intervention policy has been highly changeable over the past 30 years (see Figure 13–3). Official attitude toward the dollar has swung from benign neglect, to active encouragement of a weaker dollar, to active intervention to stop the dollar from falling, and most recently to acknowledge that a strong dollar is in the U.S. national interest.

Intervention was most pronounced in the late 1970s, the late 1980s, and in 1994–1995 (see Figures 13–4 to 13–7). Since 1995, the Fed has intervened on only two occasions—in mid-1998 (to guide the dollar lower versus the yen) and in the fall of 2000 (to guide the dollar lower versus the euro).

BOJ/MOF INTERVENTION POLICY

In Japan, the Ministry of Finance has the responsibility for determining the country's intervention policy, while the Bank of Japan carries out that policy in

FIGURE 13-3

Changeability of U.S. Exchange-Rate Policy

Administration	Period	Policy
Nixon	1969-71	Benign neglect.
	1971-73	Cut dollar loose from gold. Devalued dollar.
Carter	1977-78	Encouraged decline of dollar.
	1978-80	Major intervention to arrest dollar's decline.
Reagan/ Bush	1981-84	Benign neglect/laissez-faire attitude toward dollar's rise.
	1985-86	Encouraged decline of dollar (Plaza Accord).
	1987-92	Promoted dollar stability (Louvre Accord).
Clinton	1993-96	Encouraged decline of dollar.
	1997-00	Strong-dollar policy.
Bush	2001-	Strong-dollar policy.

FIGURE 13-4

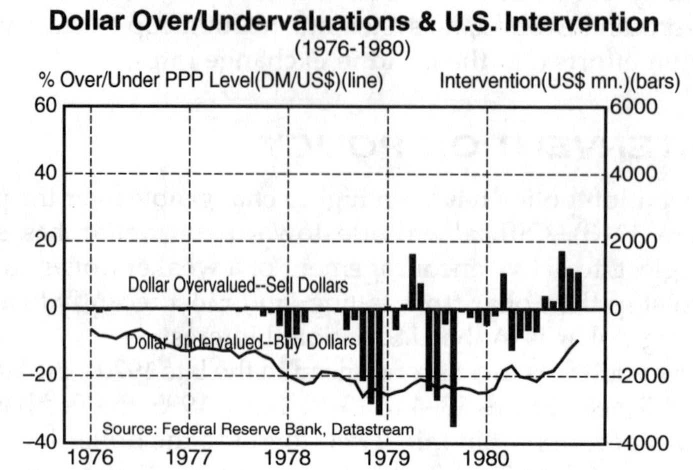

FIGURE 13-5

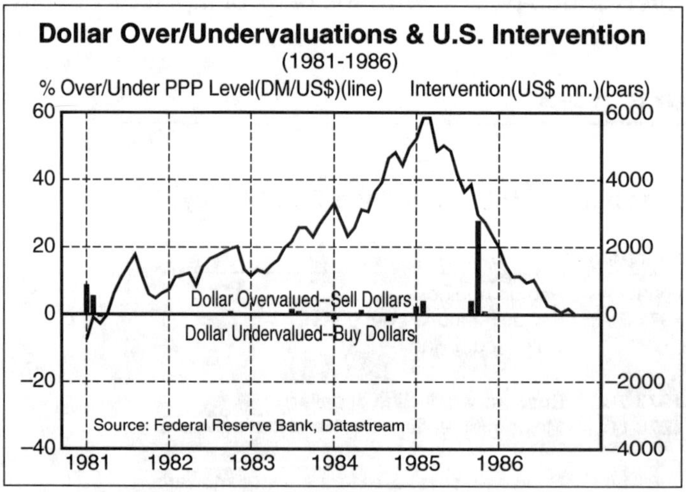

the FX market. Japanese authorities have consistently pursued a policy of "leaning against the wind" in the conduct of intervention operations. Whenever the yen has risen sharply against the dollar, the BoJ has bought dollars and sold yen to moderate the yen's rise. When the yen has fallen sharply in value versus the dollar, the BoJ has sold dollars and purchased

FIGURE 13-6

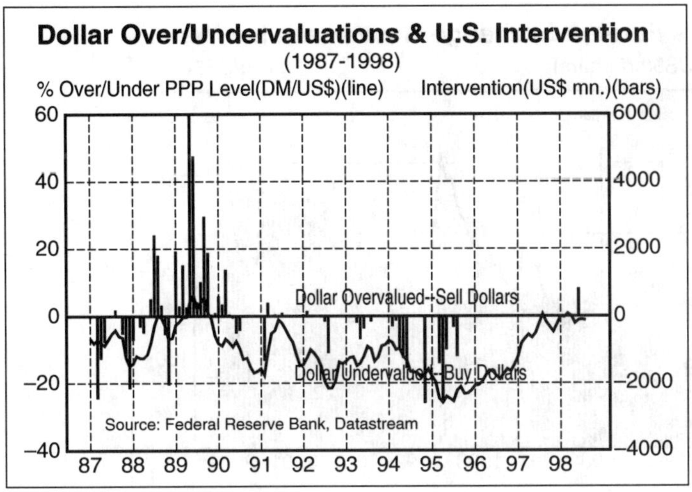

FIGURE 13-7

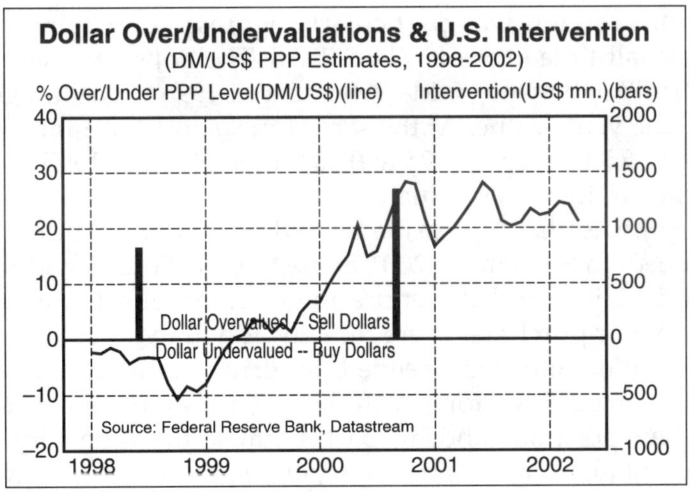

yen to moderate the yen's decline. As a result, there has been a close parallel movement between the yen's value and the BoJ's holdings of foreign-exchange reserve, with reserves rising whenever the yen has risen, and vice versa (see Figure 13–8).

Some analysts have found that the BoJ has tended to intervene more aggressively when the yen has risen sharply than when the yen has fallen

FIGURE 13-8

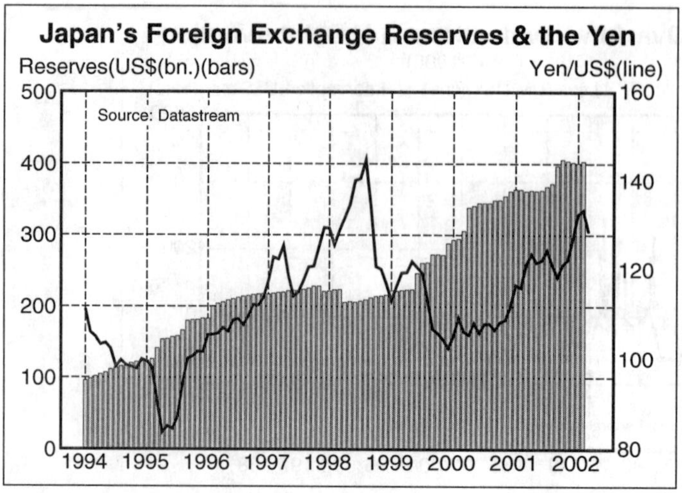

sharply. That is, BoJ intervention policy tends to be asymmetric, with greater emphasis placed on moderating yen strength than on tempering yen weakness.

BoJ intervention was particularly aggressive in 1995 when the yen soared to an all-time high of ¥/US$ 79.75. The BoJ's FX reserves soared by nearly $75 billion between mid-1995 and mid-1996 to encourage an outright decline in the yen's value. At the same time, short-term rates were guided lower from 1.75% in April 1995 to 0.50% in September 1995 to help encourage a decline in the yen's value.

The BoJ was also aggressive in 2001 as it attempted to guide the yen lower. Indeed, in September 2001 alone, the BoJ intervened to the tune of around $25 billion, and the entire intervention effort was nonsterilized, that is, its dollar purchases were directly added to Japan's monetary base. The intervention effort succeeded in driving the yen lower, in part, because it forced investors with long yen/short dollar exposures to unwind their positions and, in part, because the monetary effects were quite substantial, as Japan's monetary-base growth soared on a year-over-year basis from 9.0% to 14.2% during that month.

The BoJ has frequently geared the overall thrust of its domestic monetary policy actions with an eye toward moderating movements in the yen's value. The BoJ has often cut short-term interest rates to dissuade investors from purchasing yen assets when the yen was rising sharply in value, and vice versa. This would explain why Japanese interest rates and the yen often move inversely, with the yen rising at the same time that interest rates are falling, and vice versa (see Figure 13–9).

FIGURE 13-9

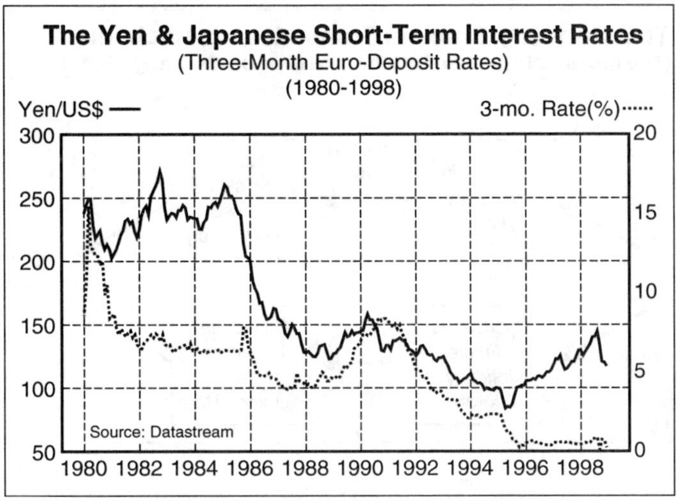

DIRECT CENTRAL BANK INTERVENTION CHANNELS: THE BALANCE-OF-PAYMENTS FLOW, MONETARY, AND PORTFOLIO-BALANCE CHANNELS

Economists have identified three *direct* channels through which central bank intervention might have an immediate impact on exchange rates.

First, intervention that alters the flow supply of foreign exchange relative to the demand for foreign exchange can directly affect the short-term trend in exchange rates. Intervention operating through that channel can be effective only if the volume of intervention is sizeable relative to the daily turnover in the foreign-exchange market.

Second, nonsterilized intervention that alters the supply of money relative to the private sector's demand for money can directly affect the medium-term trend in exchange rates (see Figure 13–10). Intervention operating through this monetary channel can be effective only if the volume of intervention is sizeable relative to the outstanding stock of domestic money holdings.

Third, sterilized intervention that alters the supply of domestic bonds relative to the supply of foreign bonds in private portfolios can also have a direct impact on the medium-term trend in exchange rates (see Figure 13–11). Intervention operating through that channel can be effective only if the volume of intervention is sizeable relative to the stock of publicly traded domestic and foreign bonds held in private portfolios.

FIGURE 13-10

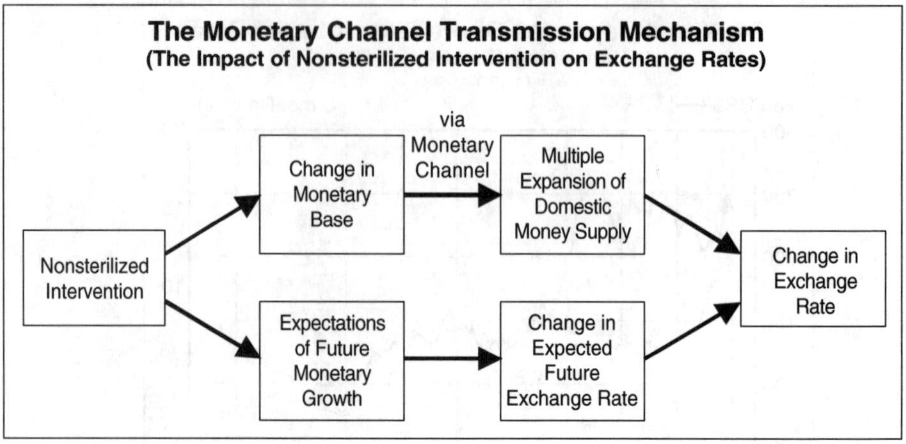

Unfortunately, the weight of evidence suggests that the volume of intervention is often quite small relative to the daily turnover of foreign-exchange activity, the stock of money held by the private sector, and the stock of publicly traded domestic and foreign bonds in private portfolios. Thus, most studies conclude that the direct effect of intervention on exchange rates is either statistically insignificant or quantitatively unimportant.

INDIRECT CENTRAL BANK INTERVENTION CHANNELS: SIGNALING AND NOISE-TRADING CHANNELS

Economists have also identified a number of *indirect* channels through which intervention can alter investors' expectations and positioning and, in so doing, help push currency values in the direction desired by monetary officials.

First, a central bank may use intervention as a signal of its monetary-policy intentions. To the extent that expectations of future monetary growth are altered, intervention could have an immediate impact on exchange rates.

Second, a central bank may use intervention as a signal to the market that an exchange rate is deviating too far from its long-run equilibrium value (see Figure 13–12). To the extent that intervention helps anchor market expectations to the true long-run equilibrium exchange rate, it can have a stabilizing influence.

FIGURE 13-11

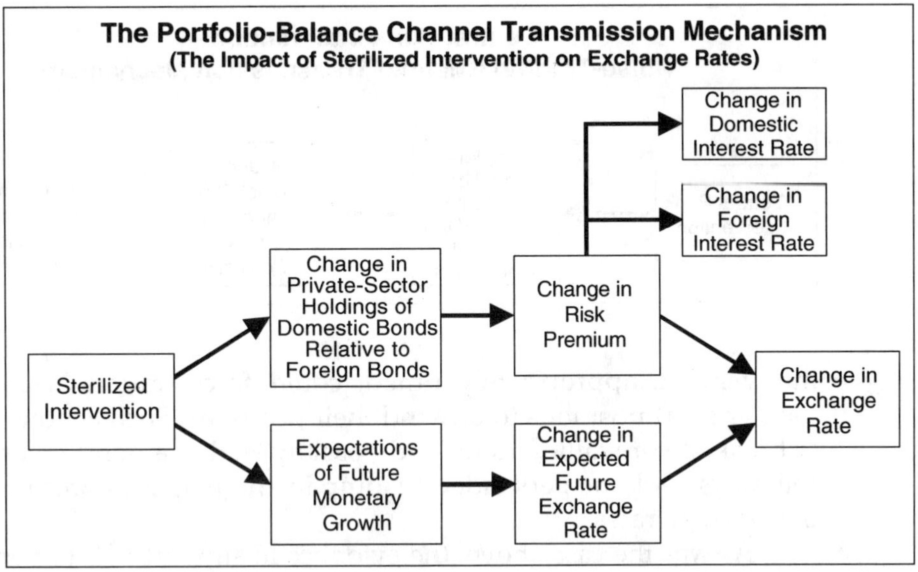

FIGURE 13-12

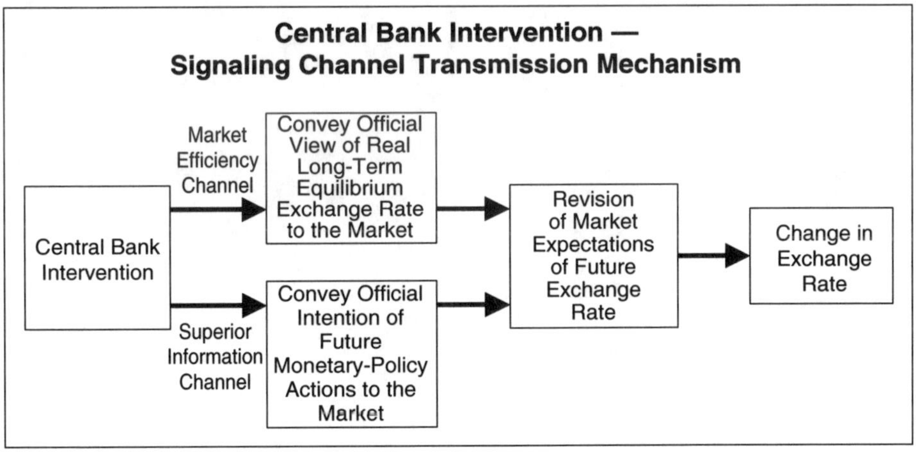

Third, a central bank may want to take advantage of the element of surprise and intervene when exchange rates have overshot their equilibrium level and the market is heavily overbought or oversold (see Figure 13–13). If trend followers dominate foreign-exchange activity and drive exchange rates far from their true long-run equilibrium values, a surprise round of

FIGURE 13-13

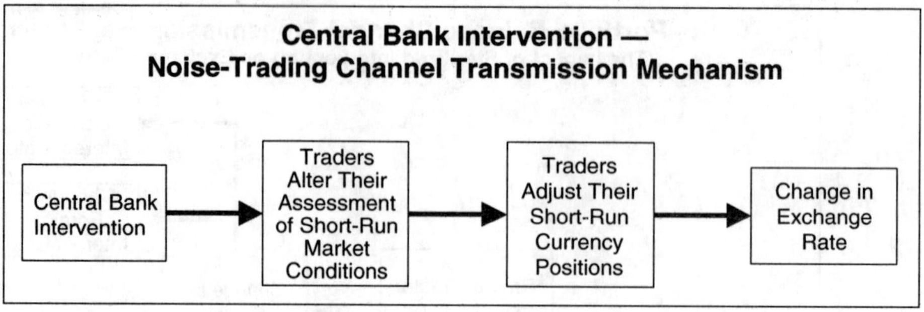

intervention, appropriately timed, could force traders with vulnerable long or short positions to unwind their positions. Such actions could serve to break the prevailing trend and possibly lead to a trend reversal if trend-followers could be persuaded to jump in and help reinforce the new trend in exchange rates.

As was the case above, the evidence in support of intervention operations working through one of these indirect channels is mixed. There have clearly been selected episodes of successful intervention operations, but most studies conclude that central banks cannot unduly influence exchange rates on a sustained basis.

PART FOUR

Anticipating Currency Crises in Emerging Markets

The first half of the 1990s witnessed a strong and growing interest on the part of global fund managers in emerging-market investments. But a series of financial crises during the second half of the decade significantly reduced global fund managers' appetite for such investments. Indeed, net private capital flows into developing countries swung from an inflow of $233.2 billion in 1996 to a mere $8.9 billion in 2000, according to IMF estimates, as overseas investors shied away from emerging-market investments following the Mexican peso crisis of 1994–1995, the Asian currency crisis of 1997, and the Russian crisis of 1998.

While the potential rewards from investing in emerging markets can be quite attractive, these crisis episodes highlight that the risks can be quite great as well. From a strategic standpoint, the issue is whether these currency crises could have been adequately anticipated ahead of time to allow investors to hedge or unwind their emerging-market currency exposures before the collapse in currency values actually took place.

Views on the underlying causes of currency crises differ greatly. One school of thought contends that currency crises tend to be precipitated by deteriorating economic fundamentals. If so, and the trend in those economic fundamentals weakens steadily and predictably, then it should be possible to construct an early-warning system to anticipate when a currency might be vulnerable to a speculative attack.

An alternative school of thought argues that while evidence of deteriorating economic fundamentals might explain a relatively large number of currency collapses, there might also be cases where economies with relatively sound fundamentals could see their currencies come under attack because of a sudden adverse shift in market sentiment or mood swing that is totally unrelated to economic fundamentals. If attacks can occur out of the blue when economic fundamentals are not offering any warning of an impending attack, then there may simply be no way for fundamental-based models to predict the onset of currency crises.

CHAPTER 14

Leading Indicators of Currency Crises

Crisis-prone currencies typically display a number of classic symptoms that warn of an impending speculative attack. These symptoms include the following:

- Excessive real appreciation of the emerging-market currency.
- Weak domestic economic growth.
- Rising unemployment.
- A deteriorating current-account balance.
- Excessive domestic credit expansion.
- Banking-system difficulties.
- Unsustainably large government budget deficits.
- Overly expansionary monetary policies.
- A high ratio of M2 money supply to reserves.
- Foreign-exchange reserve losses.
- Falling asset prices.
- A huge buildup in short-term liabilities by either the private or public sector.

While not all of these symptoms are present in each and every currency crisis, most crises display a number of these symptoms, enough to at least warn of the possibility of an impending speculative attack.

Typically, analysts will look for evidence of deteriorating fundamentals to determine whether an emerging-market currency might be vulnerable to a speculative attack. One can visualize that there exist critical threshold levels for economic vulnerability indicators where, if economic fundamentals deteriorate beyond those threshold levels, an attack on the currency will inevitably be waged.

The seeds of an inevitable currency collapse are planted when a policy shift or an economic or financial shock gives rise to a serious deterioration in one or more key economic variables (see Figure 14–1). Once economic fundamentals deteriorate beyond critical threshold levels (point *A* in the middle diagram), a currency will naturally collapse under its own weight.

FORWARD-LOOKING INVESTORS MAY WAGE AN ATTACK BEFORE FUNDAMENTALS DETERIORATE BEYOND THRESHOLD LEVELS

Since speculators, investors, and borrowers tend to be forward looking, they will recognize before the fact that a steady deterioration in economic fundamentals will lead to an inevitable currency collapse (see Figure 14–2). By looking ahead and reasoning backward, speculators, investors, and borrowers will not wait for point *A* to be reached to capitalize on or to hedge against a possible currency collapse. Instead, forward-looking market participants will begin to sell the vulnerable currency well ahead of the inevitable collapse at point *A*. By doing so, heavy selling pressure will occur well before point *A* is reached. Such selling might trigger a currency collapse in the vicinity of point *B*.

UNCERTAINTY AND THE TIMING OF SPECULATIVE ATTACKS

In a world where there is complete certainty regarding the future path that economic fundamentals will take, it should be possible to pinpoint exactly when a speculative attack might occur. However, in a world where there is less-than-complete certainty, it might not be possible for a leading-indicator model to correctly anticipate the onset of all currency crises.

Consider the case where economic fundamentals do not deteriorate in a steady and predictable manner. Assume that the trend in economic fundamentals is gradually weakening, but there comes a point (such as point C in Figure 14–3) where a sudden, unexpected improvement in one or more key fundamental indicators permanently alters the long-term trend in economic fundamentals in a favorable direction. The danger here is that prior to point C being reached, an early-detection system might have prematurely warned of an inevitable currency collapse at point *B* when no such warning was truly called for.

FIGURE 14-1

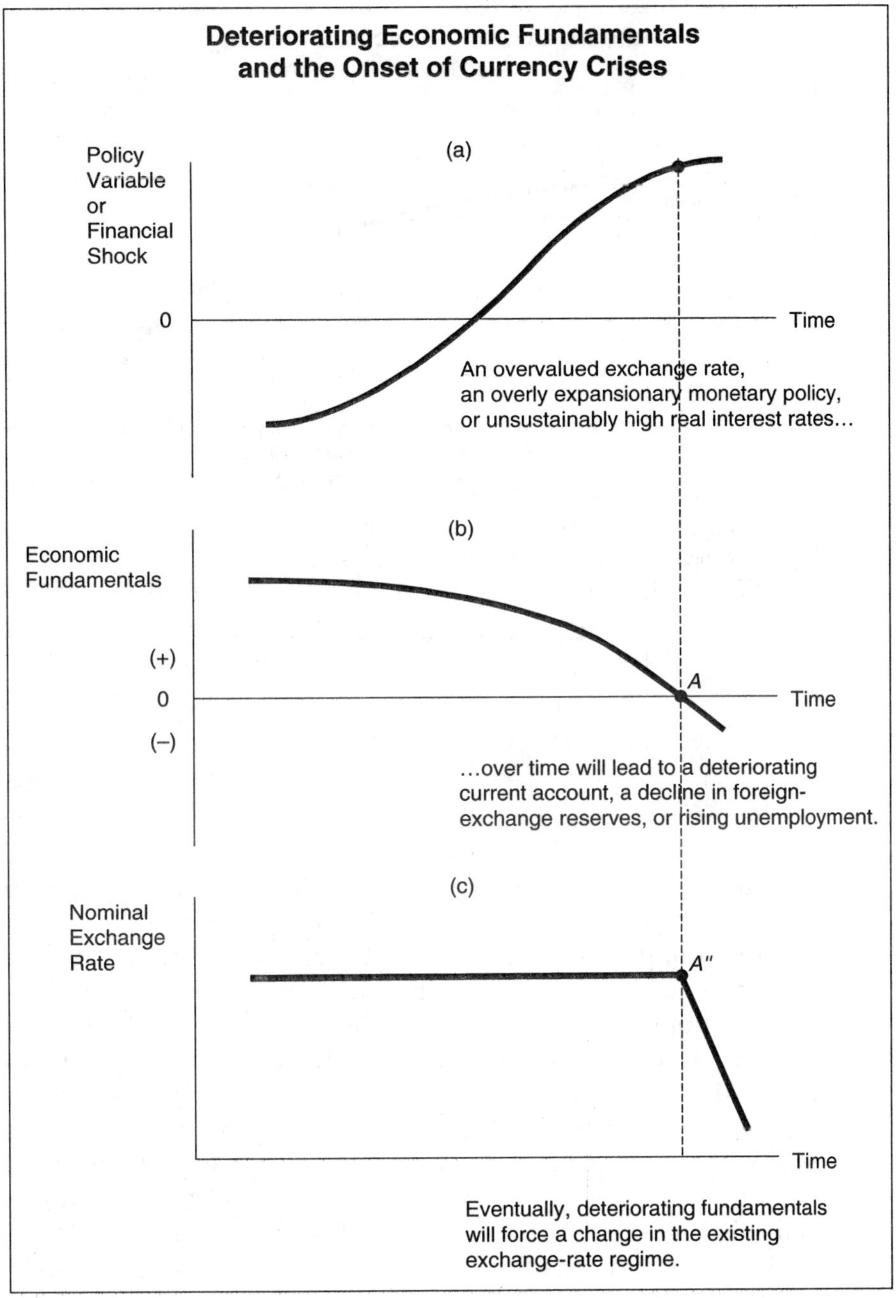
Deteriorating Economic Fundamentals
and the Onset of Currency Crises
(a)
Policy Variable or Financial Shock
0
Time
An overvalued exchange rate,
an overly expansionary monetary policy,
or unsustainably high real interest rates...
(b)
Economic Fundamentals
(+)
0
(–)
A
Time
...over time will lead to a deteriorating
current account, a decline in foreign-
exchange reserves, or rising unemployment.
(c)
Nominal Exchange Rate
A''
Time
Eventually, deteriorating fundamentals
will force a change in the existing
exchange-rate regime.

FIGURE 14-2

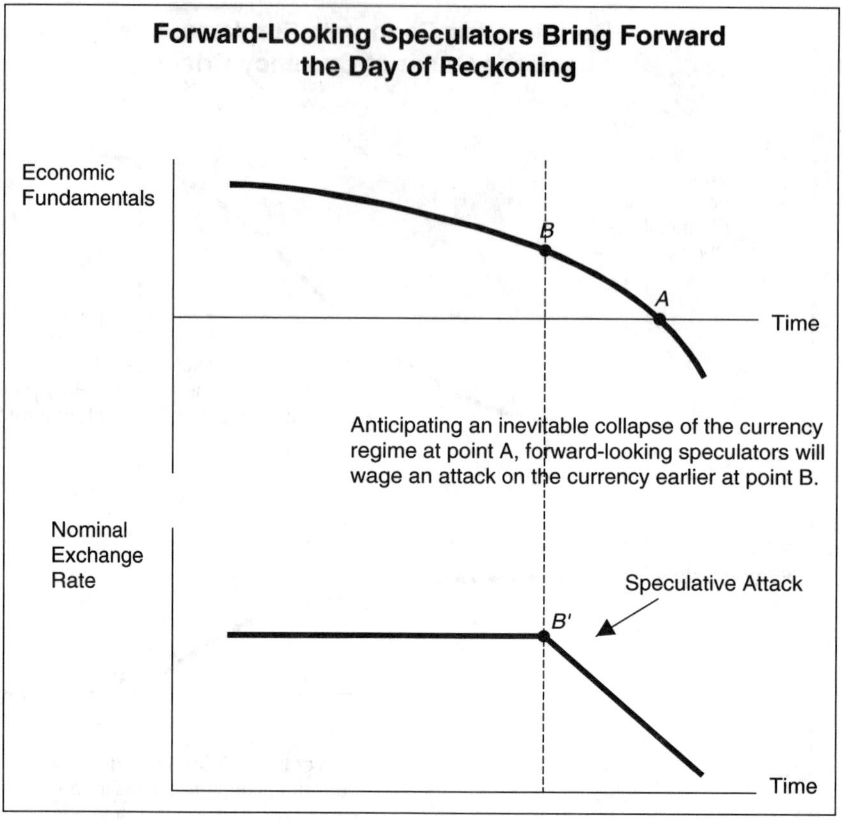

In contrast to situations where leading-indicator models might falsely warn of an attack that does not in fact occur, there might be situations where leading-indicator models fail to correctly warn market participants of an actual attack. Consider a situation where the trend in economic fundamentals appears to be sound and displays no sign of serious deterioration right up until the time of a speculative attack. Just prior to the point of attack, the trend in economic fundamentals is shown to suddenly deteriorate as shown in Figure 14–4, perhaps because of an adverse terms-of-trade shock, a sudden collapse of a large corporation or bank that undermines business confidence, or because of contagion effects stemming from financial crises in neighboring markets. The deterioration in the fundamental backdrop and the attack on the now vulnerable, but previously sound, currency occur virtually simultaneously with little or no warning.

FIGURE 14-3

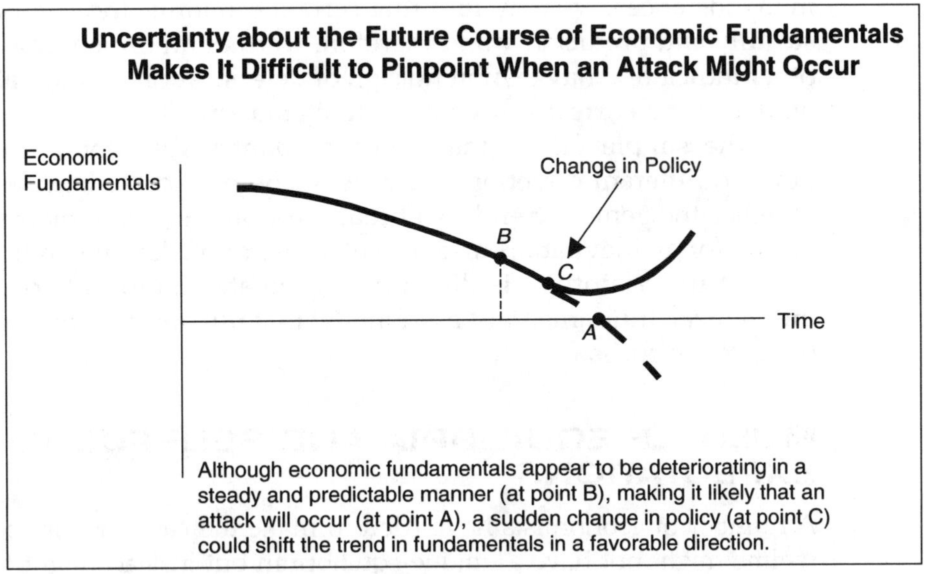

FIGURE 14-4

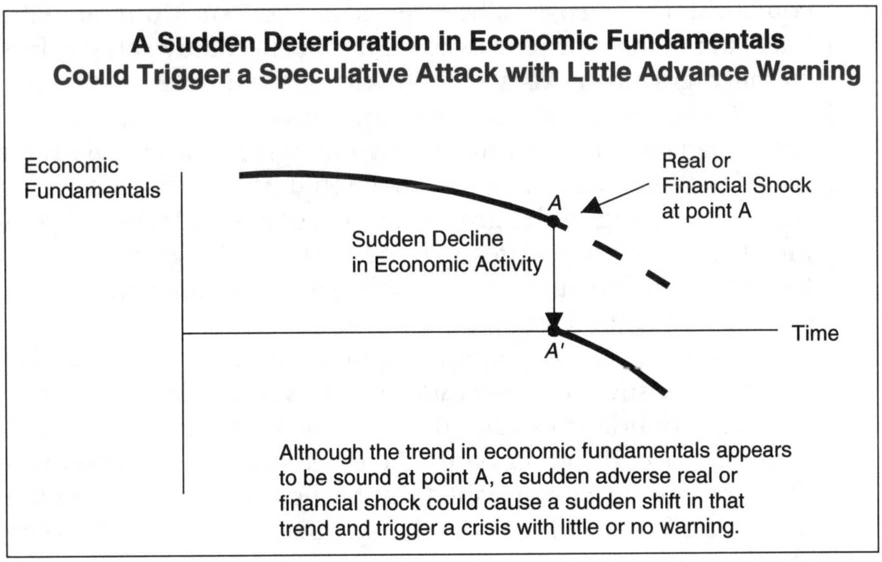

One additional problem that model builders face is that not all leading indicators of currency crises point in the same direction at the same time. In many instances, we may find that certain economic indicators deteriorate steadily and predictably and therefore warn of an impending crisis, while other indicators may exhibit no sign of deterioration and therefore suggest no need for a corrective exchange-rate adjustment.

The simple fact is that when a country's economic fundamentals point in different directions, there is likely to be considerable uncertainty whether the general trend in a broad grouping of fundamental indicators argues for an inevitable currency collapse or not. And when there is a high level of uncertainty, it is difficult to generate significant confidence in a mechanical, fundamental-based model that purportedly predicts the onset of currency crises.

MULTIPLE EQUILIBRIA AND SELF-FULFILLING EXPECTATIONS

A number of economists have tried to make the case that an exchange-rate regime might not have a unique equilibrium but instead might face multiple equilibria. Figure 14–5 illustrates the possible range of equilibrium settings that might exist for a particular exchange rate. At the right end of the fundamental economic spectrum, a unique equilibrium exists, since countries with strong fundamentals are unlikely to see their currencies come under speculative attack. At the left end of the fundamental economic spectrum, a unique equilibrium also exists, since countries with weak fundamentals are highly likely to see their currencies come under speculative attack. In the middle, a so-called gray area exists where exchange-rate crises may or may not occur.

It is in this gray area where multiple equilibria may exist—economic fundamentals are either not strong enough that a speculative attack can be completely avoided or not weak enough that a crisis is an inevitable outcome. Operating in the gray area, speculative attacks are possible but not inevitable. Exchange rates may be stable in the gray area for a while, but they can easily be pushed over the edge by a sudden adverse shift in market sentiment or mood swing.

Should a currency operating in the gray area come under speculative attack, domestic economic fundamentals could deteriorate unexpectedly if business confidence suddenly sours or if foreign-currency debt burdens suddenly rise. If the fundamental economic deterioration is truly serious, the currency could be pushed out of the gray area toward the "weak fundamentals" area where attacks are inevitable. By so doing, the initial attack, which occurred when the currency was still in the gray area, would prove to have been a self-fulfilling prophecy.

FIGURE 14-5

Multiple Equilibria and the Probability of Exchange-Rate Crises

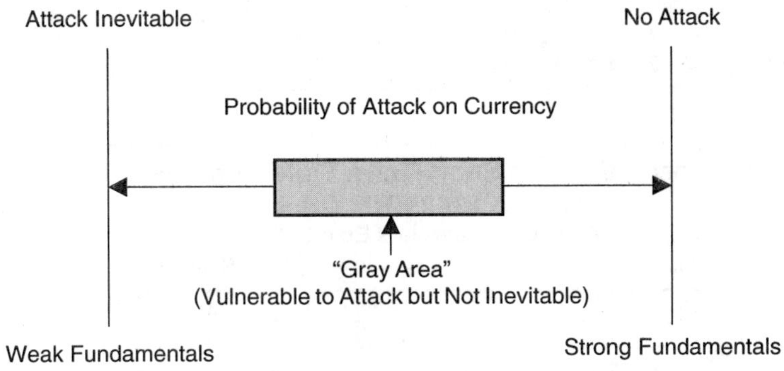

Countries with weak fundamentals are more likely to see their currencies come under speculative attack than countries with strong fundamentals. Many countries find themselves in a "gray area," where attacks are possible but not inevitable.

CAN THE MARKETPLACE ADEQUATELY ANTICIPATE THE ONSET OF CURRENCY CRISES?

If market participants were truly forward looking, interest-rate differentials would tend to widen as an impending currency crisis drew nearer and investors demanded a higher return or risk premium to cover the expected currency loss on their investment. However, a careful reading of the history of speculative attacks, particularly the crises of the 1990s, suggests that this has not been the case.

For example, interest-rate differentials failed to widen measurably in anticipation of the ERM currency crisis of 1992–1993 (see Figure 14–6), the Mexican peso crisis of 1994–1995 (see Figure 14–7), or the Asian currency crisis of 1997–1998 (see Figure 14–8). Not only did interest-rate differentials fail to widen but the consensus forecasts of private economists, the risk assessments by credit rating agencies, and the economic outlook reports of the IMF and the World Bank also failed to provide adequate warning of the impending currency crises. Even in those cases where doomsayers might have correctly anticipated the onset of an impending currency crisis, the eventual exchange-rate collapse often exceeded the direst projections of doom-and-gloom analysts.

If anything, the evidence seems to be more consistent with the view that market participants are more often than not taken by surprise when an attack occurs. Indeed, investors and borrowers often tend to be leaning the wrong way in terms of their portfolio positioning at the time of an

FIGURE 14-6

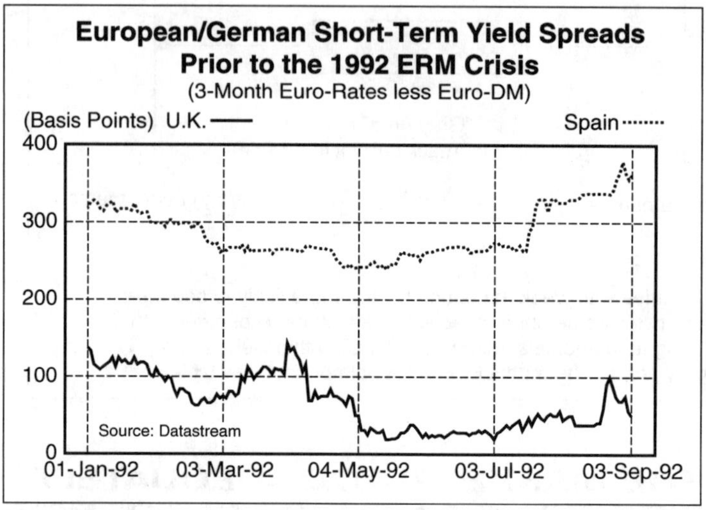

FIGURE 14-7

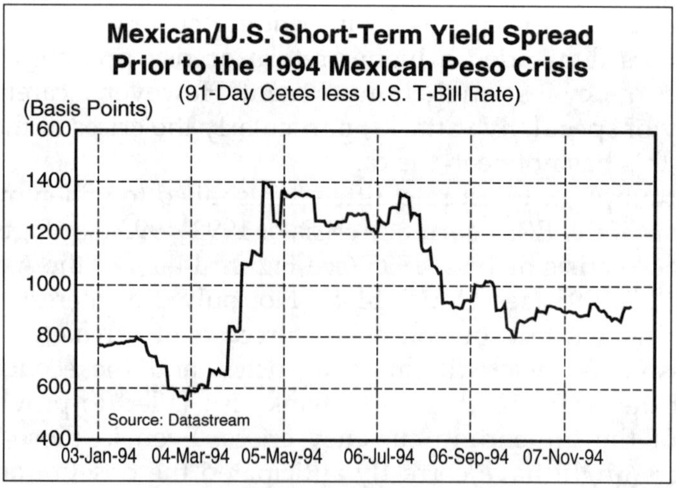

FIGURE 14-8

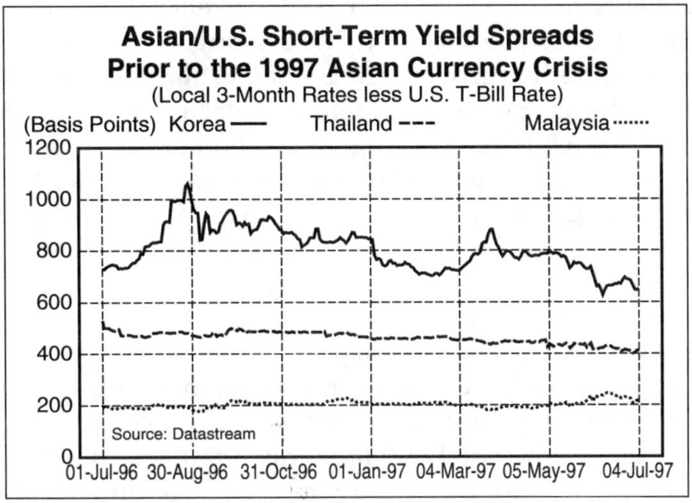

attack. Once an attack is waged, investors and borrowers are immediately forced to reposition their portfolios to avoid excessive currency losses, and such portfolio repositioning works to intensify selling pressure on the currency under attack. It is this massive liquidation of vulnerable positions that is largely responsible for the seemingly excessive exchange-rate moves that typically occur during speculative attacks.

EXCHANGE-RATE EXPECTATIONS AND THE ANTICIPATION OF CURRENCY CRISES

Why does the market fail to adequately anticipate the onset of currency crises? To answer this question one needs to develop a model of investor and borrower behavior that explains why market participants might assign decreasing weight to the probability of a currency collapse at a time when the actual probability of a currency collapse is rising. A variant of the model developed by Frankel and Froot (1990) may help explain this phenomenon.

The Frankel-Froot model can be applied to the case of an emerging-market economy that is maintaining a fixed exchange rate and where there may be some question whether the fixed exchange-rate regime will prove to be sustainable. Let's assume that investors' expectations regarding the outlook for an emerging-market currency ($\dot{e}^e_{EM}$) that is pegged to the U.S. dollar are determined as a weighted average of two possible outcomes: (1) the fixed exchange-rate regime continues to survive ($\dot{e}^e_{EM} = 0$), and (2) the fixed exchange-rate regime comes under attack, where the currency is expected to collapse at a rate equal to $\dot{e}^e_{EM} = k$ (k being the expected percentage rate collapse of the emerging-market currency). Investors are assumed to assign a certain probability, w, to the existing exchange-rate regime staying intact and another probability, $1 - w$, to the regime collapsing. Let's assume that the interest-rate differential between the emerging-market country and the United States, $i_{EM} - i_{US}$, equals the market's "average" expected change in the emerging-market exchange rate. Mathematically, the average change in the expected exchange rate can be expressed as the weighted-average probability of the two possible exchange-rate outcomes:

$$\dot{e}^e_{EM} = i_{EM} - i_{US} = w(0) + (1 - w)k$$

Investors are assumed to vary the weights, w and $1 - w$, that they attach to the two possible exchange-rate outcomes, depending on how successful the authorities are in preserving a stable, fixed exchange-rate regime. The longer the fixed exchange-rate regime survives, the more confident investors will be that the regime will continue to survive in the future. In other words, investors are prone to extrapolate favorable past behavior into the future much like chartists do.

Hence, the longer a fixed exchange-rate regime survives, the more weight investors will assign to the likelihood of no exchange-rate change in the future (that is, w will rise) and less weight to the likelihood of a currency collapse (that is, $1 - w$ will decline) (see Figure 14–9). As w rises and $1 - w$ declines, the interest-rate differential, $i_{EM} - i_{US}$, will tend to decline over time. This implies that the market will assign less weight to the possibility of a future currency collapse over time.

Thus, the long-term success of an existing exchange-rate regime might in and of itself encourage investors to assign less weight to the likelihood of a crisis even if the existing regime is enjoying unwarranted excess credibility. As the exchange-rate misalignment builds, the market "expectation" of a possible currency collapse could diverge sharply from the actual risk of such a collapse (see Figure 14–10).

THE TYPICAL PATH TO A CURRENCY CRISIS: PERSISTENT REAL APPRECIATION, OVERVALUATION, AND COLLAPSE

Currencies that undergo large and persistent real appreciations are often vulnerable to a speculative attack. Indeed, empirical studies find that overly appreciated real exchange rates are the best single leading indicator of currency crises in emerging markets. How do real appreciations get started?

FIGURE 14-9

The Longer a Fixed Exchange-Rate Regime Stays Intact, the Less Weight Investors Assign to the Likelihood of a Crash

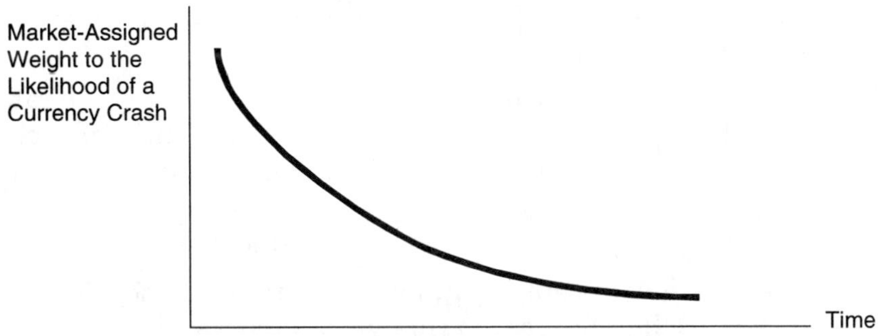

Investors tend to extrapolate favorable behavior from the past into the future. Hence, the longer a fixed exchange-rate regime stays intact, the more weight investors tend to assign to the likelihood of the regime staying intact, and less weight to the likelihood of a crash. This implies that interest-rate differentials should decline over time to reflect the sentiment change.

FIGURE 14-10

The Market's Assessment of the Risk of an Imminent Currency Crisis Might Differ Greatly from the True Risk

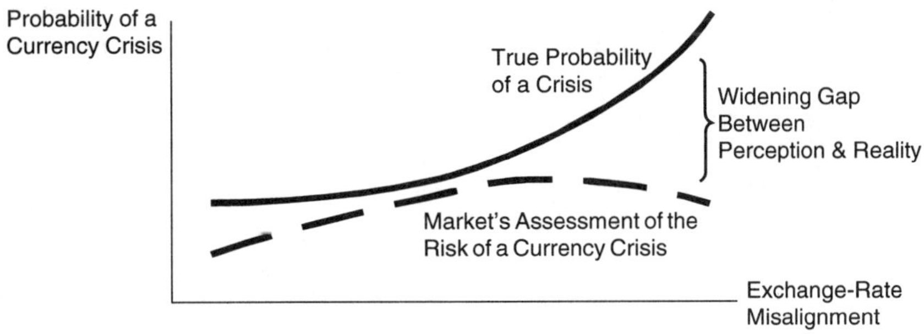

The long-term success of an existing exchange-rate regime encourages investors to assign less weight to the likelihood of a crisis, even as an exchange-rate misalignment builds.

This question can be answered with the assistance of a simple stylized diagram of the equilibrium and disequilibrium forces that contribute to large and persistent real exchange-rate appreciations over time (see Figure 14–11).

We break the typical causes of a sustained real exchange-rate appreciation episode into four phases:

1. The correction of a currency's initial undervaluation (from point *A* to point *B*)
2. A rise in the real long-run equilibrium exchange rate (from point *B* to point *C*, with the combined rise in the real exchange rate from point *A* to point *C* considered an equilibrium phenomenon)
3. Inflation inertia that contributes to a cumulative rise in inflation that is not offset by a change in the nominal exchange rate
4. A surge in capital inflows that drives the nominal exchange rate, and thus the real exchange rate, higher (from point *C* to point *D*, with the rise in the real exchange rate from point *C* to point *D* considered to be a disequilibrium phenomenon)

EXCHANGE-RATE TARGETING, INFLATION INERTIA, AND CURRENCY OVERVALUATION

One of the primary factors responsible for disequilibrium increases in the real exchange rate has been inappropriate exchange-rate policies. For instance, not allowing the nominal exchange rate to depreciate to offset a persistently high underlying inflation rate can lead to a disequilibrium rise

FIGURE 14-11

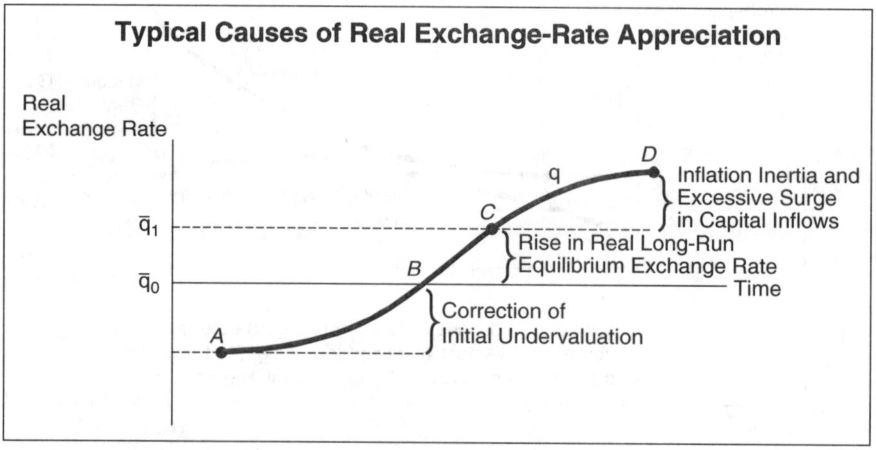

in the real exchange rate. An overvalued exchange rate will threaten the competitiveness of an emerging-market country and make its currency vulnerable to a speculative attack.

Many emerging-market countries use the nominal exchange rate as an anchor to help bring their inflation rates down to those prevailing in the rest of the world. The intent is to buy credibility with a hard-currency posture. By pegging the nominal exchange rate or limiting its flexibility, the authorities are compelled to adjust their monetary policies to satisfy their nominal exchange-rate objective. As a result, they are restricted from pursuing overly expansionary policies for purely domestic reasons.

In theory, a rigid nominal exchange-rate peg should allow an emerging-market nation to bring its inflation rate down rapidly to match the inflation performance of hard-currency industrial countries. In practice, however, this seldom happens. Instead, backward-looking expectations, particularly if the emerging-market country has a long history of failed stabilization efforts, and structural impediments—such as wage-indexation programs—work to prevent prices and wages from falling rapidly into line with those in the industrial world.

Combining an inertia-laden decline in emerging-market/industrial-country inflation differentials with a pegged nominal exchange rate, will give rise to a disequilibrium increase in the real exchange rate (see Figure 14–12). Policy decisions that permit a buildup in the cumulative inflation gap without an offsetting depreciation of the nominal exchange rate are a recipe for a currency crisis.

SURGES IN CAPITAL INFLOWS AND REAL APPRECIATION

Surges in capital inflows have also been an important source of real appreciation for many emerging-market currencies. Surges in capital inflows affect the real exchange rate via two channels (see Figure 14–13). First, where there is scope for nominal exchange-rate flexibility, a surge in private capital inflows will directly drive the value of the nominal exchange rate higher and, in the process, drive the real exchange rate higher in tandem. Second, a surge in capital inflows can indirectly drive the real exchange rate higher if the authorities intervene to stabilize the nominal exchange rate and the resulting increase in the central bank's foreign-exchange reserves fuels a major increase in the domestic money supply (assuming the intervention move is not completely sterilized). An increase in domestic money-supply growth will then tend to fuel a rise in domestic demand and in the process drive domestic inflation higher. A rise in domestic inflation without an offsetting depreciation of the domestic currency will then drive the real

FIGURE 14-12

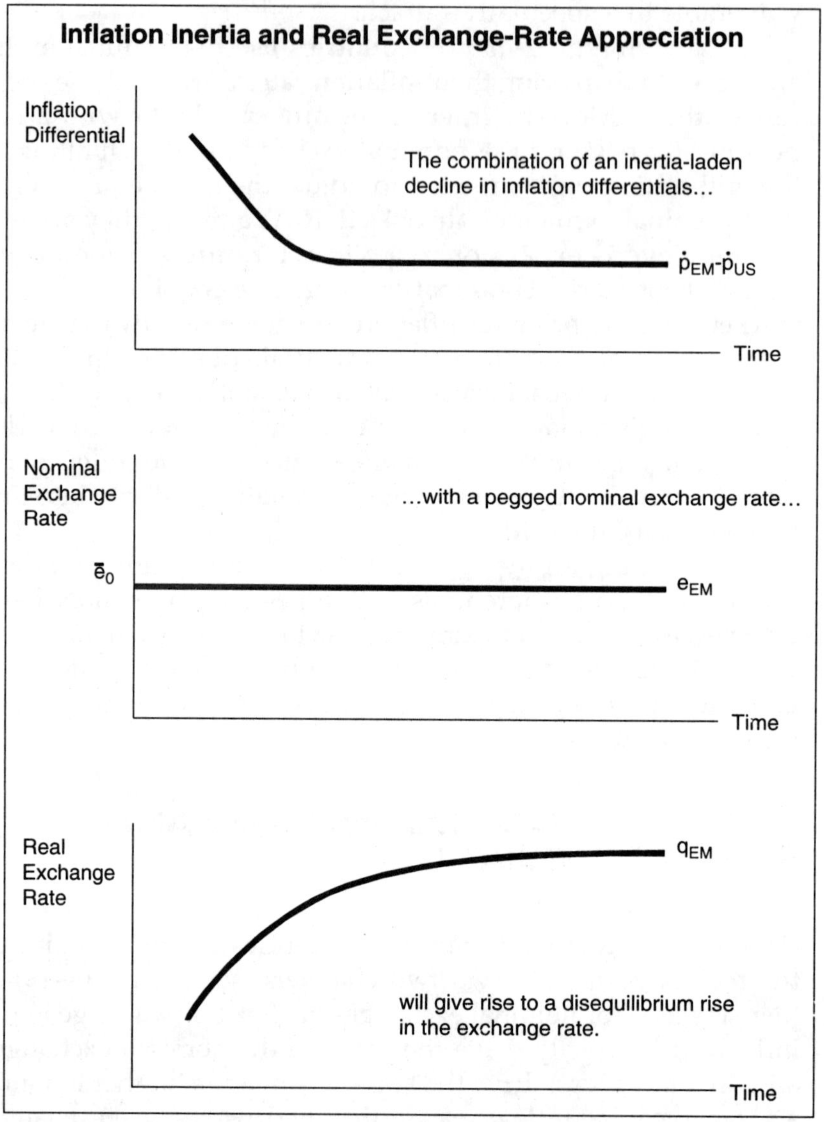

exchange rate higher. Hence, both directly and indirectly, a sustained surge in capital inflows is likely to drive the real exchange rate higher in emerging markets.

In many episodes of significant real appreciation in emerging markets, excessive optimism on the part of international investors and domestic

FIGURE 14-13

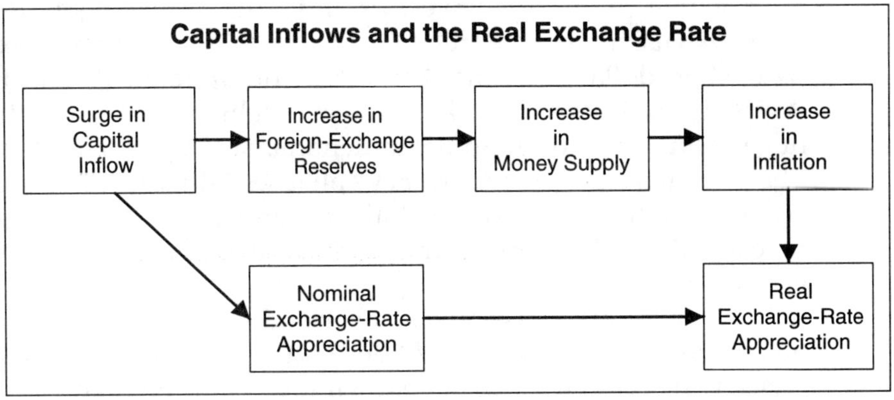

borrowers has led to excessive surges in capital inflows that have caused real exchange rates to overshoot their long-run equilibrium levels by a wide margin. At times, a speculative bubble in the real exchange rate might form, making the emerging-market currency vulnerable to a possible collapse in the event of a speculative attack. When a currency moves along a bubble path, its rise into deeply overvalued territory is clearly not sustainable in the long run, but positive feedback trading and bandwagon effects are capable of sustaining an exchange-rate overshoot for short- and medium-term periods.

CAPITAL FLOWS, EXCESSIVE LEVERAGE, AND CRISIS VULNERABILITY

An excessive surge in capital inflows can plant the seeds of a currency crisis by contributing to (1) an unwarranted real appreciation of the emerging-market currency, (2) a huge buildup in external indebtedness, (3) a financial asset or property-market bubble, (4) a consumption binge that contributes to an explosive growth in domestic credit and/or the current-account deficit, or (5) overinvestment in risky projects and questionable activities.

It is no accident that the ERM, Mexican, and Asian currency crises were all preceded by a surge in capital inflows. In each case, the surge in capital inflows led to a buildup of huge, highly leveraged, long speculative positions by local as well as international investors in the currencies that eventually came under heavy attack. For example, in the run-up to the ERM crisis, investors, believing that European yield convergence would occur as the European Monetary Union (EMU) approached, took on highly leveraged long positions in the high-yielding European currencies and short positions in the lower-yielding Deutschemark. Likewise, in the run-up to the Mexican peso crisis, investors and banks were highly leveraged and made extensive use of derivative products in taking on speculative long-peso/short-dollar positions. And in the run-up to the Asian currency crisis, it was Asian firms and banks that were highly leveraged as they took on a huge volume of short-term dollar-denominated debt to fund local activities. The seemingly excessive currency collapses (at least relative to underlying economic fundamentals) that followed in each of those episodes simply reflected the sudden unwinding of those leveraged positions at the time of each attack.

When investors assign a smaller-and-smaller probability to an imminent currency collapse, they often tend to become overconfident that no attack will occur and thus appear willing to take on highly leveraged, long speculative positions in currencies that are in reality vulnerable to a sudden collapse. What actually triggers a collapse is less important than the fact that at the time of an attack investors tend to be leaning, perhaps heavily, the wrong way in terms of their portfolio positioning (see Figure 14–14). When the attack comes, fear takes over, as highly leveraged investors need to unwind their vulnerable long positions. It is the unwinding of those long positions that causes exchange rates to depreciate violently at the time of an attack.

REAL EXCHANGE-RATE MISALIGNMENT AND COLLAPSE

A currency that undergoes significant real appreciation will be vulnerable to a speculative attack only if the actual real exchange rate (q) rises relative to its real long-run equilibrium value ($\overline{q}$). In such cases, the resulting overvaluation of the real exchange rate relative to its long-run equilibrium level should be viewed as a *disequilibrium* rise in the real exchange rate that would call for an eventual correction of the misaligned exchange rate.

Since the real long-run equilibrium exchange rate, $\overline{q}$, is not directly observable, it will never be known for sure whether a rise in the actual real exchange rate, q, is an "equilibrium" or a "disequilibrium" phenomenon. This will be especially true for small- and medium-sized real appreciations. However, for large and sustained real appreciations, the odds of a persistent rise in q being a purely equilibrium phenomenon are likely to be small. Instead, large and persistent real appreciations are more likely to be disequilibrium phenomena in need of correction. Indeed, in a recent exhaustive study of real appreciation episodes in 93 countries over the 1960–1994 period, Goldfajn and Valdes (1996) found that virtually all currencies that underwent real appreciations exceeding 35% from trough to peak eventu-

FIGURE 14-14

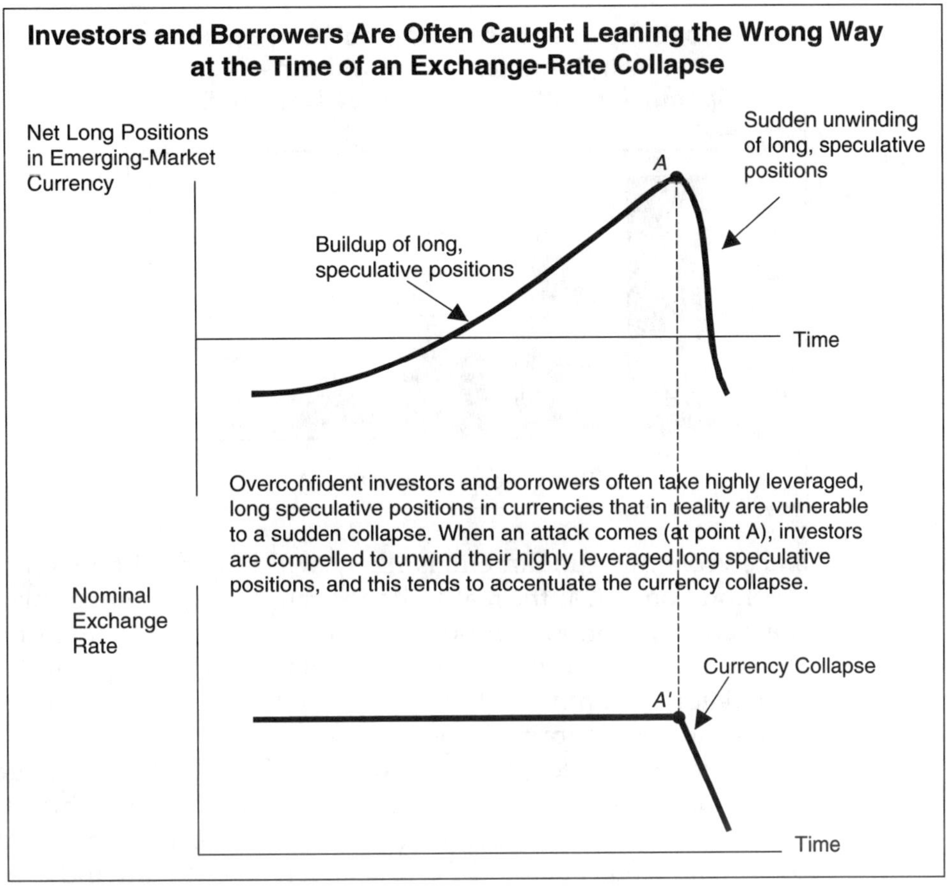

ally collapsed either through a speculative attack or a surprise devaluation (see Figure 14–15).

Views on what real exchange-rate level constitutes a currency's real long-run equilibrium value often differ among market participants. Hence, views on the magnitude of the prevailing real exchange-rate misalignment will differ as well. Given such high levels of uncertainty, the market will generally presume that a sustained increase in the real exchange rate is an equilibrium phenomenon unless convinced otherwise. Hence real exchange-rate misalignments are unlikely to be corrected until there are visible signs of fundamental economic deterioration.

In a typical real appreciation/misalignment episode, real appreciation tends to proceed gradually (see Figure 14–16). As the exchange-rate misalignment builds, there will probably be no corrective adjustment early on,

FIGURE 14-15

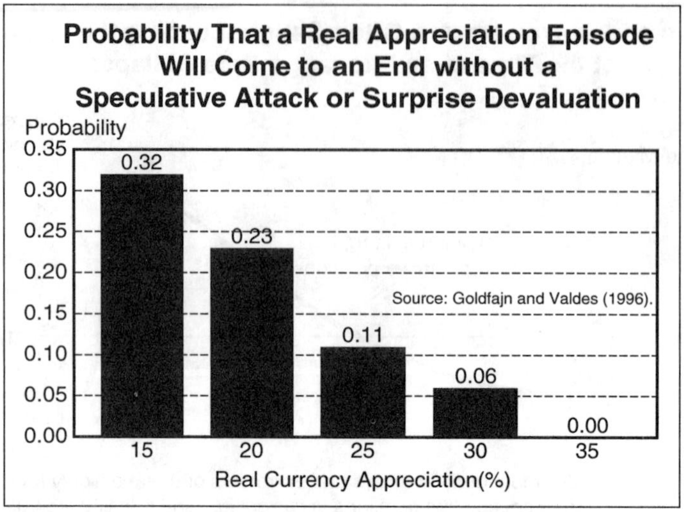

since economic fundamentals likely will display little sign of significant deterioration. But as the real exchange-rate misalignment grows and persists, the trend in economic fundamentals will gradually begin to deteriorate. When the deterioration in fundamentals reaches a point that convinces speculators that remedial action is called for, then and only then will they attack the overly appreciated currency.

Evidence presented by Goldfajn and Valdes (1996) suggests that real appreciations tend to build up gradually and then end abruptly. They find that there is a large asymmetry between the average duration of real appreciation episodes and the time that it takes to unwind the appreciation of the real exchange rate. Goldfajn and Valdes estimate that the average duration of real appreciation episodes is about twice as long as the time that it takes to unwind the real appreciation.

CURRENT-ACCOUNT IMBALANCES AND CURRENCY CRISES

Countries that run large and persistent current-account deficits are likely to see their currencies become vulnerable to a speculative attack. That appeared to be the case for European countries prior to the ERM crises of the early 1990s.

When a country is running a large and persistent current-account deficit, it must attract continual capital inflows to finance the deficit. Over time, this will give rise to a large and growing external debt. If this external

FIGURE 14-16

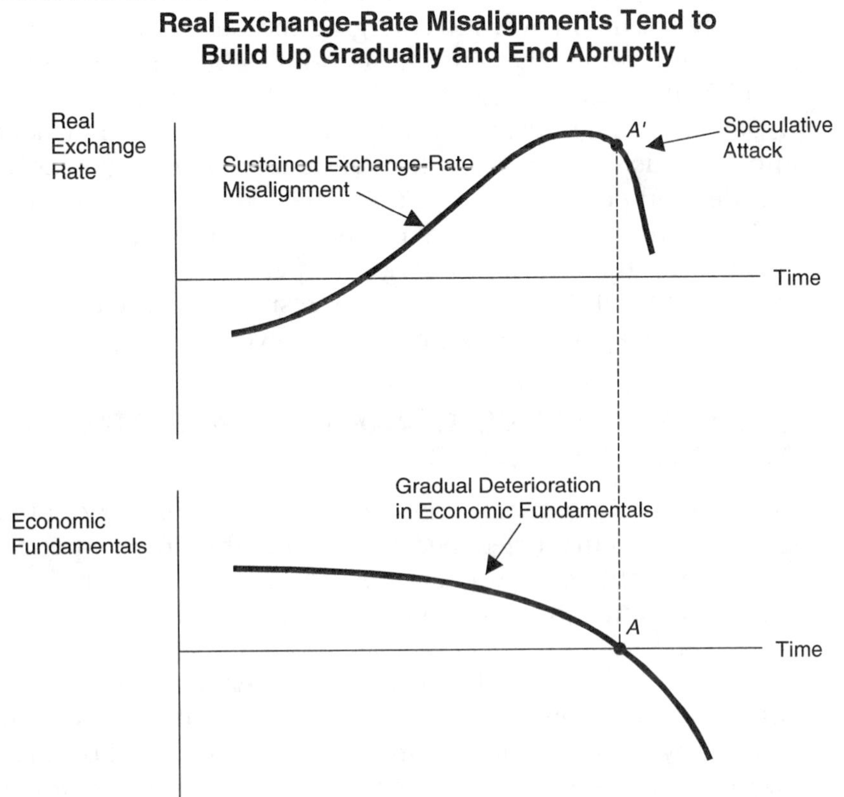

Economic fundamentals tend to deteriorate gradually in response to sustained exchange-rate misalignments. An attack will occur only when the trend in economic fundamentals is expected to deteriorate beyond point A.

debt burden becomes inordinately large, it might raise questions about the solvency of the indebted nation. If the market suspects that the indebted nation does not have the ability to generate sufficient trade surpluses in the future to repay its debt, they might reason that exchange rates will need to be adjusted downward to boost the competitiveness of the indebted nation.

While current-account imbalances may have played an important role in triggering the Mexican peso and Asian currency crises in the 1990s, most international economists would argue that the violent character of those currency-crisis episodes could be explained only by financial-sector weaknesses and not by external-balance considerations.

What does the empirical evidence suggest about the role of current-account imbalances in triggering currency crises in emerging markets? Frankel and Rose (1996) examined the fundamental forces that triggered currency crashes in over 100 emerging-market countries over the 1971–1992 period, and found that current-account imbalances were not statistically significant in predicting currency crashes. Sachs, Tornell, and Velasco (1996) found that current-account imbalances were not helpful in determining which currencies were vulnerable to contagion effects following the Mexican peso collapse in 1994–1995. However, Goldstein et al. (2000) and the IMF (1998) found that current-account deficit/GDP ratios have, on average, been significantly larger in periods leading up to a crisis than during tranquil periods. The latter results suggest that current-account imbalances may have some predictive power in anticipating currency crises.

OVERLY EXPANSIONARY MONETARY POLICY AND CURRENCY CRISES

Countries that pursue overly expansionary monetary policies are likely to see their currencies become vulnerable to a speculative attack. History is replete with examples where domestic credit creation by a central bank in excess of money demand has planted the seeds of a speculative attack.

If a central bank wished to peg its currency to a hard currency, it would need to pursue monetary policies consistent with that exchange-rate objective. An overly expansionary monetary policy would be inconsistent with the maintenance of stable nominal exchange rates in the long run. Examples of inconsistent policies would be situations in which a central bank felt compelled to monetize a large and persistent budget deficit or had to inject massive sums of liquidity to prop up an ailing banking system. In both cases, such policy stances would inevitably lead to a collapse of a pegged exchange-rate regime.

We can illustrate the inherent inconsistency between the pursuit of a stable nominal exchange rate, on the one hand, and an excessively expansionary monetary policy, on the other, with a simple model. We start by assuming that changes in a currency's value, $\dot{e}$, are inversely related to changes in that country's monetary base, $\dot{m}$.

$$\dot{e} = -\dot{m} \tag{1}$$

That is, an expansion of the monetary base will lead to an equiproportionate decline in a currency's value, while a contraction of the monetary base will lead to an equiproportionate rise in a currency's value. In this simplified model, it is assumed that a fixed exchange rate can be maintained over time only if the monetary base is kept constant over time. That is, if:

$$\dot{m} = 0 \tag{2}$$

then, from (1) above

$$\dot{e} = 0 \tag{3}$$

The level of a country's monetary base (M) consists of domestic credit issued by the central bank, D, and the central bank's holdings of foreign-exchange reserves, R:

$$M = D + R \tag{4}$$

If a central bank attempted to monetize a large budget deficit by expanding domestic credit, D, that would lead to a corresponding rise in the monetary base, M, unless the central bank's holdings of reserves, R, were run down by an amount equal to the rise in D. If the central bank's holdings of foreign-exchange reserves, R, were run down by an amount equal to the increase in domestic credit, D, the monetary base would be held constant and the nominal exchange rate would remain fixed.

Since a central bank's holdings of foreign-exchange reserves are finite, there is a limit to how much a central bank can continuously run down its reserves to offset a continuous expansion of domestic credit. At the point where the central bank's holdings of foreign-exchange reserves approach zero (shown as t_1 in Figure 14–17), an exchange-rate peg would collapse on its own accord because at that point the monetary base would begin to expand at the same rate as domestic credit was expanding. That is, if

$$R = 0 \tag{5}$$

then changes in the monetary base, M, would be entirely determined by changes in domestic credit, D:

With both D and M rising at the same rate, the rise in M would no longer be consistent with the maintenance of a stable exchange rate. Once M starts to expand, the exchange rate would begin to decline at the same rate that M is rising. In practice, if forward-looking investors saw that the central bank's FX reserves were falling to dangerously low levels, they would, in all likelihood, wage an attack on the vulnerable currency prior to point t_1 being reached.

M2/FX RESERVE RATIO AS A LEADING INDICATOR OF CURRENCY CRISES

The ratio of M2 money supply to the central bank's holdings of foreign-exchange reserves has been found to be a reliable leading indicator of currency crises in emerging markets in a number of recent empirical studies. Kaminsky, Lizondo, and Reinhart (1998) found that large increases in a country's M2/reserve ratio tended to precede currency crises in a majority

FIGURE 14-17

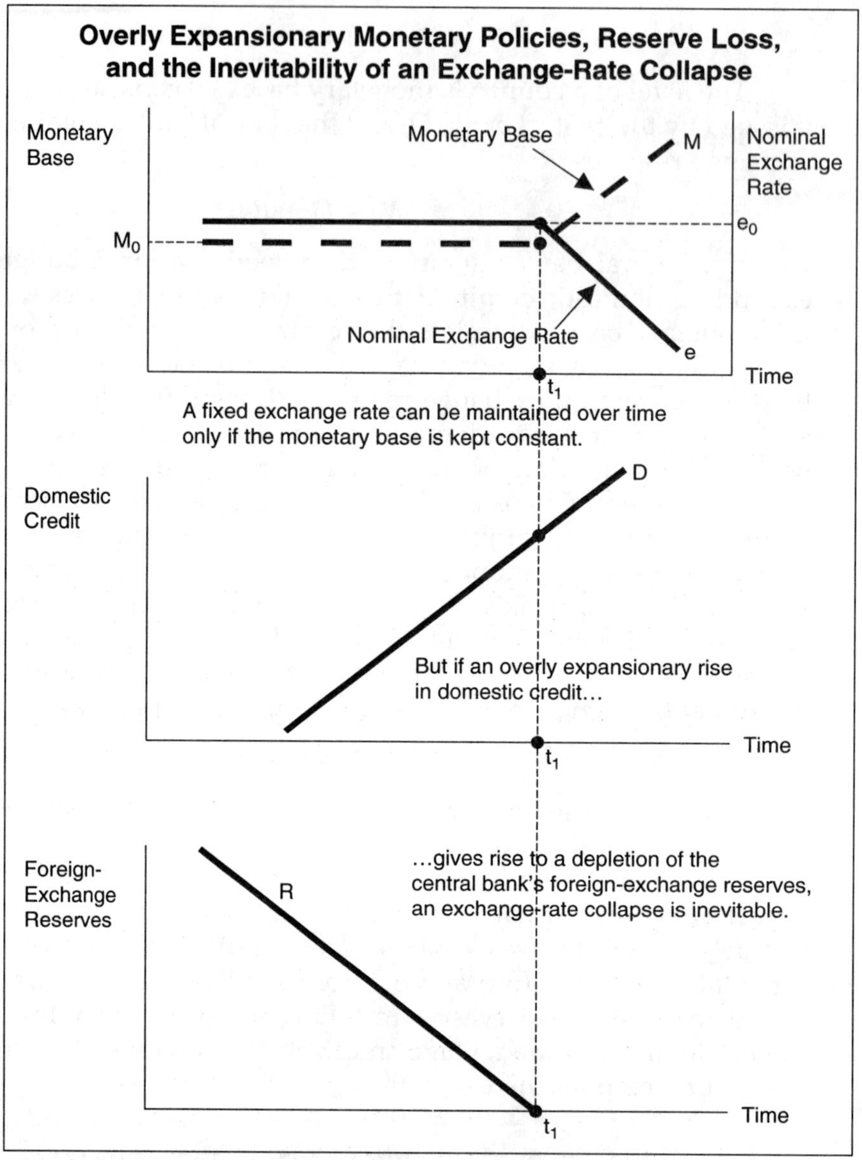

of cases studied. In addition, Sachs, Tornell, and Velasco (1996) found that countries with relatively high M2/reserve ratios tended to be more vulnerable to the contagion effects associated with the Mexican peso crisis (the so-called Tequila effect) than those countries with relatively low M2/reserve ratios. Furthermore, Goldstein and Hawkins (1998) found that

Asian countries had considerably higher M2/reserve ratios than their Latin American counterparts in mid-1997, just prior to the Asian financial crisis. This made the Asian currencies more vulnerable to a speculative attack. Finally, the International Monetary Fund (IMF), in its May 1998 World Economic Outlook report, noted that the M2/reserve ratio displayed a "remarkable pattern around the time of a crisis." According to the IMF, the M2/reserve ratio tended to rise sharply in the 24 months leading up to a crisis and then fell sharply once a crisis got underway.

What makes the M2/reserve ratio attractive as a leading indicator is that it captures the extent to which a central bank has sufficient foreign-exchange reserves on hand to absorb a run by deposit holders out of local-currency deposits into foreign currency. If the M2/reserve ratio is relatively high, it would suggest that a central bank may not have sufficient resources to directly satisfy all of the demands of deposit holders if everyone attempted to move out of domestic-currency deposits at the same time. Without sufficient reserve backing, the emerging-market currency would be vulnerable to an attack. In contrast, if an emerging-market country had a relatively low M2/reserve ratio, that would imply that the central bank had sufficient reserves to back the domestic-currency liabilities of the banking system. As the IMF notes, the M2/reserve ratio "can be viewed as an indicator of investor confidence in the domestic financial system."

HIGH UNEMPLOYMENT AS A LEADING INDICATOR OF CURRENCY CRISES

A deterioration in domestic economic activity can also act as an early-warning sign of a currency crisis. For instance, substantial increases in unemployment rates to unacceptably high levels appeared to be a key factor in precipitating the collapse of two major fixed exchange-rate regimes in the twentieth century—the collapse of the Gold Standard in the 1930s and the collapse of the ERM in 1992–1993.

If a country's unemployment rate rises to levels that are deemed to be politically unacceptable, the monetary authorities may face a major policy dilemma: Interest rates may need to be lowered to stimulate growth and alleviate the unemployment problem but, at the same time, interest rates may need to be raised to defend a potentially vulnerable exchange rate.

Recognizing that policymakers may face a growing dilemma in an environment of weak domestic demand, speculators will reason that the authorities' commitment to defend the exchange rate may gradually wane as the unemployment rate marches steadily higher. As the credibility of an exchange-rate commitment wanes, higher interest rates may be needed to persuade skeptical investors that the existing exchange-rate regime is still viable. Unfortunately, since higher interest rates will act to slow domestic demand and aggravate the unemployment problem, attempts to boost credibility through higher interest rates may actually backfire and undermine the credibility of the exchange-rate peg even further.

Since forward-looking market participants will recognize that a high and rising unemployment rate will erode the credibility of an existing exchange-rate regime, they are likely to test policymakers' resolve and wage an attack before the authorities voluntarily abandon their exchange-rate commitment. In fact, if policymakers are put to the test by a speculative attack, they may abandon their defense of the existing exchange-rate regime because an interest-rate defense likely will prove to be too costly.

DEBT CRISES AND CURRENCY CRISES

When an emerging-market country's government or private sector amasses a large volume of short-term debt, it places its currency in a vulnerable position where a self-fulfilling panic can lead to a sudden and massive speculative attack. For example, a country that issues a lot of short-term local-currency debt could run into problems if, for whatever reason, domestic and foreign creditors refuse to roll over the existing stock of debt.

In such a case, the local monetary authorities might feel compelled to push domestic short-term interest rates up sharply to induce the investment community to buy and hold the large stock of short-term debt. Unfortunately, high and rising short-term interest rates can place the highly indebted public or private sectors of an emerging market in a vulnerable position directly (by increasing the cost of servicing the large stock of local-currency debt) or indirectly (by leading to a slowdown in domestic economic activity). An interest rate hike-induced slowdown in domestic economic activity would, in turn, act to reduce both public and private sectors' revenue intake and thereby make it even more difficult to service their debts.

A rising local-currency debt-service burden poses three major risks for an emerging-market currency. First, it might raise questions about long-term solvency, which could spark a sudden panic withdrawal of funds by local and foreign creditors. Second, it might raise fears that the local authorities will attempt to reduce the real value of the debt burden by inflating. Third, a large local-currency debt-service burden could constrain the local authorities from pursuing a tight monetary policy that might be necessary to defend their currency from speculative attack. All of these risk factors highlight the fact that currency vulnerability is likely to rise when local-currency debt-service burdens are large and growing.

Currency vulnerability is also likely to be high when an emerging-market economy amasses a large volume of short-term foreign-currency debt.

Indeed, short-term foreign-currency debt has the potential to impose a greater burden on an emerging-market country than local-currency debt because the local authorities cannot reduce the real burden of a foreign-currency debt obligation by inflating. In addition, given that the local-currency value of a foreign-currency debt obligation is sensitive to changes in the exchange rate, currency depreciation could be extremely costly, since that would directly raise the local-currency value of the foreign-currency debt. Crisis-prone currencies are therefore likely to be in an especially vulnerable state when short-term foreign-currency debt obligations are high and rising.

A large buildup in short-term foreign-currency debt, by itself, will not precipitate a currency crisis if foreign creditors are willing to extend new loans and roll over any existing loans. However, if for whatever reason fear strikes in the hearts of foreign creditors, and foreign funds are withheld, the emerging-market currency could come under heavy downward pressure. If so, the local-currency value of the short-term foreign-currency debt could soar, possibly throwing otherwise viable local entities into insolvency (see Figure 14–18).

The importance of short-term foreign-currency debt as a measure of financial vulnerability is highlighted by the fact that debt crises played an important role in the currency crises in both Mexico and Asia. Indeed, the buildup of a large volume of short-term foreign-currency debt by the public sector in Mexico and the private sector in Asia is widely credited with planting the seeds of the Mexican peso and Asian currency crises. In both situations, the local-currency value of the foreign-currency debt soared as the peso and Asian currencies came under heavy downward pressure.

The local-currency value of foreign-currency debt is highly sensitive to changes in the exchange rate. A sudden sharp depreciation of an emerging-market currency will instantly raise the local-currency value of all short-term foreign-currency-denominated debt, and by so doing, will dramatically increase the burden of servicing that debt. For example, indebtedness soared in Mexico and Asia following the collapse of the peso and Asian currencies. As dept burdens increased, default risk rose sharply and, as a result, overseas private capital was no longer forthcoming. With no funds forthcoming, the trend in economic fundamentals deteriorated suddenly and markedly.

A sharp rise in the local-currency value of short-term foreign-currency debt places a nation's economy in a vulnerable position if soaring debt burdens make it difficult for local firms to service their debts. Right up until the time of a speculative currency attack, a highly indebted nation may not show any visible signs of economic weakness. But once an attack takes place and the local-currency value of short-term foreign-currency debt soars, the trend in economic fundamentals is likely to suddenly deteriorate as firms go bankrupt, banks fail, and the government's fiscal balance deteriorates.

A country's economic vulnerability might not reveal itself prior to a debt-induced attack, and there may be few signs suggesting that an attack is

FIGURE 14-18

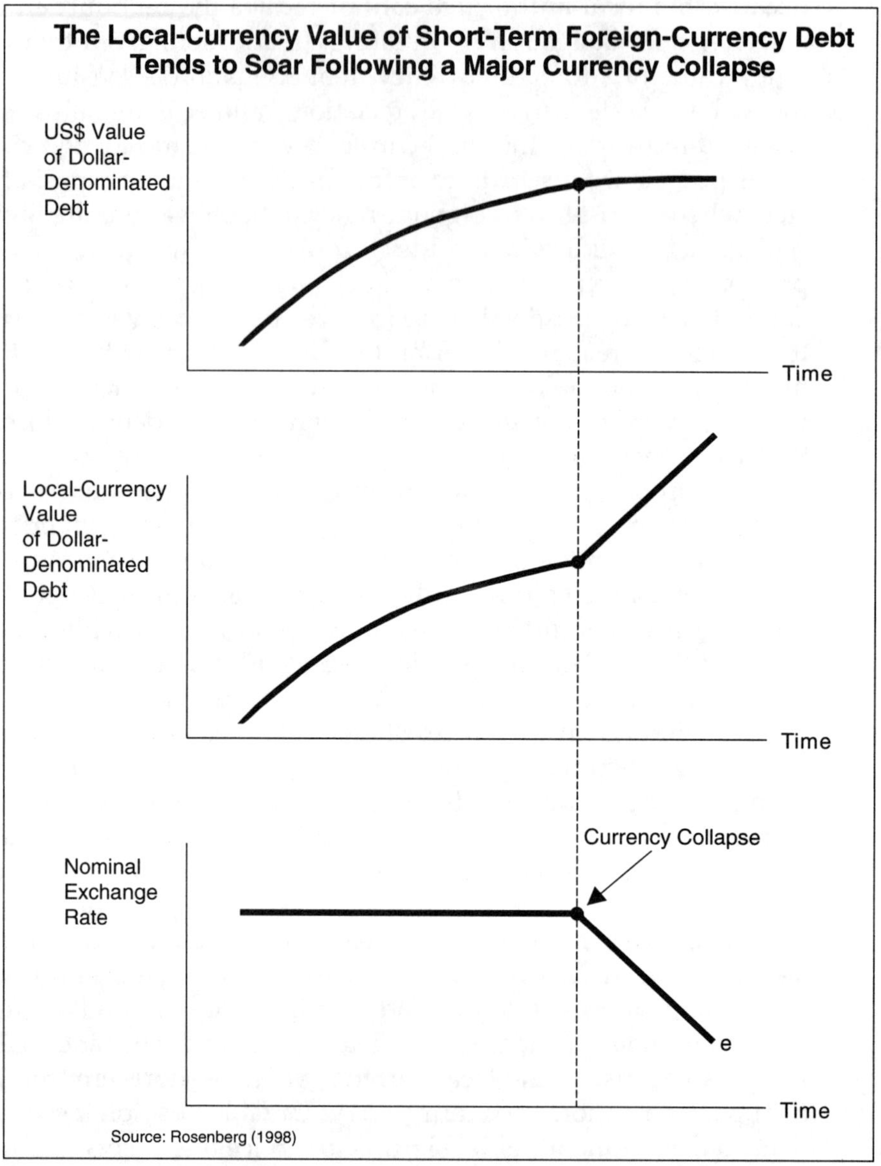

imminent. An emerging-market economy might successfully leverage off of relatively cheap short-term foreign-currency debt and post an impressive growth performance for a long while without triggering a crisis, much as Asia did in the decade leading up to the crisis in 1997. In fact, Asia's solid growth performance in the decade leading up to the 1997 crisis might have deluded the majority of market participants into believing that Asia's underlying fundamentals were sound when, in fact, they were all the time vulnerable if the value of the Asian currencies, for whatever reason, suddenly declined.

This has important implications for modeling currency crises in emerging markets. Signs of fundamental economic deterioration may not be visible going into a crisis. While evidence of deteriorating fundamentals may be useful in predicting certain currency crises, there may be few reliable guideposts available to predict when a debt-driven currency crisis might occur. A large foreign-currency debt burden may be a sign of currency vulnerability in the long run, but there may simply be no way of knowing beforehand when an attack might actually be waged.

BANKING CRISES AND CURRENCY CRISES

Many countries that have faced serious currency crises in recent years have also experienced severe banking crises at the same time. This is no mere coincidence. Recent empirical work conducted by Kaminsky and Reinhart (1997) finds that banking crises are a good leading indicator of currency crises (see Figure 14–19). According to Kaminsky and Reinhart, more than 50% of all banking crises in the past 25 years have been followed by a currency crisis within 3 years, while about 25% of all banking crises were followed by a currency crisis within 1 year. The fact that banking crises tend to lead currency crises does not imply that banking crises are the primary cause of currency crises. What the evidence does suggest is that a common set of fundamental economic factors determines whether a banking system and a currency might both be vulnerable to a crisis. When the trend in economic fundamentals is inexorably deteriorating, banking systems have tended to experience greater stress early on, followed by the currency market.

Not all currency crises are preceded by a banking crisis. However, when banking crises are present, they do tend to aggravate and accentuate the crisis on the currency front. This is true of both developed and developing countries. Banking system problems in Scandinavia in the early 1990s and in Japan in the second half of the 1990s accentuated their exchange-rate depreciations during those periods. Banking crises in Mexico and Asia are widely credited with accentuating the slide of the Mexican peso and Asian currencies during their crisis periods in the 1990s.

In a typical banking/currency crisis, the seeds of a banking crisis are often planted when an emerging-market country takes steps to liberalize its financial markets. When financial market liberalization is accompanied by other economic reforms, capital inflows from abroad often increase substantially. This surge in capital inflow is then intermediated by the banking sector to the rest of the emerging-market economy via a lending boom. The lending

FIGURE 14-19

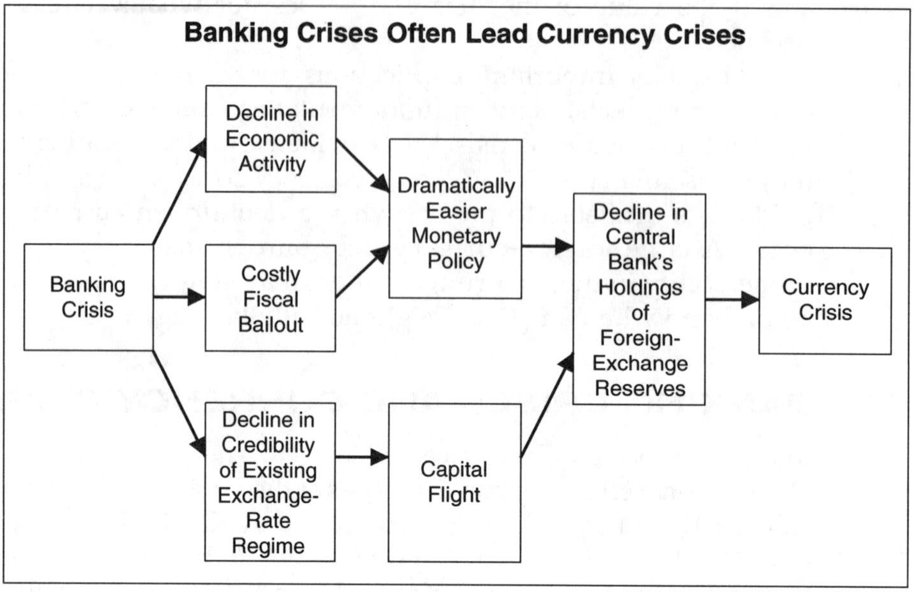

boom typically gives rise to an asset-price bubble in the equity and/or property market and often encourages over-investment or over-consumption. Given that emerging-market banks on average are less regulated and not as adequately supervised as their counterparts in the industrial world, they are more likely to engage in questionable and risky lending activities.

The excesses in a typical banking crisis are ultimately unwound when the asset-price bubble bursts and bankruptcies climb. As bankruptcies climb, this gives rise to an increase in nonperforming loans on emerging-market banks' books. If nonperforming loans are large relative to the aggregate loan portfolio, banks may become technically insolvent, which in turn may prompt a run on the banking system. In a panic phase, depositors are prone to flee both weak and healthy banks, thereby placing a strain on the entire banking system.

A banking crisis is likely to lead to a significant downturn in economic activity. As economic activity weakens, there will be great pressure on the monetary authorities to take corrective action to stimulate monetary policy. If the resolution of a banking crisis requires a costly fiscal bailout, the monetary authorities may be called upon to monetize part or all of any increase in deficit financing. Hence, a banking crisis may indirectly set off a currency crisis by requiring the monetary authorities to pursue an excessively expansionary monetary policy.

CONTAGION: HOW CURRENCY CRISES SPREAD FROM ONE MARKET TO ANOTHER

Each of the major currency crises of the 1990s has had an element of contagion that saw speculative pressures spread rapidly from one currency to another. For example, in the ERM crisis of 1992–1993, the collapse of the Italian lira spread rapidly to the United Kingdom, Spain, and Scandinavia, and then, after a 1-year respite, spread to France and Belgium. During the Mexican peso crisis of 1994–1995, speculative pressures spread rapidly to a number of markets, with Argentina the most adversely affected. In the case of the Asian currency crisis of 1997–1998, the collapse of the Thai baht spread both north and east to affect most countries in the region.

While economists agree that currency crises often contain a powerful contagion element, there is disagreement as to the underlying causes of contagion. There are actually several channels through which contagion effects can cause speculative attacks to spread from one currency to another (see Figure 14–20). First, strong bilateral or third-party trade links can be an important source of contagion. For example, if the currency of country A declines and this adversely affects the competitiveness of country B, this might raise the vulnerability of country B's currency to speculative attack.

Second, similar macroeconomic performances might lie behind contagious speculative attacks. If country A's currency came under attack because of poor current-account balance or economic growth prospects, this might lead investors to believe that country B, which might have similar weak macroeconomic prospects, could also see its currency come under attack.

FIGURE 14-20

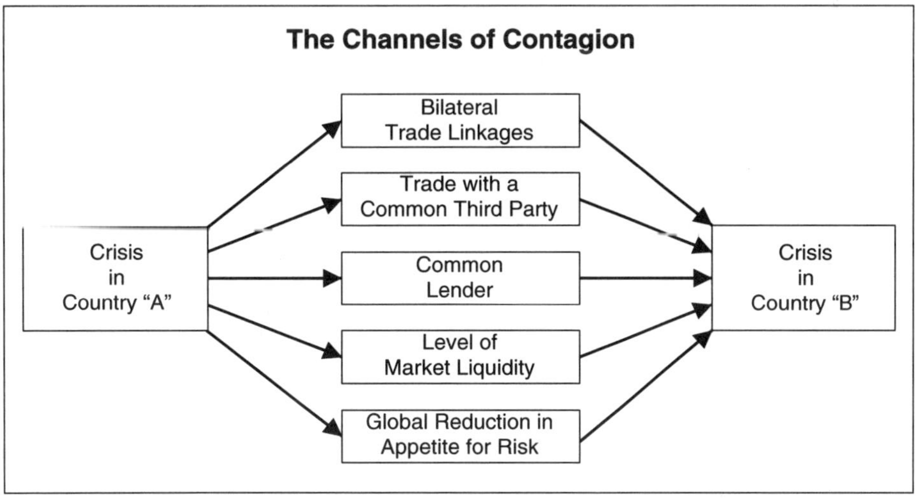

Third, financial linkages in the form of common lenders/creditors, market liquidity, and investor risk appetite can be important sources of contagion. For example, asset-allocation shifts by global investors might play a role in the spillover of currency crises from one country to another. Global fund managers with exposure to the emerging markets often diversify their investments among several emerging markets. If one of the currencies in a fund manager's emerging-market portfolio were to come under heavy speculative attack, the fund manager—concerned about the possibility of fund withdrawals by individual investors—might decide to build up cash positions and to reduce the fund's overall exposure to the entire basket of emerging-market currencies in his portfolio. If other fund manager portfolios are rebalanced in a similar fashion, this may place downward pressure on a large number of emerging-market currencies.

Fourth, a general decline in global investors' appetite for risk might generate contagion among emerging-market currencies if investors reduce their exposure to all risky assets. This typically occurs during times of global financial or economic stress.

Finally, if policymakers in an individual emerging market abandon the defense of a pegged exchange rate because the cost of defending the exchange rate against attack proves to be too great, then this action might contain information on the ability and willingness of policymakers in other countries to withstand the pressures of speculative attacks.

According to a recent IMF analysis of emerging-market contagion effects, trade linkages probably played a small role in the spread of currency crises from one country to another in the 1990s (see Figure 14–21). In contrast, financial linkages appear to have played a larger role, particularly through changes in investor risk appetite and the existence of common lenders.

FIGURE 14-21

Contagion and Its Causes

(Contagion Effects after the Mexican, Thailand, and Russian Financial Crises)

	Bilateral Trade with Initially Affected Country[1]	Trade with a Common Third Party[2]	Level of Market Common Lender[3]	Global Reduction in Liquidity[4]	Appetite for Risk[5]
Mexico (December 1994)					
Argentina	—	Low	Yes, little exposure	Low	Moderate decline in risk appetite in January 1995.
Brazil	—	Low	Yes, little exposure	High	
Thailand (July 1997)					
Hong Kong SAR	—	Low	No	High	Modest decline in risk appetite in May 1997, but not sustained.
Indonesia	—	Low	Yes, moderate exposure	Low	
Malaysia	Low	High	Yes, moderate exposure	Moderate	
Philippines	Low	Moderate	No	Low	
South Korea	—	Moderate	Yes, high exposure	Moderate	
Russia (August 1998)					
Brazil	—	—	No	High	Marked decline in risk appetite in August and September.
Hong Kong SAR	—	—	No	High	
Mexico	—	—	No	Moderate/High	

Sources: IMF World Economic Outlook (December 2001); Kaminsky and Reinhart (2000); Kumar and Persaud (2001); and Glick, and Rose, 1999.

1 Exposure through bilateral trade is measured by the share of the country's total exports destined to the initial crisis country.

2 Trade with a common third party in the same commodities is measured as the percentage of total exports competing with the top exports of initial crisis country.

3 For a discussion of how Bank of International Settlements data can be used to identify common bank lender clusters, see Kaminsky and Reinhart (2000). For bonds, see J. P. Morgan's EMBI+ weights.

4 Market liquidity is roughly proxied by the country's representation (its share) in the global mutual funds' emerging market portfolio. High, moderate, and low classifications are comparisons with respect to other emerging markets.

5 For a description of the methodology used to estimate risk appetite, see Kumar and Persaud (2001).

Source: International Monetary Fund, *World Economic Outlook*, December 2001, page 11.

CHAPTER 15

Devising an Early-Warning System to Anticipate Currency Crises

Since currency crises tend to be triggered in countries with a number of economic problems, not just one problem, an ideal early-warning system should be broad-based, incorporating a wide range of symptoms that crisis-prone currencies might exhibit prior to a speculative attack (see Figure 15–1). For instance, a typical crisis-prone currency might exhibit a number of symptoms such as an overly appreciated real exchange rate, a major terms-of-trade shock, a deteriorating current account, weak economic activity and rising unemployment, an overly expansionary fiscal policy, an overly expansionary monetary policy, an excessive increase in bank lending, declining foreign-exchange reserves at the central bank, a high ratio of M2 money supply to central bank reserves, falling equity and property prices, a sharp increase in nonperforming loans on bank books, and/or a sharp increase in short-term debt incurred by the domestic private or public sector.

Kaminsky and Reinhart (1998) argue that an ideal early-warning system should focus on the behavior of a group of indicators, and not on the behavior of a single indicator to predict the onset of currency crises. They found that currency crises in Latin America and Asia over the 1970–1995 period were preceded by a multitude of economic and financial problems, not just one (see Figure 15–2). Examining the behavior of 15 macroeconomic indicators prior to the onset of the currency crises in Latin America, Kaminsky and Reinhart found that in 44% of the crisis episodes, 80% to 100% of the indicators were flashing a warning signal prior to each crisis episode. In another 39% of the crisis episodes, 60% to 80% of the indicators were flashing prior to each attack. Similar results were found for currency crisis episodes in Asia and elsewhere.

FIGURE 15-1

Indicators of Currency Crisis Vulnerability

Symptoms	Indicators
Real Exchange Rate Overvaluation	Behavior of real exchange rate relative to trend, exports, imports, trade balance.
Terms of Trade Shock	Price of exports, price of imports, commodity prices.
Current Account Imbalance	Real exchange rate, savings, investment.
Weak Economic Activity/ Rising Unemployment	Real GDP, output gap, unemployment rate, real interest rate.
Overly Expansionary Fiscal Policy	Government spending, budget deficit, volume of credit extended to public sector.
Overly Expansionary Monetary Policy	Domestic credit expansion, reserves, money-supply growth, money multiplier.
High Ratio of M2 to Reserves	M2, international reserves.
Banking Crises	Equity and property prices, nonperforming loans, lending/deposit rate spread, bank share prices.
Debt Crises	Total debt, domestic debt, foreign-currency debt, short-term/total debt.
Contagion	Foreign growth, foreign interest rates, crises elsewhere.

Figure 15–2 provides an extensive list of indicators that can help detect whether potentially vulnerable currencies have become "symptomatic" in terms of displaying signs that a currency crisis might be imminent. Considering the broad range of symptoms that a potentially vulnerable currency might exhibit, a rule of thumb might be that the probability of an imminent currency crisis would be considered to be high if a relatively large number of indicators started flashing. An absence of flashing indicators would suggest that the probability of an imminent crisis was low.

HOW WELL DO LEADING INDICATORS PERFORM IN ANTICIPATING THE ONSET OF CURRENCY CRISES?

Kaminsky, Lizondo, and Reinhart (1998) examined the behavior of 16 macroeconomic and financial indicators around the time of a currency crisis for 76 currency-crisis episodes in 15 developing and five industrial countries over the 1970–1995 period. They established a ranking for each

FIGURE 15-2

Performance of Leading Indicators Prior to Currency Crisis

Quintiles	Percentage of Indicators Showing Anomalous Behavior Prior to Crisis		
	Latin America	Asia	Others
80%-100%	44%	28%	32%
60%-79%	39%	42%	39%
40%-59%	8%	28%	18%
20%-39%	8%	0%	11%
less than 20%	0%	0%	0%
	100%	100%	100%

Source: Kaminsky and Reinhart (1998)

FIGURE 15-3

Leading Indicators of Currency Crises
Ranked by Highest Percentage of Good Signals Issued

Indicator	Actual Good Signals/ Possible Good Signals
Real Exchange Rate	25
International Reserves	22
M2/Reserves	21
M2 Multiplier	20
Banking Crisis	19
Terms of Trade	19
Exports	1
Stock Prices	1
Output	16
Excess M1 Balances	16
Bank Deposits	16
Real Interest Rate	15
Domestic Credit/GDP	14
Lending Rate/Deposit Rate	13
Real Interest-Rate Differential	11
Imports	9

Source: Kaminsky, Lizondo, and Reinhart (1998).

FIGURE 15-4

Leading Indicators of Currency Crises
Ranked by Lowest Percentage of Bad Signals Issued

Indicator	Actual Bad Signals/ Possible Bad Signals
Real Exchange Rate	5
Banking Crisis	6
Exports	7
Stock Prices	8
Output	8
Excess M1 Balances	8
Domestic Credit/GDP	9
M2/Reserves	10
Real Interest Rate	11
Real Interest-Rate Differential	11
Imports	11
International Reserves	12
M2 Multiplier	12
Terms of Trade	15
Bank Deposits	19
Lending Rate/Deposit Rate	22

Source: Kaminsky, Lizondo, and Reinhart (1998).

indicator in terms of the largest number of good signals issued, the fewest number of false signals issued, and the average lead time between the point in time when a signal was first issued and the onset of a crisis (see Figures 15–3 to 15–5).

The real exchange rate was rated the best indicator, both in terms of issuing the highest percentage of good signals and the fewest number of false signals. Other indicators that performed well in terms of issuing a large number of good signals with few false signals included banking crises, the ratio of M2 to reserves, the trend in equity prices, exports and output. All of the indicators studied provided a warning window of 1 to 1½ years, with banking crises providing the longest lead time.

FIGURE 15-5

Leading Indicators of Currency Crises
Ranked by Longest Lead Time between
Date of Signal and the Onset of a Crisis

Indicator	Months of Lead Time
Banking Crisis	19
Real Exchange Rate	17
Real Interest Rate	17
Imports	16
M2 Multiplier	16
Output	16
Bank Deposits	15
Excess M1 Balances	15
Exports	15
Terms of Trade	15
International Reserves	15
Stock Prices	14
Real Interest Rate	14
M2/Reserves	13
Lending Rate/Deposit Rate	13
Domestic Credit/GDP	12

Source: Kaminsky, Lizondo, and Reinhart (1998).

REFERENCES

Aziz, Jahangir, Francesco Caramazza, and Ranil Salgado (2000), "Currency Crises: In Search of Common Elements," *IMF World Economic Outlook Supporting Studies*, 2000, pp. 86–128.

Bank for International Settlements (1999), "The Yen Carry Trade and Recent Foreign Exchange Market Volatility," *BIS Quarterly Review*, March 1999, pp. 33–37.

Berg, Andrew, Eduardo Borensztein, Gian Maria Milesi-Ferretti, and Catherine Pattilo (1999), *Anticipating Balance of Payment Crises: The Role of Early Warning Systems*, IMF Occasional Paper No. 186, Washington, D.C.

Bernard, Henri J., and Gabriele E.B. Galati (2000), "The Co-Movement of U.S. Stock Markets and the Dollar," *BIS Quarterly Review*, August 2000, pp. 31–34.

Bernhardsen, Tom, and Oistein Roisland (2000), "Factors That Influence the Krone Exchange Rate," *Norges Bank Economic Bulletin*, Fourth Quarter 2000.

Bilson, John F.O. (1984), "Purchasing Power Parity as a Trading Strategy," *Journal of Finance*, Vol. 39, No. 3, pp. 715–725.

Brooks, Robin, Hali Edison, Manmohan S. Kumar, and Torsten Slok (2001), "Exchange Rates and Capital Flows," *IMF Working Paper*, WP/01/190.

Cheung, Yin-Wong, Menzie D. Chinn, and Ian W. Marsh (2000), "How Do UK-Based Foreign Exchange Dealers Think Their Market Operates," *NBER Working Paper*, No. 7524, February 2000.

Chinn, Menzie D., and Ron Alquist (2000), "Tracking the Euro's Progress," *International Finance*, Vol. 3, No. 3, November 2000, pp. 357–373.

Clostermann, Jorg, and Bernd Schnatz (2000), "The Determinants of the Euro-Dollar Exchange Rate: Synthetic Fundamentals and a Non-Existing Currency," *Deutsche Bundesbank Discussion Paper*, 2/00.

Cooper, Neil, and James Talbot (1999), "The Yen/Dollar Exchange Rate in 1998: Views from Options Markets," *Bank of England Quarterly Bulletin*, February 1999, pp. 68–77.

Copeland, Laurence S. (2000), *Exchange Rates and International Finance*, Third Edition, Pearson Education Limited, Essex.

DeGrauwe, Paul (1996), *International Money: Postwar Trends and Theories*, 2nd Edition, Oxford University Press, Oxford.

Dominguez, Kathryn M., and Jeffrey Frankel (1993), *Does Foreign Exchange Intervention Work?*, Institute for International Economics, Washington, D.C.

Dornbusch, Rudiger (1976), "Expectations and Exchange Rates Dynamics," *Journal of Political Economy*, Vol. 84, pp. 1161–1176.

Dunis, Christian, and Pierre Lequeux (2001), "The Information Content of Risk Reversals," *Derivatives Use, Trading and Regulation*, Vol. 7, No. 2, pp. 98–117.

European Central Bank (2002), "Economic Fundamentals and the Exchange Rate of the Euro," *ECB Monthly Bulletin*, January 2002.

Fender, Ingo, and Gabriele Galati (2001), "The Impact of Transatlantic M&A Activity on the Dollar/Euro Exchange Rate," *BIS Quarterly Review*, December 2001, pp. 58–68.

Fleming, J. Marcus (1962), "Domestic Financial Policies Under Fixed and Floating Exchange Rates," *IMF Staff Papers*, Vol. 9, November 1962, pp. 369–379.

Frankel, Jeffrey (1979), "On the Mark: A Theory of Floating Exchange Rates Based on Real Interest Rate Differentials," *American Economic Review*, Vol. 69, September 1979, pp. 610–622.

Frankel, Jeffrey, and Kenneth Froot (1990), "Chartists, Fundamentalists and the Demand for Dollars," in *Policy Issues in Interdependent Economics*, edited by T. Courakis and M. Taylor, Clarendon Press, Oxford.

Frankel, Jeffrey A., and Andrew K. Rose (1996), "Currency Crashes in Emerging Markets: Empirical Indicators," *NBER Working Paper*, No. 5437.

Freund, Caroline L. (2000), "Current Account Adjustments in Industrial Countries," *Federal Reserve Board, International Finance Discussion Paper*, No. 692.

Froot, Kenneth A., and Richard H. Thaler (1990), "Anomalies: Foreign Exchange," *Journal of Economic Perspectives*, Vol. 4, No. 3, Summer 1990, pp. 179–192.

Gehrig, Thomas, and Lukas Menkhoff (2002), "The Use of Flow Analysis in Foreign Exchange," *CEPR Discussion Paper Series*, No. 3221.

Goldfajn, Ilan, and Rodrigo O. Valdes (1996), "The Aftermath of Appreciations," *NBER Working Paper*, No. 5650.

Goldstein, Morris, Graciela L. Kaminisky, and Carmen M. Reinhart (2000), *Assessing Financial Vulnerability: An Early Warning System for Emerging Markets*, Institute for International Economics, Washington, D.C.

Goldstein, Morris, and John Hawkins (1998), "The Origin of the Asian Financial Turmoil," *Reserve Bank of Australia, Research Discussion Paper*, No. 9805.

Gruen, David (2001), "Some Possible Long-Term Trends in the Australian Dollar," *Reserve Bank of Australia Bulletin*, December 2001, pp. 30–41.

Gust, Christopher, and Jaime Marquez (2000), "Productivity Developments Abroad," *Federal Reserve Bulletin*, October 2000, pp. 665–681.

Hallwood, C. Paul, and Ronald MacDonald (2000), *International Money and Finance*, 3rd Edition, Blackwell Publishers, Malden, Massachusetts.

IMF, *World Economic Outlook Reports*, May 1998, December 2001.

Isard, Peter, and Hamid Faruqee, editors (1998), "Exchange Rate Assessment: Extensions of the Macroeconomic Balance Approach," *IMF Occasional Paper*, No. 167.

Isard, Peter, Hamid Faruqee, G. Russell Kincaid, and Martin Fetherston (2001), "Methodology for Current Account and Exchange Rate Assessments," *IMF Occasional Paper*, No. 209.

Kaminsky, Graciela L., and Carmen M. Reinhart (1997), "The Twin Crises: The Causes of Banking and Balance of Payments Problems," *University of Maryland Working Paper*, No. 37.

Kaminsky, Graciela L., and Carmen M. Reinhart (1998), "Financial Crises in Asia and Latin America: Then and Now," mimeo.

Kaminsky, Graciela L., Saul Lizondo, and Carmen M. Reinhart (1998), "Leading Indicators of Currency Crises," *IMF Staff Papers*, Vol. 45, No. 1, March 1998, pp. 1–48.

Koen, Vincent, Laurence Boone, Alain de Serres, and Nicola Fuchs (2001), "Tracking the Euro," *OECD Economic Department Working Paper*, No. 298.

Kritzman, Mark P. (1998), "The Forward Rate Bias," *AIMR Conference Proceedings, Currency Risk in Investment Portfolios*, Charlottesville, VA.

Krugman, Paul (1998), "It's Baaack: Japan's Slump and the Return of the Liquidity Trap," *Brookings Papers on Economic Activity*, 1998, Vol. 2.

Laidler, David, and Shay Aba (2002), "Productivity and the Dollar: Commodities and the Exchange Rate Connection," *C.D. Howe Institute Commentary*, No. 158, February 2002.

Lyons, Richard K. (2000), "Multiple Currency Investment Strategies to Take Advantage of the Forward Discount Bias," class project for International Finance 285 course, (http://haas.berkeley.edu/~Lyons/285.html).

Lyons, Richard K. (2001), *The Microstructure Approach to Exchange Rates*, MIT Press, Cambridge, Mass.

MacDonald, Ronald, and J. Nagayasu (2000), "The Long-Run Relationship Between Real Exchange Rates and Real Interest Rate Differentials: A Panel Study," *IMF Staff Papers*, Vol. 47, No. 1, pp. 116–128.

MacDonald, Ronald, and Jerome L. Stein (1999), *Equilibrium Exchange Rates*, Kluwer Academic Publishers, Dordrecht, Netherlands.

MacDonald, Ronald, and Philip Swagel (2000), "Business Cycle Influences on Exchange Rates: Survey and Evidence," *IMF World Economic Outlook Supporting Studies*, 2000, pp. 129–160.

Mann, Catherine L. (1999), *Is the US Trade Deficit Sustainable?*, Institute for International Economics, Washington, D.C.

Mark, Nelson C. (2001), *International Macroeconomics and Finance: Theory and Econometric Methods*, Blackwell Publishers, Malden, Mass.

McGuckin, Robert H., and Bart Van Ark (2001), *Making the Most of the Information Age: Productivity and Structural Reform in the New Economy*, The Conference Board, Inc., New York.

McKinsey Global Institute (2001), *US Productivity Growth, 1995–2000*, McKinsey and Co., Washington D.C.

McKinnon, Ronald I. (1979), *Money in International Exchange: The Convertible Currency System*, Oxford University Press, New York.

McKinnon, Ronald I., and Kenichi Ohno (1997), *Dollar and Yen: Resolving Economic Conflict Between the United States and Japan*, MIT Press, Cambridge, Mass.

Meredith, Guy (2001), "Why Has the Euro Been So Weak?" *IMF Working Paper*, WP/01/155.

Meese, Richard, and Kenneth Rogoff (1983), "Empirical Exchange Rate Models of the Seventies: Do They Fit Out of Sample," *Journal of International Economics*, Vol. 14, No. 1, pp. 3–24.

Mundell, Robert A. (1963), "Capital Mobility and Stabilization Policy Under Fixed and Flexible Exchange Rates," *Canadian Journal of Economics and Political Science*, Vol. 29, November 1963, pp. 475–485.

Neely, Christopher J. (1997), "Technical Analysis in the Foreign Exchange Market: A Layman's Guide," *Federal Reserve Bank of St. Louis Review*, September/October 1997, pp. 23–38.

Obstfeld, Maurice, and Kenneth Rogoff (1994), "The Intertemporal Approach to the Current Account," *NBER Working Paper*, No. 4893.

Osler, Carol, and P.N. Kevin Chang (1995), "Head and Shoulders: Not Just a Flaky Pattern," *Federal Reserve Bank of New York Staff Reports*, No. 4.

Pilbeam, Keith (1998), *International Finance*, 2nd Edition, Macmillan Press LTD, London.

Posen, Adam S. (1998), *Restoring Japan's Economic Growth*, Institute for International Economics, Washington, D.C.

Rogoff, Kenneth (1996), "The Purchasing Power Parity Puzzle," *Journal of Economic Literature*, Vol. 34, June 1996, pp. 647–668.

Rosenberg, Michael R. (1998), *Currency Crises in Emerging Markets: A Guide to Speculative Attack Models and Early Warning Systems*, Merrill Lynch Research Report.

Rosenberg, Michael R. (1996), *Currency Forecasting: A Guide to Fundamental and Technical Models of Exchange Rate Determination*, Richard D. Irwin Co., Chicago, IL.

Sachs, Jeffrey, Aaron Tornell, and Andres Velasco (1996), "Financial Crises in Emerging-markets: The Lessons from 1995," *Brookings Papers on Economic Activity*, 1996, No. 1, pp. 147–215.

Sarno, Lucio, and Mark P. Taylor (2001), "Official Intervention in the Foreign Exchange Market: Is It Effective and, If So, How Does It Work?," *Journal of Economic Literature*, Vol. 34, No. 3, September 2001, pp. 839–868.

Tille, Cedric, et al. (2001), "To What Extent Does Productivity Drive the Dollar?," *Federal Reserve Bank of New York Current Issues in Economics and Finance*, Vol. 7, No. 8, August 2001.

Van de Gruen, Liesbeth, and Peter Vanden Houte, "The New Economy and the Foreign Exchange Market," Economic Research, Bank Brussels Lambert, August 2001.

Williamson, John, editor (1994), *Estimating Equilibrium Exchange Rates*, Institute for International Economics, Washington, D.C.

INDEX

About the Author

Michael R. Rosenberg is Managing Director and Global Head of Foreign Exchange Research at Deutsche Bank. Deutsche Bank's FX Research Group has been ranked #1 in a number of prominent global investor polls, including *Institutional Investor* magazine and the Pan-European Extel Survey. Michael Rosenberg holds a Ph.D. in economics from Penn State University.